# AMBEDKAR ON LAW, CONSTITUTION AND SOCIAL JUSTICE

# AMBEDKAR ON LAW, CONSTITUTION AND SOCIAL JUSTICE

Akhlakh Ahmad

CENTRUM PRESS
NEW DELHI-110002 (INDIA)

**CENTRUM PRESS**
**H.O.:** 4360/4, Ansari Road, Daryaganj,
New Delhi-110002 (India)
Tel: 23278000, 23261597, 23255577, 23286875
**B.O.:** No. 1015, Ist Main Road, BSK IIIrd Stage,
IIIrd Phase, IIIrd Block, Bangalore-560085 (INDIA)
Tel: 080-41723429
*Email:* centrumpress@gmail.com
*Visit us at:* www.centrumpress.com

*Ambedkar on Law, Constitution and Social Justice*



First Edition, 2011
ISBN 978-93-80836-49-2

PRINTED IN INDIA

*Printed at* Mehra Offset Press, Delhi

# Contents

# Preface

Some parts of the Constituent Assembly Debates make fascinating reading. One is struck by the high quality of the debates and the breadth of vision and farsightedness of the Founding Fathers. The contribution of Dr. B. R. Ambedkar, the principal architect of the Constitution, was outstanding.

Article 32 of the Constitution guarantees to every person the right to move the Supreme Court directly for enforcement of fundamental rights. It provides an inexpensive and expeditious remedy. In Ambedkar's memorable words: "If I was asked to name any particular Article in the Constitution as the most important — an Article without which this Constitution would be a nullity— I could not refer to any other Article except this one. It is the very soul of the Constitution and the very heart of it."

The secretion of Ambedkar's statute was reprehensible. But the reaction of violence and the resort to vandalism and scorching the famous Deccan Queen was more reprehensible. It was a gross insult to the memory of Babasaheb, who strongly disapproved of 'the Grammar of Anarchy' and attached great importance to constitutional morality and its diffusion not merely among the majority of any community but throughout the whole. Babasaheb must have turned in his grave at these occurrences and their condonation by the political leaders and his admirers who profess to follow his teachings and in effect worship him as a deity.

The book, which provides a rare opportunity to debate and discuss the contribution of Dr. Ambedkar in nation-building, will be great interest to all sections of people.

*—Akhlakh Ahmad*

# 1

# Constitution and Dr. Ambedkar

"Without going into the merit of constitution, however good and faultless a constitution may be, but if those who implement it are incompetent and useless, that constitution results in an evil. Similarly however defective a constitution may be, but if its executors are good the same constitution results in the good of the people", such was the view expressed by Dr. Baba Saheb Ambedkar while replying to the discussion on the Constitution on November 26, 1949. How prophetic were his statement! The, Congress rulers during the last 40 years have made a travesty of the Constitution. They needlessly amended the original charter several times to perpetuate their single-party rule. Actually the Congress rulers have no moral right to speak on the sanctity of the Constitution.

***Hindutva Challenge and Congress:*** In recent years the Congress has been facing a formidable challenge from the protagonists of Hindutva. It must be noted that the Hindutva challenge is to the Congress, and not to the Constitution, the judiciary or the democratic system. But a systematic Goebellsian propaganda blitzkrieg is conducted by the Congress and those whose vested interests lie in perpetuating the Congress rule and the Congress culture to present Hindutva as the worst challenge to the Constitution. The vilification campaign is joined by all those who have an eye on the main chance, and the Congress party is the highest bidder.

The Congress hangers-on have formed a Constitution Preservation committee as a part of this anti-Hindu propaganda campaign. Anything is grist for their propaganda mill. No falsehood or abuse is too base or too mean for them. They have no compunction to use shady methods. They argue: (1) The Sangh Parivar is out to scrap the Indian Constitution. (2) Its aim is to establish the system propounded by Manu. (3) If elected to power, Bharatiya Janata Party will rescind all legal provisions giving certain social rights to the dalits. (4) The dalits will again be dumped in the traditional ditch of untouchability and all the disabilities associated with it. The source of this offensive of falsehoods is far from any love for the Constitution. The whole business springs from the single-point programme of perpetuation of the Congress rule, the sole host of these parasites. Political propaganda should be matched on a political plane.

Yet there is enough occasion to have a hard look at the issue in dispute, "Dr. Baba Saheb Ambedkar, Constitution and Hindutva". Let us first consider Hindutva.

Hindutva is, these days, being discussed from various angles. The dominant being the accusation that Hindutva is none else than the abuse of Hindutva for political mileage by Sangh Parivar. Even the courts of law have taken the stand that Hindutva is a religious concept. And following this, elections of several Members of Parliament and State Legislative Assemblies have been declared void. But Hindutva is not a mere religious concept. At least the Sangh Parivar does not subscribe to this view. Hindutva is a concept that is related to nationhood. The part "Hindu" in the word "Hindutva" is not used to denote a group of people following any particular way of worship. The late V.D. Savarkar has defined the word "Hindu" as "the one whose country, India, spreads between the two seas and who regards it as his fatherland and sacred land".

RSS has not defined Hindu, and Hindutva. But what the Sangh understands by these words has been amply clarified. Sangh believes Hindu to be a way of life. Guruji has stated regarding this way of life: "We have perceived the entire society as a body. It is the great social person (virat samajapurush).

All men are indeed limbs and organs of the great social corpus spiritualis. Society as a mammoth humanoid body and the eternal undying spirit that dwells in that body and this realization is the specific and unique aspect of the Indian spiritual thinking. All existent objects, including all human beings are parts of that eternal existence. And that is the fount of the basic unity. Since the eternal spirit inform everyone in equal measure, the social system should be so organised as to make everyone happy. A social order where all will have equal self-interest."

Shri Guruji calls these "the principles of Hindu way of life". He further says: "The ever present principle of Hindu life, that one truth pervades in all, is the ultimate truth. That alone is the link that joins all. The selfsame truth appears in diverse forms. Therefore it is our natural duty to create all manner of scope for all to lead their life according their diverse tastes".

It should be, noted that Shri Guruji does not define Hindu-Hindutva in religious terms. He does not link Hindutva with any specific method of worship. It should be appreciated that he sheds light on the fact that the substance of Hindutva relates to the wellbeing of mankind. The Sarsanghchalak Shri Balasaheb Deoras while addressing the Maharashtra State-level camp at Tuljai declared: "The Sangh goal is to create an egalitarian society free from exploitation."

The concept of Hindutva does not imply total trust in a single scripture, neither does it strictly adhere to a single religious regimen. It does not reserve all its faith for one Prophet, nor does it profess to tailor society to the measurements given by a religious tone. Deoras has elaborated the thoughts on social system intended in Hindutva in his book Hindu Organisation and Social Equality where he says: "Untouchability should be eradicated from our society permanently, It must go lock, stock and barrel. The Hindutva of the Sangh does not accept the sense of high and low based on caste. So there is no question of Sangh justifying the present caste inequality."

The Hindutva of the RSS-is not based on any religious sect, so it has no room for religious hatred against any sect. Guruji says: "There is a deliberate attempt to create confusion around the word Hindu. Some are driven by their selfish motives to describe Hindus as opposed to Muslims, Christians, Sikhs, Jains and dalits."

They do not do this after any serious study of the issue. The Hindu thinking and the Hindu way of life have been in the world even before Islam and Christianity were yet to emerge. How could Hindus be against a religion that was not in existence, either Islam or Christianity, Sikhs, Jains, etc. are indeed under the general conceptual umbrella of Hinduism. To oppose them is a indulge in suicidal attempt to cut one's limbs. The term Hindu is never used to oppose or discriminate against any sect. The term is a positive one and could never be construed to mean anything negative.

***Constitutional Idealism:*** While discussing the Constitution, one has to bear in mind this wider meaning of the term Hindutva. Our Constitution has three types of idealism. The political idealism, social idealism and economic idealism. The blend of these three ideals becomes the national idealism. The Constitution explains to us the objectives to be kept always before our eyes in the context of individual-society relationship.

The freedom struggle was not at all limited to political freedom only. India aimed at three kinds of freedom. The political freedom was to be followed by social and economic freedoms. The great leaders at the helm of the freedom struggle had mainly the Hindu society before, their vision. The Muslim community did not fully participate in the freedom struggle. Muslim leaders were without any big following. There was hardly any Muslim League representative in the Constituent Assembly.

The kind of political freedom the leaders in the freedom struggle had envisaged is reflected in the Constitution in the form of the fundamental rights. This freedom was not demanded by the Muslims. Because their overwhelming majority had demanded a separate land for Muslims. And the factor of social freedom in the struggle for the freedom of the country was a hundred-per-cent Hindu social reform movement. Untouchability, social inequality, traditional superstition, injustice to women, child-marriage, widow remarriage an so on and so forth were all issues of social reforms in Hindu society.

The incursion of social justice in the Constitution is the outcome of these agitations for social reforms. The demand for the country's liberation from the foreign economic yoke and all-out efforts for gaining that were the activities of Hindus. Though the Parsis like Jamshedji Tata and Dadabhoy Naoroji were at the forefront of the country's economic liberation they were different only in their manner of worship. They were in fact a factor in the all-round movement for economic emancipation carried out by Lokmanya Tilak, Mahatma Gandhi, Lalchand Hirachand in their own way. The economic ideal enshrined in the Constitution is the fruit of their efforts.

Because the ideals of political, social and economic liberaties are enshrined in the Constitution the responsibility for their fulfilment devolves on the government machinery and the citizens are granted some of these liberties in the form of the fundamental rights. All these are intended to achieve the goal of highest interests and welfare of the people, and therefore Hindutva cannot have any quarrel with these.

The noble ideals included in the Constitution, if viewed uninhibited by political considerations and those of Hindutva, would appear to have no contradictions. Hindutva does not deny individual liberty, equality and fraternity. It also does not deprive anyone of his freedom of worship. The founding fathers of our Constitution felt that such ideals must be enshrined in our Constitution, because they were deeply impressed by Indian traditions in social thought. In this context Dr. Ambedkar's interpretation is very significant. He says: "I have not borrowed liberty, equality and fraternity from the French Revolution. I have learnt them from the teachings of Lord Buddha. To allow every person to adopt a way of worship dictated by his conscience is in the best of Hindu tradition. It is not in the Hindu tradition to oppress anyone only because he happens to worship his lord in a different manner. This has been beautifully expressed in the Mahimnastotra which says: "O Lord, you are the destination of all people reaching you by various ways, straight or crooked according to their taste as waters of various rivers flowing whichever way reach the sea." The Constitution also merely paraphrases the contents of this stotra (praise to Lord).

***Social Justice :*** The social ideals of our Constitution are as important as the political ones. There was dual slavery in our country. One political and the other social. Under the social slavery it was mainly the scheduled castes which were trampled under the injustices by higher castes. They had no political or social rights. Their lowest state in society was determined by their birth. Great savants raised a relentless revolt against this social slavery prevalent in the Hindu society. Sages like Maharshi Dayanand, social reformers like Mahatma Phule, political leaders like Mahatma Gandhi and Swatantrya Veer Savarkar ceaselessly agitated against this social slavery. Ambedkar fought the final battle against the Hindu society. The strugglers reflected in our Constitution.

"I entered the Constituent Assembly to safeguard the interests of the dalits", said Dr. Ambedkar while explaining his purpose in joining the Constituent Assembly. He further stated: "I did not go there to draft the Constitution. But that responsibility crane upon me for certain reasons. It is a matter of pride for me to have been associated with the architects of the Constitution." Dr. Ambedkar's is the lion's share in clearly defining the social and economic ideals in our Constitution. Article 17 of the Constitution eradicates untouchability. Article 15 guarantees that no discrimination would be allowed on the basis of religion race, caste, gender or domicile. Article 16 guarantees that the State will grant equal opportunities to all citizens. And the same Article 16 makes provision for reservations for the backward people.

***Political Democracy:*** This is a special feature of our Constitution. All adults enjoy the right to vote. All votes are of equal weightage. This right of the citizens is very important and this has invested the common man with full control on the State power. With the ballot-power the Constitution itself grants to the majority of the citizens the power to rule. To extend the right to select their rulers to the common people is politically a revolutionary measure. Politicians playing caste-card organise their parties on various caste-lines and try to acquire majority.

The Ahirs, the Jats, the Rajputs, the Yadavs, the dalits and the Muslims are yoked together to present what is named as Bahujan Samaj. But this is an election strategy. Some others try to garner castes other than the Brahmins, the Kshatriyas and the Kayasthas, and try to present them as Bahujan Samaj.

But Hindutva is opposed to such fissiporous business of strengthening divisive caste sentiments through politician means because a very narrow sentiment is detrimental to national unity. The political organisation of the Indian society should be undertaken on the basis of the wide and comprehensive content of Hindutva. If caste is conceived as the basis of political activity the hallowed social ideals in the Constitution would be gathering dust in the statute. The protagonists of Hindutva in the widest ken of the term-aspire to bring a Hindu-again in the wide connotation-rule in the country.

The adult franchise granted in the Constitution is bound to result in the majority rule, *i.e.*, Hindu rule. No one can change this foregone conclusion. The limited demand of the Hindutva protagonists is that those politicians who play caste politics, who foster communal division for their politician ends and who deny the just share of the national life to the dalits and the backward sections of society should not be allowed to usurp power by formenting fissiparous, communal and caste passions. Hindutvists are not opposed to the principle of political democracy consecrated in the Constitution. Their objection and opposition is to the policies of implementing the democracy promoted by political parties with their eye on the main chance without any compunction regarding national interests.

***Economic Justice:*** Our Constitution has vowed to render economic justice to all citizens. The directive principles laid down in the Constitution have recorded the economic goals to be achieved by the States. Article 36 to 51 comprise such directive principles, Two of them are relevant here. Article 38 enjoins on the State to establish a social system which will ensure social, political and economic justice to its citizens. Article 39 directs the State to formulate policies of distribution of physical means which will result in the greatest good of all and will provide adequate means of livelihood to all its citizens, men and women. The principle of equal remuneration for equal work should be implemented. The States should not allow centralisation of wealth and the means of-production which harm the society.

A part from these, there are other directives which have extensively discussed the responsibilities of the States regarding adult education, unemployment, children, women, etc., and how the States should execute these responsibilities. The administrators and the government are guided by these directive principles to achieve, the goals included in the preamble of the Constitution.

Dr. Ambedkar in commenting on this says: "These directive principles are not mere decorative pieces showing noble sentiments. The executive and the judiciary should keep those principles in their minds while taking any decisions in future." The economic ideals in the Constitution guide the States in their actions in the relevant field. In the present age the government field of action is not limited to maintaining peace and order. It will be seen that these ideals are but the concrete form of the Hindu directive principle:

Sarve Santu Sukhinah, Sarve Santu Niramayah,

Sarve Bhadrani Pashyantu ma Kashchit Duhkhabhag Bhavet.

(Let all be happy and healthy. Let all see the vision of universal wellbeing. Let no one suffer miseries.)

If liberty and equality are to materialise in the practical life of the people then economic justice should be granted to all without exception. All the rights enumerated in the Constitution are swallowed by the enormous dragon of poverty and destitution. Dr. Ambedkar says: "On 26 January 1950, India will awake in political freedom, but in the social and economic field the darkness of inequality will persist. We must strive to remove this contradiction between political freedom and economic and social bondage, as soon as possible. If we do not succeed in removing this contradiction, then those masses who are the victims of this contradiction will certainly raze to ground the lofty edifice of political democracy, the Constituent Assembly has so painstakingly and assiduously erected."

Hindutvists have never suggested that the State may deny economic equality-economic justice. On the contrary they have for so long been opposing those very policies that have impaired economic justice. Because the political policies so far carried out have denied this very economic justice to the masses, the rich have snowballed into affluent giants, the poor have been lowered into utter destitution. The directive principles have evaporated in their implementation. The State apparatus has installed and operated an economic machinery that diligently preserves the vested interests of a particular tiny but powerful group. The country is groaning under the unbearable load of foreign debt. Indigenous industries are facing insurmountable difficulties created by multinationals riding on the backs of the ruling coterie. The economic policies that help these multinationals to ascend the ruling backs are wrong. And so these policies should be opposed. Opposition to these policies cannot be construed to mean opposition to economic ideals enshrined in the Constitution.

***Framework of Constitution:*** The Hindutva ideology is not in conflict with the framework of the Constitution that lays down the political, economic and social ideals and the ideals regarding freedom of worship. The foregoing discussion would have brought to light two reasons for this. One, the framework of Constitution upholds certain guiding principles and these principles are but a reflection of the noblest ideals held dear for centuries by Indian thinkers. And two, the Hindutva philosophy has already assimilated the ideals our Constitution so explicitly proclaims. Therefore the Hindutva protagonists have no warrant to wage a war against the lofty values they have cherished all their life.

***Congress and Constitution:*** The malicious, mendacious and mean campaign to malign the Hindutva camp springs from causes that are far from the high plane of the directive principles. These are: One for the last several decades the Congress has been operating the Constitution for its narrow political ends. There is nowhere any proof of Congress efforts to bring into practice the noble values enshrined in our Constitution. Whenever their was imminent threat to the Congress hold on political power, the Congress has never flinched from abusing and wrongfully amending the Sections of the Constitution to save its rule from being overthrown. In 1969 the threat to Indira Gandhi's premiership was staring in the face. So she abused the economic ideal of the Constitution to nationalize the banks and abolish the privy purses of the native princes and shouted from the housetops the slogan of "Garibi Hatao".

In 1975 she was again threatened with loss of her seat in the Lok Sabha; she took recourse to the Emergency, abrogated fundamental rights granted by the Constitution, amended the very preamble by interpolating the words "secular" and "socialist". The Constitution cannot slap any specific restricting ideology on the society. The State cannot be bound by such partisan ideology. Dr. Ambedkar astutely skirted these two words but equally sagely incorporated the ideas of freedom of worship and economic justice. He intended to ensconce the soul of these ideas, whereas the late prime minister, Indira Gandhi wanted to use these words as catchwords to attract and abuse popular sentiments without granting anything of substance.

For, the Congress programme for the last four decades had nothing really secular or really socialistic. This travesty of the directive principles is a breach of the sanctity of the Constitution. The Hindutvists' present struggle is against the Congress. But how can the fight against the Congress be considered as a fight against Constitution? The, propaganda that the Hindutvists are opposed to the Constitution is politically motivated to save the Congress rule.

For some years now all the political parties have been celebrating 14 April,Dr. Ambedkar's birthday in a big way; for most of them it is a ritual.

Some of the major parties indulge in unalloyed hypocrisy in that they do two things simultaneously. One, their think tanks attack Dr. Ambedkar mercilessly; they are very angry that there are more statues of Dr. Ambedkar than that of Gandhiji, and that, too, of a larger size; angry because Dr.

Ambedkar is called the father/architect of the Indian Constitution. They are dismissive of the perpetual suffering and unequal status of the depressed section of our population and Dr. Ambedkar's fight for their right to be human. Two, on 14 April the leaders garland Dr. Ambedkar's "oversized" statues, hail him as the architect of the Constitution and as one who sowed the seeds of social democracy and social equality.

The think tank—the 'ideologues' of 'patriotic' political formations—shed crocodile tears over Ambedkar's disagreement with Gandhiji on a number of issues. They, however, conveniently forget what Gandhiji thought of Ambedkar: "If Ambedkar does not break our heads, it is an act of self-restraint on his part. Dr. Ambedkar has had to suffer humiliations and insults which should make any one of us bitter and resentful. Had I been in his place, I would have been as angry. We shall be unfit to gain Swaraj so long as we keep in bondage a fifth of the population. In the history of world religions there is perhaps nothing like our treatment of the suppressed classes. Caste Hindu well-wishers of untouchables have no right to speak for them."

Dr. Ambedkar was a revolutionary, rationalist-humanist, human rights intellectual-activist, a man who looked ahead of his time. He wondered "why the Hindus having traditions of charity and humanity—their regard for animal life-should behave so heartlessly towards their fellow human beings and in such unreasonable ways. The Hindu community is set in the steel frame of the caste system, in which one caste is lower than another in social gradation involving particular privileges, rights, inhibition and disabilities with regard to each caste. This system has created vested interests which depend upon maintaining the inequalities resulting from the system".

He, therefore, "unfurled the banner of equality". He was not satisfied with the abolition of untouchability only, leaving the caste system along with "the inequalities inherent in the system". Dr. Ambedkar embraced Buddhism because the Buddhist dharma is based on scientific reasoning, it seeks to achieve human freedom, equality, liberty and fraternity. According to him Buddhism is the only religion which does not sanctify poverty and inequality: nirvana is the way "to remove injustice and inhumanity that man does to man." Buddha taught "social freedom, intellectual freedom, and political freedom. He taught equality, equality not between man and man only but between man and woman. His concern was to give salvation to man in his life on earth, and not to promise it to him in heaven after he is dead".

Many progressives whisper that Dr. Ambedkar accepted a cabinet post in Pandit Nehru's government because he wanted, political, power. Like all political leaders he too wanted power, but unlike most of them he accepted a cabinet post to empower those who have remained depressed and deprived for centuries. But for him the progressive provisions in the Constitution might not have been incorporated. He devoted his whole life to the cause of human rights of the depressed; his mission in life was to restore human dignity to those who have been victims of an ugly and unjust hierarchical social order which gave rise to injustice and, inequality. "My hear breaks", he said, "to see the pitiable sight of your faces and hear your sad voices".

To the Hindus he said. "If you say that Hindu religion is our religion, then your right and ours must be equal. But is this the case?" Dr. Ambedkar fought a relentless battle against this social order and was one of the very few Indian leaders who was forthright, and called a spade a spade: "I hate all injustice, tyranny, pompousness and humbug". Dr. Ambedkar believed that if he succeeded in his struggle—struggle for a just social order—it will prove a blessing for all Indians, not merely any group or community. He wanted the dominating section of our people to adopt a strong position against the hierarchical social order.

Dr. Ambedkar will be remembered for all time to come as the architect of the Indian Constitution, specially for the Fundamental Rights and Directive Principles Chapters which, aim at eradicating "all injustice and tyranny" and ushering in social democracy and social equality. He was however, disappointed that the dominating section of our society did not rise to the occasion and did not water the plants that he had planted. Our political rulers have failed Ambedkar and his vision. It is now for human rights groups and grassroots activists to make social democracy and equality a way of life in the absence of which political democracy will always stand on a shaky foundation.

## Dr. Bhim Rao Ambedkar, "The Father of Indian Constitution"

Dr. Bhim Rao Ambedkar was the most important leader of the oppressed untouchable minority in the history of India. He acquired the honorific name Babasaheb. Fighting for his people, he angered Mohandas K. Gandhi, the revered leader of the Indian nationalist movement, as well as many Hindu traditionalists.

When India became an independent country, he served in its cabinet and drafted its constitution. Near the end of his life, he became a Buddhist and encouraged other untouchables to do likewise; he had lost hope of justice for his people within Hinduism.

In Hinduism most people belonged to four hierarchical castes, but a large minority were excluded from the caste system and were regarded as beneath it. They did jobs that other Hindus rejected as ritually unclean and were not allowed to pray in temples or to draw water from communal wells. Nearly all of them were desperately poor. In English these people often are called untouchables, or pariahs. Gandhi, wishing to improve their status, called them harijans, or children of God. To underscore their miserable condition, untouchables preferred to be called dalits, a name that means oppressed.

B. R. Ambedkar was born to an untouchable family as its 14th child. At the time of his birth his father was a soldier. Untouchables were divided into numerous hereditary subgroups, or jatis. Ambedkar belonged to the Mahar jati. Despite the disadvantages of poverty, family responsibilities, and untouchable status, he acquired an advanced education. In 1912 he earned a B.A. degree from Elphinstone College at Bombay University. The ruler of a princely state then financed his education in the United States and Britain. In 1916 Columbia

University awarded him a Ph.D. in economics. He continued his studies at the London School of Economics. In 1921 it awarded him a second doctorate. He studied law at Gray's Inn and in 1923 was called to the bar in Britain. He also studied briefly at a German university.

In India he practiced law, taught, edited newspapers, and entered politics. Although he was elected to the Bombay legislature, his real political career was as the leader of the formerly passive untouchable community. Ambedkar's nonviolent protests mobilized tens of thousands of dalits for the right to draw water from wells and public tanks and to pray in temples. Although Gandhi saw himself as a friend of the untouchables, he got along poorly with Ambedkar. They quarreled at the Round Table Conferences on India's future held in London.

When Britain decided to grant India extensive political autonomy, its government grappled with the problem of the diversity within the Indian population. In 1932 Britain offered separate electorates to the untouchables, so that this oppressed minority would control the selection of its representatives. The Indian National Congress strongly opposed any separate electorates. Gandhi began a fast to put pressure on Ambedkar to reject the special electorates for his people. Reluctantly, he did so. The Indian National Congress offered Ambedkar concessions in what was known as the Poona Pact. The number of seats reserved for untouchable candidates was increased, but the entire electorate, not just untouchables, would vote on the candidates for these seats.

In 1936 Ambedkar organized the Independent Labour Party. In contrast with Gandhi and the Indian National Congress, Ambedkar and his party supported the British government in India during World War II. In 1942 he became a member of the viceroy's executive council. In the same year he organized a new political party, the Scheduled Castes' Federation.

When India became independent, Ambedkar joined the new government that the Indian National Congress dominated. From 1947 to 1951, he was a member of the cabinet. More important, he chaired the committee that drafted the national constitution and was its principal author. In the final years of his life, Ambedkar turned to Buddhism, a religion with Indian roots that rejected the Hindu caste system and the concept of untouchability. He formally converted to Buddhism in October 1956. Hundreds of thousands of untouchables joined him in leaving Hinduism for Buddhism. A few weeks after his conversion ceremony, Ambedkar died.

## Constituent Assembly of India

The Constituent Assembly of India was elected to write the Constitution of India, and served as its first Parliament as an independent nation.

### *Election*

The Constituent Assembly of India was set up as a result of negotiations between the Indian leaders and members of the British Cabinet Mission. The constituent assembly was elected indirectly by the members of the Provincial legislative assembly. The Congress secured an overwhelming majority in the general seats while the Muslim League managed to sweep almost all the seats reserved for Muslims. The Congress had a majority of 69%. There were also members from smaller parties like the Scheduled Caste Federation, the Communist Party of India and the Unionist Party. It first met on December 9, 1946 in Delhi, while India was still under British rule. It originally included the provinces that now compose Pakistan and Bangladesh, and the representation of the princely states of India. In June 1947, the delegations from the provinces of Sindh, East Bengal, Baluchistan, West Punjab and the North West Frontier Province formed the Constituent Assembly of Pakistan in Karachi.

The final Constituent Assembly had two hundred and seven representatives, including fifteen women. Only 28 members of the Muslim League finally joined the Indian Assembly. Later, 93 members were nominated from the princely states. The Congress thus secured a majority of 82%. On August 15, 1947, India became an independent nation, and the Constituent Assembly became India's Parliament.

### *Organization*

Dr. Sachchidananda Sinha was the first president (temporary Chairman of the Assembly )of the Constituent Assembly when it met on December 9, 1946. Dr. Rajendra Prasad then became the President of the Constituent Assembly, and would later become the first President of India. The Vice President of the Constituent Assembly was Professor Harendra Coomar Mookerjee, former Vice-Chancellor of Calcutta University and a prominent Christian from Bengal who also served as the Chairman of the Minorities Committee of the Constituent Assembly. He was appointed Governor of West Bengal after India became a republic.

Constitution and elections *See Also*: Constitution of India

The Assembly approved the Constitution on November 26, 1949, making it official. On January 26, 1950, the Constitution took effect — a day now commemorated as Republic Day nationwide.

At this point, the Constituent Assembly became the Provisional Parliament of India, until the first elections under the new Constitution took place in 1952.

### *Committees Under the Constituent Assembly*

- Committee on the Rules of procedure - Rajendra Prasad
- Steering Committee *Rajendra Prasad*
- Finance and Staff Committee *Anugrah Narayan Sinha*
- Credential Committee *Alladi Krishnaswamy Iyer*
- House Committee *B. Pattabhi Sitaramayya*
- Order of Business Committee *K.M. Munshi*
- Ad hoc Committee on the National Flag *Rajendra Prasad*
- Committee on the Functions of the Constituent Assembly *G.V. Mavalankar*
- States Committee *Jawaharlal Nehru*
- Advisory Committee on Fundamental Rights, Minorities
- Tribal and Excluded Areas Vallabhbhai Patel
- Minorities Sub-Committee *H.C. Mookherjee*

- Fundamental Rights Sub-Committee *J.B. Kripalani*
- North-East Frontier Tribal Areas and Assam. Excluded & Partially Excluded Areas Sub-Committee *Gopinath Bardoloi*
- Excluded and Partially Excluded Areas (Other than those in Assam) Sub-Committee *A.V. Thakkar*
- Union Powers Committee *Jawaharlal Nehru*
- Union Constitution Committee *Jawaharlal Nehru*
- Drafting Committee *B.R. Ambedkar.*

## Members of the Indian Constituent Assembly

### *Indian National Congress*

- Pandit Jawaharlal Nehru, 1st Prime Minister
- Sardar Vallabhbhai Patel, Deputy Prime Minister cum Home Minister
- Maulana Azad, Minister for Education,
- Dr. Rajendra Prasad, Chairman of the Assembly
- C. Rajagopalachari, Governor General
- Sarat Chandra Bose
- Sri Krishna Sinha, Chief Minister, Bihar
- Shyam Nandan Prasad Mishra
- Anugrah Narayan Sinha, Deputy Chief Minister cum Finance Minister,Bihar
- Rafi Ahmed Kidwai
- Asaf Ali
- Syama Prasad Mookerjee, President, Hindu Mahasabha
- Rajkumari Amrit Kaur, Minister for Health
- Hansa Mehta, President, All India Women's Conference
- Prof. N.G. Ranga
- Deep Narayan Singh
- P. Subbarayan
- Kailashnath Katju
- N.G Ayyangar
- T.T. Krishnamachari

- Rameshwar Prasad Sinha
- Durgabai Deshmukh
- K.M. Munshi
- Krishana Vallabh Sahay
- Frank Anthony, Anglo Indian representative
- Sarvepalli Radhakrishnan
- Dr. John Mathai
- Pratap Singh Kairon
- Prof. Shibbanlal Saxena
- R. K. Shanmukham Chetty
- Alladi Krishnaswamy Iyer
- Jagjivan Ram, President, All India Depressed Classes League
- Pandit Govind Ballabh Pant, Premier, United Provinces
- Minoo Masani
- Renuka Ray
- Purushottam Das Tandon
- Mahavir Tyagi
- Thakur Das Bhargava
- Bhagwan Das
- Feroze Gandhi
- B. Shiva Rao
- Jairamdas Daulatram
- Pattom A. Thanu Pillai
- R. Sankar
- P. S. Nataraja Pillai
- K. A. Mohamed
- P. T. Chacko, Pullolil
- Panampilly Govinda Menon
- Annie Mascarene
- Bhograju Pattabhi Sitaramayya
- Kamraj
- Ammu Swaminathan

- Purnima Banerjee
- Vijayalakshmi Pandit
- Ramnath Goenka, Editor of the Indian Express
- Sarojini Naidu
- Jaipal Singh Munda, President, Adibasi Mahasabha
- Jagjivan Ram
- Dakshayani Velayudan
- Reverend Jerome D'Souza
- Reverend JJM Nichols-Roy
- Gopinath Bordoloi
- Dharanidhar Basumatari
- Malati Choudhury
- Homi Mody
- Leela Roy
- Biswanath Das, Premier of Orissa
- Acharya Kriplani
- Sucheta Kriplani
- Harendra Coomar Mookerjee
- Gopi Krishna Vijayvargiya
- Pandit Raghunath Vinayak Dhulekar
- D.H. Chandrasekharaiya
- Nibaran Chandra Laskar
- Ari Bahadur Gururng, Gorkha Community (Darjeeling)
- Ch. Ranbir Singh Hooda.

***Muslim League***

- Begum Aizaz Rasul, Vice President (later President) Muslim League (India)
- Maulana Hasrat Mohani
- Nawab Mohammad Ismail Khan
- Kazi Syed Karimuddin
- Chaudhry Khaliquzzaman, President, Muslim League (India)
- Naziruddin Ahmad

- Z.H. Lari
- Mohammad Saadullah, Premier of Assam
- Aziz Ahmed Khan
- Maulana Daud Ghazhnavi
- Tajamul Hussain
- Hussain Imam
- Mahboob Ali Baig Sahib Bahadur
- Pocker Sahib Bahadur.

***Others***

Scheduled Caste Federation:

- Dr. Ambedkar.

Akalis:

- Sardar Hukam Singh.

Communist:

- Somnath Lahiri.

## List of Members (According to Regions)

***Madras***

O.V. Alagesan, Mrs. Ammu Swaminathan, M. Ananthasayanam Ayyangar, Moturi Satyanarayana, Mrs. Dakshayani Velayudhan, Mrs. G. Durgabai, Kala Venkatarao, N. Gopalaswamy Ayyangar, D. Govinda Das, Rev. Jerome D'Souza, P. Kakkan, K. Kamaraj, V.C. Kesava Rao, T.T. Krishnamachari, Alladi Krishnaswamy Ayyar L. Krishnaswami Bharathi, P. Kunhiraman, M. Thirumula Rao, V.I. Muniswamy Pillay, M.A. Muthiah Chettiyar, V. Nadimuthu Pillai, S. Nagappa, P.L. Narasimha Raju, B. Pattabhi Sitaramayya, C. Perumalswamy Reddy, T. Prakasam, S.H. Prater, Raja Swetachalapati Ramakrishna Renga Roa of Bobbili, R.K. Shanmukham Chetti, T.A. Ramalingam Chettiyyar, Ramanath Goenka, O.P. Ramaswamy Reddiyar, N.G. Ranga, N. Sanjeeva Reddy, K. Santhanam, B. Shiva Rao, Kallur Subba Rao, U. Srinivasa Mallayya, P. Subbarayan, C. Subramaniam, V Subramaniam,, M.C. Veerabahu, P.M. Velayudapani, A. K. Menon, T.J.M. Wilson, Mohamed Ismail Sahib, K.T.M. Ahmed

Ibrahim, Mahboob Ali Baig Sahib Bahadur, B. Pocker Sahib Bahadur

### *Bombay*

Balchandra Maheshwar Gupte, Mrs. Hansa Mehta, Hari Vinayak Pataskar, B.R. Ambedkar, Joseph Alban D'Souza, Kanayalal Nanabhai Desai, Keshavrao Marutirao Jedhe, Khandubhai Kasanji Desai, Bal Gangadhar Kher, M.R. Masani, K.M. Munshi, Narahar Vishnu Gadgil, S. Nijalingappa, S.K. Patil, Ramchandra Manohar Nalavade, R.R. Diwakar, Shankarrao Deo, G. V. Mavalankar, Vallabhbhai Patel, Abdul Kadar Mohammad Shaikh, A.A. Khan

### *West Bengal*

Monomohan Dass, Arun Chandra Guha, Lakshmi Kanta Maitra, Mihir Lal Chattopadhyay, Satis Chandra Samanta, Suresh Chandra Majumdar, Upendranath Barman, Prabhudayal Himatsingka, Basanta Kumar Das, Mrs. Renuka Ray, H.C. Mookherjee, Surendra Mohan Ghose, Syama Prasad Mookerjee, Ari Bahadur Gurung, R.E. Platel, K.C. Neogy, Raghib Ahsan, Jasimuddin Ahmad, Naziruddin Ahmad, Abdul Hamid, Abdul Halim Ghuznavi

### *United Provinces*

Ajit Prasad Jain, Algu Rai Shastri, Balkrishna Sharma, Banshi Dhar Misra, Bhagwan Din, Damodar Swarup Seth, Dayal Das Bhagat, Dharam Prakash, A. Dharam Dass, R. V. Dhulekar, Feroz Ganhdi, Gopal Narain, Krishna Chandra Sharma, Govind Ballabh Pant, Govind Malaviya, Har Govind Pant, Harihar Nath Shastri, Hriday Nath Kunzru, Jaspat Roy Kapoor, Jagannath Baksh Singh, Jawaharlal Nehru, Jogendra Singh, Jugal Kishore, Jwala Prasad Srivastava, B.V. Keskar, Mrs. Kamala Chaudhri, Kamalapati Tiwari, J.B. Kripalani, Mahavir Tyagi, Khurshed Lal, Masurya Din, Mohan Lal Saksena, Padampat Singhania, Phool Singh, Paragi Lal, Mrs. Purnima Banerjee, Prurshottam Das Tandon, Hira Vallabha Tripathi, Ram Chandra Gupta, Shibban Lal Saxena, Satish Chandra, John Matthai, Mrs. Sucheta Kripalani, Sunder Lall, Venkatesh Narayan Tivary, Mohanlal Gautam, Vishwambhar Dayal Tripathi, Begum Aizaz Rasul, Hyder

Hussain,, Hasrat Mohani, Abul Kalam Azad, Muhammad Ismail Khan, Rafi Ahmad Kidwai, Mohd. Hifzur Rahman

***East Punjab***

Bakshi Tek Chand, Jairamdas Daulatram, Thakurdas Bhargava, Bikramlal Sondhi, Yashwant Rai, Ranbir Singh, Achint Ram, Nand Lal, Sardar Baldev Singh, Giani Gurmukh Singh Musafir, Sardar Hukam Singh, Sardar Bhopinder Singh Mann

***Bihar***

Amiyo Kumar Ghosh, Anugrah Narayan Sinha, Banarsi Prasad Jhunjhunwala, Bhagwat Prasad, Boniface Lakra, Brajeshwar Prasad, Chandika Ram, K.T. Shah, Devendra Nath Samanta, Dip Narain Sinha, Guptanath Singh, Jadubans Sahay, Jagat Narain Lal, Jagjivan Ram, Jaipal Singh, Kameshwara Singh of Darbhanga, Kamaleshwari Prasad Yadav, Mahesh Prasad Sinha, Krishna Ballabh Sahay, Raghunandan Prasad, Rajendra Prasad, Rameshwar Prasad Sinha, Ramnarayan Singh, Sachchidananda Sinha, Sarangdhar Sinha, Satyanarayan Sinha, Binodanand Jha, P.K. Sen, Sri Krishna Sinha, Sri Narayan Mahtha, Syamanandan Sahaya, Hussain Imam, Saiyid Jafar Imam, Latifur Rahman,, Mohammad Tahir, Tajamul Hussain.

***Central Provinces and Berar***

Raghu Vira, Rajkumari Amrit Kaur, B.A. Mandloi, Brijlal Nandlal Biyani, Thakur Cheedilal, Seth Govind Das, Hari Singh Gour, Hari Vishnu Kamath, Hemchandra Jagobaji Khandekar, Ghanshyam Singh Gupta, Lakshman Shrawan Bhatkar, Panjabrao Shamrao Deshmukh, Ravi Shankar Shukla, R.K. Sidhva, Shankar Trimbak Dharmadhikari, Frank Anthony, Kazi Syed Karimuddin, Ganpatrao Dani.

***Assam***

Nibaran Chandra Laskar, Dharanidhar Basu-Matari, Gopinath Bardoloi, J.J.M. NIchols-Roy, Kuladhar Chaliha, Rohini Kumar Chaudhury, Muhammad Saadulla, Abdur Rouf.

***Orissa***

B.Das, Biswanath Das, Krishna Chandra Gajapati Narayana Deo of Parlakimedi, Harekrushna Mahatab, Lakshminarayan Sahu, Lokanath Misra, Nandkishore Das, Rajkrishna Bose, Santanu Kumar Das.

***Delhi***

Deshbhandhu Gupta

***Ajmer-Merwara***

Mukut Bihari Lal Bhargava

***Coorg***

C.M. Poonacha

***Mysore***

K. Chengalaraya Reddy, T. Siddalingaiya, H.R. Guruv Reddy, S.V. Krishnamurthy Rao, K. Hanumanthaiya, H. Siddaveerappa, T. Channiah,

***Jammu and Kashmir***

Sheikh Muhammad Abdullah, Motiram Baigra, Mirza Mohmmad Afzal Beg, Maulana Mohammad Sayeed Masoodi,

***Travancore-Cochin***

Pattom A. Thanu Pillai, R. Sankar, P. S. Nataraja Pillai, Annie Mascarene, K. A. Mohamed, P. T. Chacko, Pullolil, Panampilly Govinda Menon,

***Madhya Bharat***

V.S. Sarwate, Brijraj Narain, Gopikrishna Vijayavargiya, Ram Sahai, Kusum Kant Jain, Radhavallabh Vijayavargiya, Sitaram S. Jajoo,

***Saurashtra***

Balwant Rai Gopalji Mehta, Jaisukhlal Hathi, Amritlal Vithaldas Thakkar, Chimanlal Chakubhai Shah, Samaldas Laxmidas Gandhi,

***Rajasthan***

V.T. Krishnamachari, Hiralal Shastri, Sardar Singhjhi of Khetri, Jaswant Singhji, Raj Bhadur, Manikya Lal Varma,

Gokul Lal Asava, Ramchandra Upadhyaya, Balwant Sinha Mehta, Dalel Singh, Jainarain Vyas,

***Patiala and East Punjab States Union***

Ranjit Singh, Sochet Singh, Bhagwant Roy

***Bombay States***

Vinayakrao Balshankar Vaidya, B.N. Munavalli, Gokulbhai Daulatram Bhatt, Jivraj Narayan Mehta, Gopaldas A. Desai, Paranlal Thakurlal Munshi, B.H. Khardekar, Ratnappa Bharamappa Kumbhar.

***Orissa States***

Lal Mohan Pati, N. Madhava Rau, Raj Kunwar, Sarangadhar Das, Yudhishthir Misra.

***Central Provinces States***

R.L. Malaviya, Kishorimohan Tripathi, Ramprasad Potai.

***Uunited Provinces States***

B.H. Zaidi, Krishna Singh.

***Madras States***

V. Ramaiah.

***Vindhya Pradesh***

Avdesh Pratap Singh Shambu Nath Shukla Ram Sahai Tiwari Mannulalji Dwidedi.

***Cooch Behar***

Himmat Singh K. Maheshwari.

***Tripura and Manipur***

Girja Shankar Guha.

***Bhopal***

Lal Singh.

***Kutch***

Bhawani Arjun Khimji.

***Himachal Pradesh***

Y.S. Parmar.

# 2

# Indian Legal Systems and Ambedkar

The reverence paid by the Hindus to Brahmins, and the reputed inviolability of their persons, and the loss of, or prejudice to cast(e), that ensues from proving the cause of their death, have in some places in the province of Benares, and more especially in the pergunnahs of Kuntit and Budhoe been converted by some of the more unlearned part of them, into the means of setting the laws at defiance, from the dread and apprehensions of the persons of the Hindu religion, to whose lot it must frequently fall to be employed, in enforcing against such Brahmins any process or demands on the part of Government The devices occasionally put in practice under such circumstances by these Brahmins, are lacerating their own bodies, either more or less slightly, with knives or razors; threatening to swallow, or, sometimes actually swallowing poison, or some powder which they declare to be such; or, constructing a circular enclosure called a *koorh,* in which they raise a pile of wood or of other combustible and betaking themselves to fasting, real or pretended, place within the area of the koorh, an old woman, with a view to sacrifice her by setting fire to the koorh, on the approach of any person to serve them with any process, or to exercise coercion 'over them on the part of Government, or its delegates.

These Brahmins likewise, in the event of their not obtaining relief within a given time, for any loss or disappointment that they may have justly *or* unjustly experienced, also occasionally bring out their women or children, and causing them to sit down in the view of the peon who is coming towards them on the part of Government, or its delegates, they brandish their swords, and threaten to behead, or otherwise slay, these females, or children, on the nearer approach of the peon; and there are instances, in which, from resentment at being subjected to arrest or coercion, or other molestation, they have actually not only inflicted wounds *on* their own bodies, but put to death with their swords, the females of their families, or their own female infants, or some aged female, procured for the occasion. Nor are the women always unwilling victims; on the contrary, from the prejudices in which they are brought up, it is supposed that in general they consider it incumbent on them to acquiesce cheerfully in the species of self-divulgement, either from motives of mistaken honour, or of resentment and revenge, believing that after death they shall become the tormentors of those who are the occasion of their being sacrificed.

On similar principles, these Brahmins, to realize any claim or expectation, such as the recovery of a debt, or for the purpose of extorting some charitable donation, frequently proceed either with some offensive weapon, or with poison, to the door of another inhabitant of the same town or village, and take post there in the manner called Dhurna; and it is understood, according to the received opinions on this subject, that they are to remain fasting in that place until their object be attained; and that it is equally incumbent on the party who is the occasion of such Brahmins thus sitting, to abstain from nourishment until the latter be satisfied.

Until this is effected, ingress and egress to and from his house are also more or less prevented, as according to the received opinion, neither the one nor the other can be attempted, but at the risk of the Brahmin's wounding himself with the weapon, or swallowing the powder or poison, with which he may have come provided.

These Brahmins, however are frequently obliged to desist and are removed from sitting Dhurna by the officers of the courts of justice, without any ill consequence resulting it, having been found by experience, that they seldom or ever attempt to commit suicide, or to wound themselves or others, after they are taken into the custody of Government. The rules and measures adopted for putting a stop to these abuses, and for preventing the revival of the still more savage custom, which until within these few years, had been generally prevalent amongst the tribe of Rajkumars inhabiting the borders of the province near Juanpore, of destroying their infant female children, by suffering them to perish for want of sustenance, are hereby enacted, with modifications, into a regulation.

## Slaughter his Women or Children

Upon information in writing being preferred to the magistrate of the city or a zillah court, against any Brahmin or Brahmins, for establishing a *koorh,* or for being prepared to maim, wound, or slaughter his women or children, or any, or either of them, in the manner described in the preamble to this regulation, or in any other account or manner substantially similar thereto, on account of any subject of discontent, or any other account whatsoever; in such case, upon oath being made to the truth of the information, the Magistrate is immediately to address to the said Brahmin or Brahmins, a written notice in the Persian language and character, and in the Hindustani language and Nagri character, and under his official seal, which notice is to be served on him or them, by such relations, friends, or connections of the said Brahmin or Brahmins, as the magistrate may think fit, and have an opportunity of employing for the purposes and in default of such relations, friends, or connections of the said Brahmin or Brahmins, the magistrate is to cause the notice to be served by a single peon of the same religion; and the notice shall require the said Brahmin or Brahmins to remove the *koorh,* and the women and people that may be placed in it; or to desist from any preparation towards wounding or slaughtering the women or children according as either or both of these facts shall be charged in the information.

The notice shall also contain a positive and encouraging assurance to the Brahmin or Brahmins in question, that on his or their complying with the principal exigence thereof, by removing the *koorh,* and the person or persons, or by desisting from any preparation to wound or slaughter the women and children, and thereon repairing (as such Brahmin or Brahmins may think fit) in person, or by Vakeel to the city or zillah court, proper enquiry shall be made concerning the dispute that may have given occasion to the act or acts thus prohibited.

But if the issuing of the notice shall not have the effect of inducing the said Brahmin or Brahmins to comply with the exigency thereof, a written return to that purpose is to be made and attested by the party or parties entrusted with the serving of it; and the magistrate is thereon to issue a warrant under his official seal and signature for the apprehension of the said Brahmin or Brahmins specifying the misdemeanour and contumacy with which he or they stand charged; and the execution of the warrant is to be committed to peons of the Mohammedan religion, nor is any Hindu to be sent on such duty.

On the Brahmin or Brahmins against whom the warrant shall have been issued being brought before the magistrate, he or they are to be dealt with, in the mode prescribed in Section 5, Regulation IX, 1793, respecting persons charged with crimes or misdemeanours; and if it shall appear to the magistrate on the previous enquiry, which by the said section he is himself directed to make, that the misdemeanour or misdemeanours charged, (that is, the constructing of the *koorh,* or being prepared to wound or slay the women or children, according as either or both of these acts shall have been charged) were actually committed, and that there are grounds for suspecting the prisoner or the prisoners respectively to have been concerned, either as a principal or an accomplice, in the perpetration of either or both of these acts; the magistrate shall cause him or them to be committed to prison or held to bail, (according as the parties shall appear to have been principals or accomplices) to take his or their trial at the next session of the court or circuit, and shall bind over the informant or complainant, and the witnesses, to appear at the trial, in the manner prescribed in the aforesaid section.

## Process of Trial and Punishment

The court of circuit shall conduct the trial of Brahmin or Brahmins charged with the above offences, in the manner prescribed in Regulation IX, 1793 and XVI, 1795, in respect to the other offences, but as the Mohammedan law cannot adequately apply to offences of this local nature, it is therefore hereby provided and ordered, that where in the opinion of the court of circuit, the charge of being a principal in respect to the constructing of a *koorh,* or to having been prepared to wound or slay the women or children, shall be proved, the said court shall sentence the prisoner to the payment of a fine equal to the amount of his annual income, which is to be estimated according to the best information that they may be able to procure respecting it; and on proof to the court's satisfaction of the prisoner's being guilty only as an accomplice, he shall be sentenced to the payment of a fine equal to one-fourth of his estimated annual income.

In all cases of parties being sentenced to the payment of such fines, they are to be committed to, and are to remain in jail until the amount thereof be paid, or until they shall have delivered to the court of circuit, or, after the said court's departure, to the magistrate, full and ample malzamines or security, to pay the same within six months from the date of their release; and such parties, before their enlargement, either in consequence of their having liquidated, or having entered into security for the payment for the fine imposed on them, shall deliver into the court of circuit, or, in their absence, to the *magistrate, faelzaminee,* or satisfactory security from one or more creditable persons, not to offend in like manner in future.

### *Authority Reserved to the Nizamut Adawlut to Mitigate such Fines*

All sentences passed by the court of circuit under Section 3, without however any intermediate suspension of their execution, are to be transmitted within ten days after their being passed, to the Nizamut Adawlut, which court may order such mitigation and restitution of the fine or fines thereby imposed, as may be thought proper; but until the order be issued by the Nizamut Adawlut, the sentence of the court of circuit is to be considered in full force, and to be carried into effect accordingly.

## Penalty for Brahmins Absconding

In case any Brahmin or Brahmins, against whom the city or a Zillah magistrate may issue the warrant prescribed in Section 2, shall refuse to obey, or resist or cause to be resisted, the peons deputed to serve it, or escape after being taken by them into custody, or abscond, or shut himself or themselves up in any house or building, or retire to any place, so that the warrant cannot be served upon him or them, the magistrate shall issue a precept to the Collector, requiring him to cause to the nearest Tehsildar to attach the lands that such Brahmin or Brahmins may possess in property, or in mortgage, or in farm, or *Lakharaje.*

The lands shall remain attached until he or they surrender, and the collections made during the attachment, after deducting such revenue as may fall due to Government, shall be accounted for, and paid to, the party against, or on account of, or in resentment to, whom, the *Koorh* was originally established, or the woman or women, or child or children, were to be wounded *or* slain, and after the surrender or apprehension of the Brahmin or Brahmins who set on the Koorh, or was or were prepared to wound or slay his or their women or children, or either of them, his or their lands shall be released; but he or they shall be proceeded against, in respect to his or their lands shall be released; but he or they shall be proceeded against, in respect to his or their trial for the original offence or offences, as prescribed in Sections 3 and 4. Collector to Apply to the Magistrate in Case of Brahmins Establishing a Koorh, or being Prepared to Kill or wound Women or Children, on Account of any Process from the Revenue Department

In the event of any Brahmin or Brahmins establishing a *Koorh,* or preparing to wound or slay his or their women or children, or any or either of them, with a view to prevent the serving of any *Dustuck* or writ on him or them, for arrears of revenue by the local Tehsildar, or by the Collector of Benares, in the manner in which by Regulation VI, 1795, they are respectively authorised to issue such *Dustucks,* if it be the Dustuck of the Tehsildar that is thus opposed, he is not, after being informed thereof, to persist in enforcing it, but is to report the case immediately to the Collector, accompanied by the written testimonies of the peon deputed to serve the *Dustuck;* upon receipt of which information, or in case of his own original process being in like manner resisted, the Collector is to represent; through the Vakeel of Government, the amount of the balance due by such Brahmin or Brahmins, and the circumstances attending the issuing of his own or of his Tehsildar's process for realizing it, to the judge and magistrate of the city or Zillah in whose jurisdiction the lands on account of which the arrears shall be due, may be situated; and upon the peon deputed with the Tehsildar's or the Collector's *Dustuck,* or any other creditable person or persons, attending in court, and making oath to the truth of the circumstance stated in the representation of the collector, either as to the constructing of a koorh by such Brahmin or Brahmins, or as to his or their being prepared to wound or slay the women and children, or any of them, (according as one or both of these expedients, shall be stated to have been resorted to by the Brahmin or Brahmins in question) the magistrate is thereon to issue to such Brahmins a written notice under his official seal in the Persian language and character, and in the Hindustani language and Nagri character, which is to be served on him or them by such of the relations, friends or connections, of the said Brahmin or Brahmins as the magistrate may think fit, and have an opportunity of employing for the purpose; and in default of such relations, friends, or connections, of the said Brahmin or Brahmins, the Magistrate is to cause the notice to be served by a single peon of the same religion, and the tenor of it shall require the said Brahmin or Brahmins to remove the koorh, and the women and people that may be placed in it, or to desist from any preparation for wounding or killing the women or children, (according as either or both of these offences may be charged in the information) as likewise, either to discharge the balance of rent or revenue that shall have been demanded from him or them or to appear, and entering security for such part of it as he or they may have pleas against the payment of, to file his or their objections to the payment of such part in the city or Zillah Court, that the merits of the case may be enquired into and decided, according to the principles by which other disputed demands and accounts of revenue are under Regulation VI, 1795, directed to be determined; and the said notice is also to contain a positive and encouraging assurance to the Brahmin or Brahmins in question, that on his or their employing with the exigency of it, by removing the koorh and the persons therein, or by desisting from any preparation to wound or slay the women and children, and either discharging the balance of revenue in demand, or repairing in person, or deputing a Vakeel, to the city or Zillah Court, and entering security for the amount of it, proper enquiry shall be made into the pleas that he or they may have to state against the justice of the demand.

If the issuing of the notice shall fail to induce the said Brahmin and Brahmins to comply with the requisitions of it, a written return to that effect is to be made and attested by the party or parties entrusted with the serving of it, and the magistrate is immediately to issue a warrant under his official seal and signature for the apprehension of such Brahmin or Brahmins in which shall be specified the misdemeanour, contumacy, and arrear, with which he or they stand charged; and the warrant shall be executed by peons of the Mohammedan religion, as directed in Section 2; and if the Brahmin or Brahmins shall refuse to obey or resist, or cause to be resisted, the peons deputed to serve it, or escape, after being taken by them into custody or abscond, or shut himself or themselves up in any house or building, or retire to any place, so that the warrant cannot be served on him or them; the magistrate, on information to this effect, shall issue a precept to the collector, to cause the nearest Tehsildar to attach the lands that such Brahmin or Brahmins may possess in property, or in mortgage, or in the farm, *or Lakheraje;* and the lands shall accordingly remain attached, and the profits of them be appropriated by

Government, until the liquidation of the balance shall be effected, either from the produce, or in consequence of the said Brahmin or Brahmins making good the same from his or their other means; and also, until the said Brahmin or Brahmins shall have been brought, or made his or their appearance before the court, when he or they shall be tried for being concerned either as principles or accomplices in setting up the koorh, or for having been prepared to wound *or* slay his or their women or children, or any or either of them, in the same manner, and with the same reservation as to the mitigation of the sentence, as is specified in Sections 2,3 and 4.

Brahmins Causing the Construction *of* a Koorh, and Persons Firing it, to be tried on a Charge of Murder for the Loss of the life or Lives of any Person or Persons that may be thereby Occasioned.

If any Brahmin or Brahmins, on account of any discontent or alarm, well or ill founded, either against Government, or its officers, or servants, shall establish a koorh, in which any person or persons shall, at any period from its construction until its removal, be burnt to death, or otherwise lose their lives, in consequence of such koorh's being set fire to, by any person whomsoever; the Brahmin or Brahmins who shall have caused the construction thereof, shall be held chargeable with, and made amenable for, the crime of murder; as well as the party or parties who may have been immediately employed, or aided in setting fire to the pile or combustibles in question; and upon proof of the fact to the satisfaction of the court of circuit, such Brahmin or Brahmins, and such person or persons, setting fire to the koorh, shall be sentenced on trial before the said court, to suffer the punishment of death, in the same manner as if they had committed and been convicted *of Kutl* and, or premeditated murder, according to the doctrines of the Mohammedan law; and with a view to render the example as public as possible such sentence (whether consistent with the future of the Mohammedan law officers, or otherwise) is in this case, to be accordingly formally passed by the court of circuit on the Brahmin or Brahmins thus convicted; but it is to be at the same time explained to the party or parties thus condemned, as it is also hereby expressly provided, that all such trials, and the sentences passed, are by the court of circuit to be submitted (in like manner as is prescribed in Section 47, Regulation IX, 1793,) to the Nizamut Adawlut, and the party or parties condemned under this section, are to remain in Jail to await the final judgment of that court; and if the Nizam ut Adawlut shall approve of the condemnation, it shall order the Brahmin or Brahmins in question to be conveyed to Calcutta, to be thence transported for life, in conformity to Section 23, Regulation XVI, 1795, which establishes this commutation for the legal punishment of murder perpetrated by Brahmins within the province of Benares, or, if the court of Nizamut Adawlut shall see cause for not proceeding pursuant to the sentence passed by the court of circuit either in respect of the Brahmin or Brahmins, who may have caused the construction of the *koorh,* or to the party or parties who may have been employed or aided in firing it, they shall submit the case or cases to the Governor General in Council, and either recommend a pardon, or such other commutation by way of mitigation of the punishment, as to the said court may seem proper.

## Punishment for Brahmins wounding Women and Children

If any Brahmin or Brahmins, under the circumstances, and in the manner, described in the preamble to, and the following sections of this regulation, or under such circumstances, and in such manner, as shall be substantially similar thereto, with a sword, or other offensive weapon, or otherwise, shall actually wound his or their women or children or other women or children, or any or either of them, on account of, in resentment of any real or supposed injury committed towards him or them, by aumils, tehsildars, or other officers, or servants, employed in the revenue or judicial departments; or shall so wound any of his or their own women or children, or any other woman or child, on account or in resentment of, his or their differences with any individual; he or they shall for such act or acts, be sentenced by the *court* of circuit to transportation, subject to the same reference to the Nizamut Adawlut and to the like commutation of the punishment, or pardon, as in the cases referred to in section 7.

### *Punishment for Brahmins killing Women or Children*

If any Brahmin or Brahmins, under the circumstance and in the manner, described in the preamble to, and subsequent sections of this regulation, or under such circumstances, and in such manner, as shall be substantially similar thereto, with a sword or other offensive weapon, or otherwise, shall actually put to death his or their women or children, or other women or children, or any or either of them, on account or in resentment of any real or supposed injury, committed towards him or them by aumils, tehsildars, or any other officers, or servants, employed in the revenue or judicial departments; or shall so put to death any of his or their own women or children, or any other woman *or* child, on account or in resentment of his or their differences with any individual; he or they shall be tried for such homicide and on proof of the fact or facts, be accordingly sentenced by the court of circuit to capital punishment, subject to the same reference to the Nizamut Adawlut and to the like commutation of the punishment, or pardon, as in the cases referred to in section 7; and the families of any Brahmin or Brahmins found guilty of murder under this section, shall, according to the order of the Governor General in Council under date the 17th of June 1789, and the publication made in conformity to it by the Resident at Benares under date the 7th day of July of the same year, be banished from the province of Benares, and the Company's territories; and his and their estates in land shall be forfeited and disposed of as to Government shall seem proper; and accordingly, the court of circuit is required to subjoin this order to all sentences that they may pass, on Brahmins for murder under this section, at the same time reporting such sentence and order to the Nizamut Adawlut, together with as accurate an account as they may be able to procure, of the number, sex, and age, of the persons composing the family of such Brahmin or Brahmins and annexing their opinion how far it may be advisable or otherwise, rigorously to enforce the banishment of the family of such Brahmin or

Brahmins, or to confirm, or mitigate or annul, the order for the forfeiture of their real property; and the Nizamut Adawlut, on consideration of this sentence and order, and of the opinion of the court of circuit, shall either wholly confirm, or recommend to the Governor General in Council such mitigation of the said sentence and order, as shall appear to them proper; and in all cases there the forfeiture of the landed property of such Brahmin or Brahmins, and that of his or their family, shall be confirmed by the Nizamut Adawlut, the said Court is to advise the Governor General in Council thereof, nor shall such sentence be carried into execution as far as regards the forfeiture of the landed property, without an order from the Governor General in Council approving such part of the sentence, and directing in what manner the lands thus forfeited shall be disposed of.

## *Limitation as to the Forfeiture of the Family Lands of the Offenders*

In the exercise of the discretion vested in the Nizamut Adawlut by section 9, of recommending to the Governor General in Council, the mitigation of sentences and orders passed by the Court of Circuit, under the said Section, it shall be a rule that whenever the Governor General in Council shall in consequence deem it proper to limit the banishment either to the party or parties committing the murder, or to a certain number only of his or their family or families; no confiscation or forfeiture of the landed-property shall in such instances take place, but the same shall be entirely left in the possession, and as the property, of those members of the family who shall be exempted from banishment.

## *Regulations respecting Brahmins sitting Dhurna*

***First:*** In conformity to the order of the Governor General in Council, of the 2nd of November 1792, and the publication issued in consequence at Benares on the 22nd of December of the same year, and the further order of the Governor General in Council under date the 7th November 1794, the following rules are enacted for the preventing of *dhurna;* and for the trial and punishment of Brahmins committing this offence.

### *Magistrate to cause Brahmins sitting Dhurna to be Apprehended*

***Second:*** On a complaint in writing being presented to the Magistrate against any Brahmin or Brahmins for sitting *dhurna,* the Magistrate, upon oath being made to the truth of the information, shall issue a warrant under his seal and signature for the apprehension of the person or persons thus complained against, on the prisoner or prisoners being brought before the magistrate, he shall enquire into the circumstances of the charge, and examine the prisoner or prisoners and complainant, and also such other persons (whose depositions are to be taken on oath) as are stated to have any knowledge of the misdemeanour alleged against him or them, and commit their respective depositions to writing; and after this enquiry, if it shall appear to the magistrate that the misdemeanour charged against the prisoner or prisoners was never committed, or, that there is no ground to suspect him or them to have been concerned in the committing of it, the magistrate shall cause such Brahmin or Brahmins to be forthwith discharged, recording his reasons for the information of the Court of Circuit, in the manner specified in Section 17, Regulation IX, 1793.

On the contrary, if it shall appear to the magistrate that the crime or misdemeanour was actually committed, and that there are grounds for suspecting the prisoner or prisoners to have been concerned therein as principals or accomplices, the magistrate shall cause him or them to be committed to prison or held to bail, (according as *in* his discretion he shall judge proper) to take his or their trial at the next session of the Court of Circuit, and shall bind over the complainant to appear and carry on the prosecution, and the witnesses to attend and give their evidence, in the manner required by Section 5, Regulation IX, 1793. The Trial shall take place before the court of circuit, in the manner prescribed in the said regulation, and in Regulation XVI, 1795; and after the evidence is closed, it shall be referred to the pundit of the court, to deliver in writing the *vyuvustha,* or exposition of the shaster, as to whether the facts contained in the evidence of amount to proof of the prisoner or prisoners having committed *dhurna,* and in the event of such *vyuvustha* being in the affirmative, the Court of Circuit is to sentence the prisoner or prisoners to be expelled from the province of Benares, and to forfeit all title to the right or claim for the realizing of which the misdemeanour shall have been committed; but this sentence is not to be carried into execution until it shall have been reported by the Court of Circuit to the Nizamut Adawlut, and it shall have been either wholly confirmed, or directed to be enforced under such mitigation as to the expulsion from the province, or to the forfeiture of the right or claim of the prisoner or prisoners to the property for which he or they sat *dhurna,* as to the said court shall seem proper.

Court of Circuit bow to proceed in case all the legal requisites to constitute *dhurna* shall not be found, although the offence was substantially committed

In the event of the *vyuvustha* which the *pundit* is required to deliver in Section II, not stating the circumstances sworn to in the evidence to amount to the offence of *dhurna,* and the Court of Circuit shall nevertheless be of opinion, from the evidence before them that the prisoner did in fact commit *dhurna,* according to the common construction and received meaning of the term, although the act may not have been attended with all the circumstances that may be legally required to constitute *dhurna,* according to the description of it in the books of the Hindus; the said court is, under such circumstances, (as directed by the order of the Governor General in Council, under date the 7th of November 1794) to take from the prisoner or prisoners, a *moochulka* or engagement, conditioning that if such prisoner or prisoners shall again sit *dhurna* on any one, or perform any act of a nature similar to *dhurna* as shall, on their being prosecuted before the Court of Circuit, be deemed by the judges of the said court present at the trial, or the majority of them, equivalent or tantamount to *dhurna,* the said prisoner or prisoners shall respectively for such second offence, suffer the full penalty of *dhurna,* as provided for by the order of the Governor General in Council, by being expelled from the province, and by being made to forfeit all right and title to the claim in question.

How Rajkumars are to be tried for leaving or causing their female infants to perish for want of nourishment

In the month of December 1789, the tribe of Rajkumars having bound themselves to discontinue the practice of causing their female infants to be starved to death; it is now accordingly ordained, that from the establishment and opening of the city and Zillah courts and of the Court of Circuit in Benares, if any Rajkumar shall designedly prove the cause of the death of his female child, by prohibiting its receiving nourishment, as set forth in the preamble to this regulation, *or* in any other manner, the magistrate, on receiving information thereof upon oath, or such other information or proof as he shall deem sufficient to render the charge highly probable, shall cause such Rajkumar to be apprehended in the manner prescribed, and make the enquiry ordered, in Section 5, Regulation IX, 1793; when if it shall appear to the magistrate that the crime has been actually committed, and that there are grounds for suspecting the prisoner to have been concerned in the perpetration of it, the magistrate shall cause him to be committed to prison to be tried before the Court of Circuit, and shall at the same time take all the other precautions required in the section and regulation last quoted, relative to securing the attendance of the original complainant or informant, and of the witnesses; and the prisoner shall be tried accordingly, in the manner directed in Regulation IX, 1793, and Regulation XVI, 1795, with respect to other cases of murder.

The second piece of social Legislation which the British undertook is contained in Bengal Regulation VI of 1802. It is a regulation for preventing the Sacrifice of Children at Saugor and other places. It enacted as follows:

## REGULATION VI

### *A. D. 1802*

A Regulation for preventing the Sacrifice of Children at Saugor and other Places. Passed by the Governor General in Council, on the 20th August 1802.

It has been represented to the Governor General in Council, that a criminal and inhuman practice of sacrificing children, by exposing them to be drowned, or to be devoured by sharks, prevails at the island of Saugor, and at Bansbaryah, Chaughadh, and other places on the Ganges. At Saugor especially, such sacrifices have been made at fixed periods, namely, the day of full moon in November and in January, at which time also grown persons have devoted themselves to a similar death. Children thrown into the sea at Saugor have not been generally rescued, as is stated to be the custom at other places; but the sacrifice has, on the contrary, been completely effected, with circumstances of peculiar atrocity in some instances.

This practice, which is represented to arise from superstitious vows is not sanctioned by the Hindu law, nor countenanced by the religious orders or by the people at large; nor was it at any time authorized by the Hindu or Mohammedan Governments of India. The persons concerned in the perpetration of such crimes are therefore clearly liable to punishment, and the plea of custom would be inadmissible in excuse of the offence. But, for the more effectual prevention of so inhuman a practice, the Governor General in Council has enacted the following Regulation to be in force from the promulgation of it in the provinces of Bengal, Orissa, and Benares.

If any person or persons shall wilfully, and with the intention of taking away life, throw or cause to be thrown, into the sea or into the river Ganges, or into any other river or water, any infant or person not arrived at the age of maturity, with or without his or her consent, in consequence whereof such person, so thrown into water, shall be drowned, or shall be destroyed by sharks or by alligators, or shall otherwise perish, the person or persons so offending shall be held guilty of wilful murder, and on conviction shall be liable to the punishment of death; and all persons aiding or abetting the commission of such act shall be deemed accomplices in the murder, and shall be subject to punishment accordingly. The trials of prisoners convicted as principals or accomplices of the crimes specified in this section shall be referred to the Court of Nizamut Adawlut, which is to pass sentence thereupon according to Section LXX, Regulation IX, 1793 whatever may be the futwah of the law officers of that Court. (or report to the Governor General in Council the case of any prisoner who may appear to that court to be a proper object of mercy, in conformity with Section LXXIX, Regulation IX, 1793).

If a child or any person not arrived at maturity, be thrown into water, as stated in the preceding section, and be rescued from destruction, or by any means escape from it, the persons who shall have been active in exposing him or her to danger of life, and all aiders and abettors of such act, shall be held guilty of a high misdemeanour, and on convicting shall be liable to such punishment as the Courts of Circuit, under *the futwah* of their law officers, may judge adequate to the nature and circumstances of the case.

The magistrates of districts wherein the sacrificing of children may have been hitherto particles are required to be vigilant to prevent the continuance of the practice, and shall cause the provisions of this Regulation to be from time to time proclaimed at the places, and in the season, where and when such sacrifices have hitherto been effected.

The Second piece of Social Legislation is one dealing with Suttee. It is Bengal Regulation XVII of 1829; It enacted as follows:

## REGULATION XVII

### *A. D. 1829*

A Regulation for declaring the practice of Suttee, or of Burning or Burying alive the Widows of Hindus, illegal, and punishable by the Criminal Courts. Passed by the. Governor General in Council, on the 4th December 1829.

### *Preamble*

The practice of suttee, or of burning or burying alive the widows of Hindus, is revolting to the feelings of human nature; it is nowhere enjoined by the religion of the Hindus as an imperative duty; on the contrary, a life of purity and retirement on the part of the widow is more especially and preferable inculcated, and by a vast majority of that people throughout India the practice is not kept up nor observed; in some extensive districts it does not exist; in those in which it has been most frequent, it is notorious that, in many instances, acts of atrocity have been perpetrated, which have been shocking to the Hindus themselves, and in their eyes unlawful and wicked. The measures hitherto adopted to discourage and prevent such acts have failed of success, and the Governor General in Council is deeply impressed with the conviction that the abuses in question cannot be effectually put an end to without abolishing the practice altogether.

Actuated by these considerations, the Governor General in Council, without intending to depart from one of the first and most important principles of the system of British Government in India, that all classes of the people be secure in the observance of their religious usages, so long as that system can be adhered to without violation of the paramount dictates of justice and humanity, has deemed it right to establish the following rules, which are hereby enacted to be in force from the time of their promulgation throughout the territories immediately subject to the presidency of Fort William.

The practice of suttee, or burning or burying alive the widows of Hindus, is hereby declared illegal, and punishable by the Criminal Courts.

***First:*** All zamindars, talookdars, or other proprietors of land, whether malguzarry or lakhiraj; all sudder farmers and under-renters of land of every description; all dependent talookdars, all naibs and other local agents; all native officers employed in the collection of the revenue and rents of lands on the part of Government, or the Court of Wards; and all munduls or other head men of villages, are hereby declared especially accountable for the immediate communication to the officers of the nearest police station of any intended sacrifice of the nature described in the foregoing section; and any zemindar, or other description of persons above noticed, to whom such responsibility is declared to attach, who may be convicted, of wilfully neglecting or delaying to furnish the information above required, shall be liable to be fined by the magistrate or joint magistrate in any sum not exceeding two hundred rupees, and in default of payment, to be confined for any period of imprisonment not exceeding six months.

### *Police Darogas, how to Act on Receiving the Intelligence of the Intended Sacrifice*

***Second:*** Immediately on receiving intelligence that the sacrifice declared illegal by this Regulation is likely to occur, the police darogah shall either repair in person to the spot, or depute his mohurrir or jamadar, accompanied by one or more burkundauzes of the Hindu religion, and it shall be the duty of the police officers to announce to the persons assembled for the performance of the ceremony, that it is illegal, and to endeavour to prevail on them to disperse, explaining to them that, in the event of their persisting in it, they will involve themselves in a crime, and become subject to punishment by the Criminal Courts. Should the parties assembled proceed in defiance of these remonstrances to carry the ceremony, into effect, it shall be the duty of the police officers to use all lawful means in their power to prevent the sacrifice from taking place, and to apprehend the principal person aiding and abetting in the performance of it; and in the event of the police officers being unable to apprehend them, they shall endeavour to ascertain their names and places of abode, and shall immediately communicate the whole of the particulars to the magistrate or joint magistrate for his orders.

How to act when the intelligence of sacrifice may not reach them until after it shall have actually taken place.

***Third:*** Should intelligence of a sacrifice declared illegal by this Regulation, not reach the police officers until after it shall have actually taken place, or should the sacrifice have been carried into effect before their arrival at the spot, they will nevertheless institute a full inquiry into the circumstances of the case, in like manner as on all other occasions of unnatural death, and report them for the information and orders of the magistrate or joint magistrate to whom they may be subordinate.

***First:*** On the receipt of the reports required to be made by the police darogahs, under the provisions of the foregoing section, the magistrate or joint magistrate of the jurisdiction in which the sacrifice may have taken place shall inquire into the circumstances of the case, and shall adopt the necessary measures for bringing the parties concerned in promoting it to trial before the Court of Circuit.

Persons convicted of aiding and abetting in the sacrifice of a Hindu widow, shall be deemed guilty of culpable homicide, and liable to punishment.

***Second:*** It is hereby declared, that after the promulgation of this Regulation, all persons convicted of aiding and abetting in the sacrifice of a Hindu widow, by burning or burying her alive, whether the sacrifice be voluntary on her part or not shall be deemed guilty of culpable homicide, and shall be liable to punishment by fine or by imprisonment, or by both fine and imprisonment, at the discretion of the Court of Circuit, according to the nature and circumstances of the case and the degree of guilt established against the offender, nor shall it be held to be any plea of justification, that he or she was desired by the party sacrificed to assist in putting her to death.

***Third:*** Persons committed to take their trial before the Court of Circuit for the offence above mentioned, shall be admitted to bail or not, at the discretion of the magistrate or joint magistrate, subject to the general rules in force in regard to the admission of bail.

The Court of Nizamut Adawlut not precluded from passing sentence of death in certain cases.

It is further deemed necessary to declare, that nothing contained in this Regulation shall be construed to preclude the Court of Nizamut Adawlut from passing sentence of death on persons convicted of using violence or compulsion, or of having assisted in burning or burying alive a Hindu widow, while labouring under state of intoxication, or stupefaction, or other cause impeding the exercise of her free will, when, from the aggravated nature of the offence proved against the prisoner the court may see circumstances to render him or her a proper object of mercy. The third piece of Social Legislation is the Caste Disabilities Removal Act XXI of 1850. It enacts as follows:

## The Caste Disabilities Removal Act (xxi of 1850)

*An act for extending the principle of section 9, Regulation VII, 1832, of the Bengal Code throughout the Territories subject to the Government of the East India Company.*

### *Preamble*

Whereas, it is enacted by section 9, Regulation VII, 1832, of the Bengal Code that "whenever in any civil suit the partie's to such suit may be of different persuasions, when one party shall be of the Hindu and the other of the Muhammadan persuasion, or where one or more of the parties to the suit shall not be either of the Muhammadan or Hindu persuasions, the laws of those religions shall not be permitted to operate to deprive such party or parties of any property to which, but for the operation of such laws, they would have been entitled, and whereas it will be beneficial to extend the principle of that enactment throughout the territories subject to the Government of the East India Company it is enacted as follows:

*Law or Usage which inflicts forfeiture of, or affects, rights of change of religion or loss of caste to cease to be enforced.*

So much of any law or usage now in force within the territories subject to the Government of the East India Company as inflicts on any person forfeiture of rights or property, or may be held in any way to impair or affect any right of inheritance, by reason of his or her renouncing, or having been excluded from the communion of, any religion, or being deprived of caste, shall cease to be enforced as law in the Courts of the East India Company, and in the Courts established by Royal Charter within the said territories."

The fourth piece of Social Legislation is the Hindu Widows' Remarriage Act XV of 1856. It enacts as follows:

*An Act to remove all legal obstacles to the marriage of Hindu Widows.*

### *Preamble*

Whereas, it is known that, by the law as administered in the Civil Courts re-established in the territories in the possession and under the Government of the East Indian Company, Hindu widows with certain exceptions are held to be by reason of their having been once married, incapable of contracting a second valid marriage, and the offspring of such widows by any second marriage are held to be illegitimate and incapable of inheriting property; and Whereas, many Hindus believe that this imputed legal incapacity, although it is in accordance with a true interpretation of the precepts of their religion, and desire that the civil law administered by the Courts of Justice shall no longer prevent those Hindus who may be so minded from adopting a different custom, in accordance with the dictates of their own conscience; and

Whereas, it is just to relieve all such Hindus from this legal incapacity of which they complain, and the removal of all legal obstacles to the marriage of Hindu widows will tend to the promotion of good morals and to the public welfare; it is enacted as follows:

## Marriage of Hindu Widows Legalized

No marriage contracted between Hindus shall be invalid, and the issue of no such marriage shall be illegitimate, by reason of the woman having been previously married or betrothed to another person who was dead at the time of such marriage, any custom and any interpretation of Hindu law to the contrary notwithstanding.

### *Rights of Widow in deceased Husband's Property to Cease on her Remarriage*

All rights and interests which any widow may have in her deceased husband's property by way of maintenance, or by inheritance to her husband or to his lineal successors, or by virtue of any will or testamentary disposition conferring upon her, without express permission to re-many, only a limited interest in such property, with no power of alienating the same, shall upon her remarriage cease and determine as if she had then died; and the next heirs of her deceased husband, or other persons entitled to the property on her death, shall thereupon succeed to the same.

The fifth piece of Social Legislation prescribed an age limit for, sexual intercourse with a woman., It is Act XLV of 1860 (Penal Code) Sec. 375. It enacted as follows: "A man is said to commit ' rape ' who except, in the case hereinafter excepted, has sexual intercourse with a woman under circumstances falling under any of the five following:

***First:*** Against her will.

***Secondly:*** Without her consent.

***Thirdly:*** With her consent, when the man knows that he is not her husband, and that her consent is given because she believes that he is another man to whom she is or believes herself to be lawfully married.

***Fifthly:*** With or without her consent, when she is under ten years of age.

***Exception:*** Sexual intercourse by a man with his own wife not being under ten years of age, is not rape."

## What about the Untouchables?

Caste and Untouchability are the two great social evils in India. Caste has disabled the whole Hindu Society. Untouchability has suppressed a large class of people. And yet the British Government has completely ignored the two evils. One may search in vain the Indian Code to find any law dealing with Caste or with Untouchability. It is true that caste and untouchability are social matters.

They will vanish when people will begin to interdine and intermarry. Law cannot compel a person to dine with another. It is true, law cannot compel a person to marry with another. But it is also true that Law can prohibit a Caste from preventing a person from marrying a person outside his caste. Caste continues because a Caste can conspire to punish its members if they break the rules of caste by declaring a social boycott against him. It would have been perfectly possible to have enacted a law declaring such social boycott to be a crime. Again in the matter of Untouchability the disabilities are not merely social. They are fundamentally civic. Inability to I get admission to school, to be able to take water from a public well, to be able to get into a public conveyance, to be able to get into public service, are all civic disabilities. It was the duty of the British Government to legislate at least to the extent necessary to protect their civic rights. It was possible to do so. A short Enactment on the lines of Caste Disabilities Removal Act would have been sufficient. Yet the British Government has gone on as though these two evils did not exist at all. Indeed it is most extraordinary thing to note that although Legislative Bodies were established in India in 1861 and have been passing laws on every social questions and discussing public questions, yet except on two occasions the Untouchables were not even mentioned. The first "occasion on which they were mentioned was in 1916, when one Parsi gentleman Sir Maneckji Dadabhoy moved the following Resolution in the Central Legislature:

> *"That this Council recommends to the Governor General in Council that measures be devised with the help, if necessary, of a small representative committee of officials and non-officials for an amelioration in the moral, material and educational condition of what are known as the Depressed Classes, and that, as a preliminary step the Local Government and Administrations be invited to formulate schemes with due regard to local conditions."*

There was no sympathy to this resolution. The Hindu members of the Legislature were angry with the mover for his having brought such a subject before the Legislature.

Pandit Madan Mohan Malviya said: "Sir, it seems rather ungracious to say so, but a sense of the dignity of the proceedings of this Council compels me to utter a protest against the manner in which sometimes subjects are brought before it for consideration............ "In moving the Resolution the object of which I may at once say, has my wholehearted support, my friend, the Hon'ble Mr. Dadabhoy, went out of his way to make remarks against the Hindu community which, I think, he ought to have avoided............I am not here to defend everything Hindu that exists. I am not here to apologise for the many prejudices or superstitions, which I am sadly conscious are to be found among one portion or another of our community.

But it is not the Hindu community alone which finds it difficult to get rid of prejudices....... Without meaning the smallest disrespect, I would instance the case of the marriage with a Deceased Wife's Sister Bill......... We Hindus have got some much worse prejudices to fight against.......... But I do not think it is within the province of a member of this Council either to lecture to the Hindus present here or to those outside as to the socio-religious disabilities among themselves which they might fight against and remove. I think the province of Members of this Council is limited to dealing with matters of legislation or other administrative matters which may properly be taken up by the Government.

As has been already pointed out, the Government have, in pursuance of a wise and liberal policy, laid it down that they shall not interfere in matters of a religious or socio-religious character, and accusations of the character in question ought, therefore, to be avoided there............... I do not wish to descend into a disputation as to the merits of the imputations or the justification for the general observations that have been made......... And yet, if I do not, I am left in the position that I have heard without protest remarks showing that the Hindu Community from one end of the country to the other was guilty of all that my friend, the Hon'ble Mover of the Resolution, has suggested............ I am conscious that we Hindus have many prejudices to fight against and conquer; but I submit that this is not the place to tell us of them."

Even a social Reformer like Sir Surendranath Bannerjee was not happy. He said:

I regret very much that my Hon'ble friend the Mover of this Resolution went somewhat out of his way to level (I do not think he did it intentionally) an attack against the Hindu Community. He must bear in mind that we are the inheritors of past traditions, of a civilization as ancient as the world. That civilization undoubtedly had its defects,' but that civilization in the morning of the world was the guarantee for law and order and social stability. In the past it afforded consolation to millions. We are trying to evolve a national system in conformity with our present environments, but we cannot push aside all those things which have come down to us from the past.

We reverence the venerable fabric which has been built up by our ancestors. We notice their defects, and we are anxious to get rid of them gradually and steadily, not by any revolutionary movement, but the slow, steady process of evolution. My friend must have a little sympathy with us; he must extend to us the hand of generosity in our efforts to deal with the problems. My Hon'ble friend suggests that Government should take measures........ We welcome the action of Government in a matter of this kind, but after all, if you analyse the situation, it is a social problem, and the British Government, very properly, as I think, in conformity with its ancient traditions, holds aloof from all interference with social questions.

> *"Government can do a great by way of education, a great deal by helping forward the industrial movement among the Depressed Classes. But the vital problem, the problem of problems, is one of social uplifting, and there the Government can only afford to be a benevolent spectator. It may sympathize with our efforts, but it cannot actively participate in them........"*

The Hon'ble Mr. Dadabhoy had to defend himself. In his reply he said:

> *"Sir, I find myself in a very peculiar and unfortunate position. There are two parties in this Council, and they are both on the defensive on this occasion. My justification for bringing in this Resolution, if any justification were needed, is to be found in the unenthusiastic and half-hearted support which I have received from my non-official colleagues. It was no pleasure, I assure you. Sir, to me to bring in this*

*Resolution. If I could possibly have avoided it, I would have very cheerfully and very willingly done so. This is the sixth year of the life of this Reformed Council, as Hon'ble Members are aware, and the second term is now approaching expiration. During the major portion of that time—the five years that I have been on this Council—1 anticipated that the champions of public liberty, public spirit and public enterprise and culture—men like my friends the Hon'ble Surendra Nath Bannerjee or the Honourable Pandit Madan Mohan Malaviya—would take the trouble of moving a Resolution to this effect. I waited all this time to see if one of these enthusiastic members would bring in a Resolution for the amelioration of the Depressed Classes, but when I found that none of them had taken up the matter—though at times this matter is discussed even in the Congress Pandal in a certain manner; when I found that it was not taken up in this Council—............ I, as a Parsee, representing a Hindu constituency thought it my duty to bring this matter for public discussion in this Council."*

The Government naturally felt relieved by this quarrel. Resting behind the moral support of the Hindu members of the Legislature for covering up their delinquency Sir Reginald Crad-dock speaking on behalf of the Government disposed off the Resolution in the following terms:

*"Sir, we sympathize with the objects of the Hon'ble Mr. Dadabhoy's Resolution. We are willing to go so far as to ask Local Governments to put on record what they have done, are doing, and what further they can do, to improve the condition of these people. But we can place no faith in special committees. Have I not indicated to the Council how wide are the problems, and how impossible it would be to deal with them by means of Committees? The problems extend over the whole range of Government from top to bottom. What I say is that, while extending our sympathy to the objects aimed at by the Hon'ble Mr. Dadabhoy, we can go no further than*

*promise to refer the question to Local Governments, and ask them whether they can do more than they are doing. That is as far as we can go, and with that assurance, I will ask the Hon'ble Member to withdraw his Resolution."*

The second time the Untouchables are mentioned in the proceedings of the Legislature was in 1928 when Mr. M. R. Jayakar moved the following Resolution:

*"This Assembly recommends to the Governor-General in Council to issue directions to all Local Governments to provide special facilities for the education of the Untouchables and other depressed classes, and also for opening all public services to them, specially the Police."*

On this occasion the Government of India was no more enthusiastic than it was in 1916. Mr. G. S. Bajpai, speaking on behalf of the Government of India said:

*"The Local Governments are alive to their responsibility, they are doing what they can. It is not my privilege to claim for them that they have achieved the ideal, but I do claim that there is an awakening and an awakened and roused sense of responsibility and a roused sense of endeavour for improving the position of these depressed classes. That being so, it is no function to interfere by direction or by demand. They (i.e. the Government) can, if the House wishes, communicate to them the views of the House on this very national problem."*

For this speech, Mr. Bajpai, according to the official report of the proceedings, was cheered!

Such is the record of the British Government in the matter of social Reform. What a miserable record it is? How meager a record it is; Six social Laws in sixty years of legislative activity!! From the very beginning, its attitude to social reform has been of a very halting character. It kept on some mask of a responsible Government up to 1860. After 1860 it threw off the mask. The Government would not move and reform came to a dead stop. In 1881 a great agitation was started in favour of legislation prohibiting child marriage. Rather than be pestered with social reform, it took courage to announce publicly and once for all its policy of opposition to reform. In a Government Resolution of that year, the British Government proclaimed:

> *"In dealing with such subjects as those raised in Mr. Malabari's Notes, the British Government in India has usually been guided by certain general principles. For instance, when caste or custom enjoins a practice which involves a breach of the ordinary criminal law, the State will enforce the law. When caste or, custom lays down a rule which is of its nature enforceable in the Civil Courts, but is clearly opposed to morality or public policy, the State will decline to enforce it. When caste or custom lays down a rule which deals with such matters as are usually left to the option of citizens, and which does not need the aid of Civil or Criminal Courts for its enforcement. State interference is not considered either desirable or expedient."*

In the application of such general principles to particular cases, there is doubtless room for differences of opinion; but there is one common-sense test which may often be applied with advantage in considering whether the State should or should not interfere in its legislative or executive capacity with social or religious questions of the land now under notice. The test is, ' Can the State give effect to its commands by the ordinary machinery at its disposal? ' If not, it is desirable that the State should abstain from making a rule which it cannot enforce without a departure from its usual practice or procedure.

If this test be applied in the present case, the reasons will be apparent why His Excellency in Council considers that interference by the State is undesirable, and that the reforms advocated by Mr. Malabari, which affect the social customs of many races with probably as many points of difference as of agreement, must be left to the improving influence of time and to the gradual operation of the mental and moral development of the people by the spread of education.

It is true that the British Government in India has by its legislation set up a standard of morality independent of, and in some material respects differing from, the standard set up by caste; and it may be that the former standard has had some beneficial effect in influencing native customs, practices, and modes of thought. But legislation, though it may be didactic purposes; and in the competition of influence between legislation on the one hand, and caste or custom on the other, the condition of success on the part of the former is that the Legislature should keep within its natural boundaries, and should not, by overstepping those boundaries, place itself in direct antagonism to social opinion.

The policy laid down in this Resolution has ever since remained the policy of the British Government in the matter of Social Reform.

Why did the British Government leave the Untouchables in the cold without any care or attention?

The explanation for so criminal a neglect was furnished by Sir Reginald Craddock. In replying on behalf of the Government of India on the Resolution moved by Sir Maneckji Dadabhoy in the Imperial Legislative Council in 1916, he stated what the position of the British Government took with regard to the Untouchables in the following terms:

> *"With regard to them (i.e. the Untouchables) the difficulty is not that Government does not recognize them, but that, until the habits and prejudices of centuries are removed, the hands of their neighbours must necessarily press upon them............. you must remember that these people live mostly in villages and very often in the back lane of towns, and that their neighbours have not yet come under these broad and liberal minded influences. Therefore, as many speakers have indicated, the problem in dealing with this question is more social and religious than purely administrative."*

I know myself of many difficulties in the matter of schools. There are many places where the Maharboys will not be allowed into the school; they may be allowed in the Verandah and get only a small part of the master's attention there, or they may be entirely excluded. But it is only gradually that the difficulty can be met. I have constantly dealt with this very problem on the spot. I have reasoned with people; I have said to them. There are tax payers like yourselves, either let them come into the school, or if you wish to indulge in your own prejudices—they may be reasonable prejudices, as you consider them—but if you wish to indulge them, should you not contribute something in order that these boys may have a school of their own?

In that what some of the better people have come forward to help in the matter of wells, and schools for the low castes; they have assisted, and the difficulties have been got over. But of course if is a matter which must take time, and Government itself cannot use compulsion. They go rather near to it sometimes, for example, in travelling by railway: and when petitions are presented in Court. But they cannot ensure that these people shall always be well treated in their offices. Very often, I think, some of these classes refrain from seeking service they might otherwise wish to secure, because their neighbours are not likely to treat them warmly. Although the Hon'ble mover described the statement made by the Government of Bombay as a ' magnificent *non-possumus*', I think that it very accurately describes that the real difficulties of the situation are. Even though Government is willing to help in every way these unfortunate people, yet it remains true that ' the position of these castes and tribes in the future depends partly on their own selves, and partly those more favoured Indian Communities, which by extending the hand of human comradeship or hardening their hearts and averting their faces, have it in their power to elevate or to degrade them.'

> *"That Sir, I think, represents very truly and accurately the position of affairs as regards these Depressed Classes."*

The same attitude was reiterated in 1928 when the resolution of Mr. Jayakar was discussed in the Central Legislative Assembly. Mr. Bajpai speaking on behalf of the Government said:

> *"It is not by increasing the number of special schools or by providing special facilities that you are going to solve this problem (of the Untouchables). You will solve this problem only by a quickening and broadening the*

*spirit of all sections of the community towards the so called depressed classes."*

Leaving the problem to be solved by the quickening of the consciences of the Hindus, the British Government just neglected the Untouchables and believed that as a Government they were I not called upon to do anything to help to improve the lot of the Untouchables. How did the British justify this neglect of so helpless and so downtrodden a class of their subjects as the Untouchables? The answer is very clear. They did it by taking the view that the evil of Untouchability was not of their making. They argued that if they did not deal with the evil of untouchability, they are not to be blamed for it because the system did not originate with them. This was clearly enunciated by the Government of Bombay in 1856. In June 1856 a petition was submitted on behalf of a Mahar boy to the Government of Bombay complaining that though willing to pay the usual Schooling fee, he had been denied admission to the Dharwar Government School. In disposing of the application, the Government of Bombay thought the matter so important that it issued a Resolution dated 21st July 1856 of which the following is the full text:

1. The question discussed in the correspondence is one of very great practical difficulty.
2. There can be no doubt that the Mahar petitioner has abstract justice on his side; and Government trust that the prejudices which at present prevent him from availing himself of existing means of education in Dharwar may be ere long removed.
3. But Government are obliged to keep in mind that to interfere with the prejudices of ages in a summary manner, for the sake of one or few individuals, would probably do a great damage to the cause of education. *The disadvantage under which the petitioner is not one which* I *has originated with the Government,* and it is one which Government cannot summarily remove by interfering in his favour, as he begs them to do."

This is of course an easy view of the duties of a Government. It is not a responsible view. It is certainly not a view which a civilized Government would take. A Government which is afraid to govern is not a Government. It is only a corporation formed to collect taxes. The British Government undoubtedly meant to be more than a mere tax gathering machinery. It claimed to be a civilized Government. Then why did it not act to prevent wrong and injustice? Was it because it had no power or was it because it was afraid to use them or was it because it felt that there was nothing wrong in the social and religious system of India?

The answer is that it had the power, the amplest power. It did not use it because for a part of the period it did not think that there was anything wrong in the social system of the Hindus and during the period when it became convinced that things were wrong it was overpowered by sense of fear. It is notorious that the beginning of its career the British had a dread and a horror of the consequences of permitting the diffusion of "Christian truth". But it is not quite as notorious that the British at the same time were showing a corresponding respect for native prejudices. Mr. Ward, a Missionary in Calcutta records in his journal for 1802 the following fact:

> *"Last week a deputation from the Government went in procession to Kali Ghat, and made a thank offering to this Goddess of the Hindus, in the name of the Company, for the success which the English have lately obtained in this country. Five thousand rupees were offered. Several thousand natives witnessed the English presenting their offerings to this idol. We have been much grieved at this act, in which the natives exult over us."*

Another illustration of the same is furnished by Mr. Robert Lindsay who was a civilian in the employment of the East India Company in the time of Warren Hastings. Describing his initiation into his new office of Resident at Sylhet he says:

> *"I was now told that it was customary for the new Resident to pay his respects to the shrine of the tutelary saint, Shaw Jullol. Pilgrims of the Islam faith flock to this shrine from every part of India, and afterwards found that the fanatics attending the tomb were not a*

*little dangerous. It was not my business to combat religious prejudices, and I therefore went in state, as others had done before me, left my shoes on the threshold, and deposited on the tomb five gold mohurs as an offering. Being thus purified I returned to my dwelling and received the homage of my subjects."*

How much the British Government had become associated with and interested in supporting native prejudices can be seen from the following memorial which was submitted to the Government of Madras by Bishop Corrie in 1833. The instances cited in the Memorial were these:

*"First, that it is now required of Christian servants of the Government, both civil and military, to attend to Heathen and Mohammedan religious festivals, with the view of showing them respect Second, that in some instances they are called upon to present offerings, and to do homage to idols. Third, that the impure and degrading services of the pagodas are now carried on under the supervision and control of the principal European, and therefore, Christian officers of the Government, and the management and regulation of the revenues and endowments, both of these pagodas and mosques, so vested in them, under the provision of regulation vii of 1817, that no important idolatrous ceremony can be performed, no attendant of the various idols, not even the prostitutes of the temple, be entertained or discharged, nor the least expense incurred, without the official concurrence and orders of the Christian functionary. Fourth, that British officers, with the troops of the Government, are also now employed in firing salutes and in otherwise rendering homage to Mohammedan and idolatrous ceremonies, even on the Sabbath day; and Christians are thus not unfrequently compelled by the authority of Government to desecrate their own most sacred institutions and to take part in unholy and degrading superstitions."*

This is enough to show that the British Government in India "not content with their exertions to suppress the diffusion of the saving truths of the Gospel was openly and authoritatively aiding and abetting the worst forms of devil-worship; that they were taking all the hideous indecencies and revolting cruelties of Hinduism under their especial patronage; sending their own masters-of-the-ceremonies to preside over the hellish orgies; and with paternal tenderness managing the property of the idol temples pampering the priests, cherishing the dancing girls, and doing such honour to heathen is generally as was best calculated to maintain it in a high state of exultant obesity.

It was not till 1841 that Government dissociated itself from actual participation in the Hindu and Mohammedan religions I ceremonies and that too after a great deal of agitation by the Missionaries.

> *"In a circular letter signed by the Military Secretary to the Government of Fort St. George, and addressed to the Commander-in-Chief, under date of July 6, 1841, it is intimated," under instructions from the Court of Directors, conveyed through the Government of India ", that "the attendance of troops or of military bands at native festivals or ceremonies, and the firing of salutes on occasions of that nature," were "in future to be discontinued, with the object of separating the Government and its officers, as far as possible, from all connection with the ceremonies of the Hindu and Mohammedan religions. "The ordinary marks of respect paid to native princes on the occasions of their going forth or returning from such festivals or religious observances were, however, to be paid; and the change was to be effected "in a manner calculated not to alarm the minds of the natives or to offend their feelings. "These orders were circulated by the Commander in Chief to the Generals commanding divisions, and by them to the regiments under their several commands."*

What reform could be expected from a Government which had become so steeped in native prejudices and which wasted such official resources to tend them and keep them up?

It was stricken and paralysed by sympathy. When it ceased to sympathise with the prejudices it was overtaken by fear.

This fear arose out of two considerations. The first consideration related to the promises it had made to the people of India.

On assuming the Government of any new territory, previously under native rule, it was the practice of the British Government to announce to the people that they would be protected in the free exercise of their religions and that neither their institutions nor their usages would be assailed.

Thus in 1801 a solemn declaration was made, in the following terms to the people of the Carnatic:

> *"Although the Right Honourable the Governor in Council trusts that the experience which the inhabitants of the Carnatic have already had, will have rendered it unnecessary for His Lordship to explain the general principles of moderation, justice, protection, and security, which form the characteristic features of the British Government, yet His Lordship in accepting the sacred trust transferred to the Company by the present engagements, invites the people of the Camatic to already and cheerful obedience to the authority of the Company, in a confident assurance of enjoying, under the protection of public and defined laws, every just and ascertained civil right, with a free exercise of the religious institutions and domestic usages of their ancestors".*

In may 1834 the following proclamation was issued to the people of Coorg when it was conquered:

> *"Whereas it is the unanimous wish of the inhabitants of Coorg to be taken under the protection of the British Government, His Excellency the Right Honourable the Governor-General has been pleased to resolve that the territory heretofore governed by Veer Rajunder Woodyer shall be transferred to the Honourable Company. The inhabitants are hereby assured that they shall not again be subjected to native rule; that their civil rights and religious usages, will be respected, and the greatest desire will invariably be shown by the British Government to augment their security, comfort, and happiness."*

In 1849, on the annexation of the Punjab, the following assurance was given to the people:

> *"The British Government will leave to all the people whether Mussulman, Hindu, or Sikh, the free exercise of their own religions; but it will not permit any man to interfere with the other in the observance of such forms and customs as their respective religions may either enjoin or permit."*

Other similar proclamations may be cited. They were treated as pledges. Whether it was just and politic that such pledges should have been given, it was felt that it was impolitic to ignore them once they were given. This was the general view. But there were always some who construed them literally and whose point of view was not to draw any distinction and make any reservations and who wished to interpret the pledges as amounting to saying to the Indians, "You have enjoyed it undisturbedly under the new "and who argued that "any departure from this would be a breach of faith. "Fear of breach of faith was one consideration. Fear of open rebellion was another. Fear of rebellion so far as the British Government in India was concerned was not a fear of the unknown. It was a fact of experience. There was one rebellion in 1801 which was known as the Vellore Mutiny. There was another rebellion in 1857.

It was known as I the Sepoy Mutiny. The Vellore Mutiny was a small flame. But I the Sepoy Mutiny was a conflagration. In both cases the cause alleged was an interference with the religious practices of the Hindus. Two rebellions are enough to teach a lesson and the lesson of these two rebellions was not lost upon the British Government. The Vellore Mutiny of 1801 had made the British Government cautious in the matter of social innovations. The Sepoy Mutiny of 1857 made hostile to any kind of social reform. The British did not want to take any risk and from their point of view the risk was very great. The Mutiny made them so panicky that they felt that loss of India was the surest consequence of social reform and as they were anxious to keep India they refused to look at any project of Social Reform.

This attitude of the British Government to Social reform is quite understandable. However sovereign a Government may be its authority as pointed out by Prof. Dicey is circumscribed by two limitations:

> *"There is first of all the internal limitation which arises from the character, motives and interests of those who are in power. If the Sultan does not abolish Mahomedanism, Pope ban Catholicism, the Brahmin condemn caste, or the British Parliament declare the preservation of blue-eyed babies illegal, it is not because they "cannot" do things, but it is because they "will "not do those things. In the same way if the Executive in India did not do certain things most conducive to progress, it I was because by reason of its being imperial and also by reason of its character, motives and interests, it could not sympathize with the living forces operating in the Indian Society, was not charged with its wants, its pains, its carvings and its desires, was inimical to its aspirations, did not advance Education, disfavoured Swadeshi or snapped at anything that Smacked of nationalism, it was because all these things went against its grain. But an irresponsible government is powerless to do even such things as it may like to do. For its authority is limited by the possibility of external resistance. There are things which it would do but dare not do for the fear of provoking thereby resistance to its authority. Ceaser dare not subvert the worship of the Roman people, a modern parliament dare not tax the Colonies, however much they would. For the same reason the Government of India dared not abolish the caste system, prescribe monogamy, alter the laws of succession, legalize intermarriage or venture to tax the tea planters. Progress involves interference with the existing code of social life and interference is likely to cause resistance. None the less a Government which is of the people and is not detached from them can venture on the path of progress, because it is in a position to know where the obedience will end and resistance will begin. But the Indian Executive, not being of the people, could not feel*

*the pulse of the people. The gist of the matter is that the irresponsible Executive which had been in power in India was paralysed between these two limitations on its authority and much of what to make life good was held up. Part of the programme it would not undertake and the other part it could not undertake. That there was some advancement in material progress is not to be denied. But no people in the world can long remain contented with the benefits of peace and order, for they are not dumb brutes. It is foolish to suppose that a people will indefinitely favour a bureaucracy because it has improved their roads, constructed canals on more scientific principles, effected their transportation by rail, carried their letters by penny post, flashed their messages by lightening, improved their currency, regulated their weights and measures, corrected their notion of geography, astronomy and medicine and stopped their internal quarrels. 'Any people, however patient, will sooner or later demand a Government that will be more than a mere engine of efficiency."*

People wanted freedom political, economic and social. This the British Government declined to create:

*"As a result of this, so far as the moral and social life of the people was concerned, the change of Government by the Mughals to a Government by the British was only a change of rulers rather than a change of system. Owing to the adoption of the principle of non-interference partly by preference and partly by necessity by the British ' the natives of India found themselves under a Government distinguished in no vital respect from those under which they had toiled and worshipped, lived and died through all their weary and forgotten history. From a political standpoint, the change was but the replacement of one despotism by_ "another. It accepted the arrangements as it found them and preserved them faithfully in the manner of the Chinese tailor who, when given an old coat as a pattern, produced with pride an exact replica, rents, patches and all.'"*

This policy of nonintervention though understandable, was so far as the Untouchables were concerned, mistaken in its conception and disastrous in its consequences. It may be granted that Untouchables can only be lifted up by the Hindus recognizing his human rights and him as a human being as correct. But that does not dispose of the matter. Question remains how is this recognition of his rights as a human being to be secured. There are only two ways of helping to realize this object. One way is to make him worthy of respect and the other is to punish those who disrespect him and to deny him his rights. The first way involves the duty to educate him and to place him in positions of authority. The other way involves social reform by making recognition of Untouchability a penal office. Neither of this the British Government was prepared to do.

It would not give the Untouchables any preferential treatment in public service. It I would not undertake to reform Hindu Society. The result was that _ Untouchable has remained what he was before the British, namely an Untouchable. He was a citizen but he was not given the rights of a citizen. He paid taxes out of which schools were maintained but his children could not be admitted into those schools. He paid taxes out of which wells were built but he had no right to take water from them. He paid taxes out of which roads were built. But he has no right to use them. He paid taxes for the upkeep of the State. But he himself was not entitled to hold offices in the state. He was a subject but not a citizen.

The Untouchable stood most in need of education and supply of water. He stood mostly in need of office to protect himself. Owing to his poverty he should have been exempted from all taxes. All this was reversed. The Untouchable was taxed to pay for the education of the touchable. The Untouchable was taxed to pay for the water supply of the touchable. The Untouchable was taxed to pay for the salary of the touchables in office.

What good has British conquest done to the Untouchables? In education, nothing; in service, nothing; in status, nothing. There is one thing in which they have gained and that is equality in the eye of the law. There is of course nothing special in it because equality before law is common to all. There is of course nothing tangible in it because those who hold office often prostitute their position and deny to the Untouchables the benefit of this rule. With all this, the principle of equality before law has been of special benefit to the Untouchables for the simple reason that they never had it before the days of the British.

The Law of Manu did not recognize the principle of equality. Inequality was the soul of the Law of Manu. It pervaded all walks of life, all social relationships and all departments of state. It had fouled the air and the Untouchables were simply smothered. The principle of equality before law has served as a great disinfectant. It has cleansed the air and the Untouchable is permitted to breath the air of freedom. This is a real gain to the Untouchables and having regard to the ancient past it is no small gain.

# 3

# Ambedkar Notes on Acts and Laws

## The Common Law

1. In the English system. Equity has acquired a technical connotation and we are accustomed to think of it as a whole jurisdiction distinct from Common Law principles.
2. For better or for worse, the stream of English Law divided into two channels, not without considerable disturbance of the soil and morbidity of the waters.
3. But the interdependence of Law and Equity has never wholly disappeared.
4. We ought not to think of Common Law and Equity as rival systems. Equity was not a self-contained system, at every point it presupposed the existence of Common Law.

The principle on which the Court of Equity granted relief:

1. If we look for one general principle which more than any other influenced the Equity developed by the Chancery, we find it in a philosophical and theological conception of *conscience.*
2. The English Equity begins to be systematised under the guidance of a governing moral principle of conscience.

3. Not that we can suppose that all the Chancellors were assiduous and consistent in the pursuit of that principle. Under the Tudors, some of them behaved with complete arbitrariness. These occasional aberrations may have inspired Seldon's oft quoted, but probably only half serious quip about the length of the Chancellor's foot. But they were not typical, the 'conscience' which the Chancellor set before him was normally something more constant and imperishable than the mere caprice of his own whim. A 'hardening' process sets in. By 1676 we find Lord Nottingham expressly repudiating the notion that the conscience of the Chancellor is merely *naturalis etinterna,* and in 1818, Lord Seldon summarily repudiates any notion of mere individual discretion being open to an Equity Judge. Equity is a settled system of conscience.

The limits of the Chancellor's authority:

This prerogative to grant relief had certain limits':

(i) It could be exercised only where law gave no rights but where conscience required that certain rights should be given—This was known as the *Exclusive* jurisdiction of Equity.

(ii) It could be exercised only where law gave rights required by conscience but the remedies which it gave were insufficient to satisfy justice—This was known as the *concurrent* jurisdiction of Equity.

(iii) It could be exercised in matters in which the law gave rights required by conscience and remedies sufficient to satisfy the ends of justice but as to which its process was too defective to secure the remedies without the assistance of Equity—This was known as the *auxiliary* jurisdiction of Equity.

The nature of an equitable right:

1. The nature of an equitable right will be better understood if it was studied in contrast with a moral right and a legal right. A mere definition would be very little use.

2. By way of introduction we may begin by seeking to have a precise conception of a right. What do we mean when we say that any given individual has a right:
   (i) If a man by his own force or persuasion can carry out his wishes, either by his own accord or by influencing the acts of others, he has the 'might' so to carry out his wishes.
   (ii) If, irrespectively of having or not having this night, public opinion would view with approval or at least with acquiescence, his so carrying out his wishes, and with disapproval any resistance made to his so doing then he has a '*moral right*' *so* to carry out his wishes.
   (iii) If, irrespectively of the approval or disapproval, acquiescence or non-acquiescence of public opinion, the State would support him in carrying out his wishes then he has a *legal right* so to carry out his wishes.
3. Whether it is a question of might, depends upon a man's own powers of force or persuasion. Whether it is a question of moral right depends on the readiness of public opinion to express itself on his side. Whether it is a question of legal right, depends upon the readiness of the State to exert its force on his behalf. A *legal right* exists where one course of action is enforced, and the other prohibited by that organised society which is called the State. A legal right is, therefore, an interest which is recognised and protected by the State. Right is any interest, respect for which is a duty and the disregard for which is a wrong.

The Characteristics of a legal right:

1. A legal right is a right which unlike moral right is enforced by the State.
2. A legal right is founded in a title which must be shown to have been acquired in any one of the modes of acquiring title recognised by law—*e.g.* possession, prescription, agreement and inheritance, etc.

3. A vestitive fact which creates a title to a right in one person destroys the title of another to the same right.
4. A legal right creates an obligation which is either an obligation *in rem* or an obligation *in personam.*

In what respects does an equitable right resemble, in what respects does it differ, from a legal right:

1. Equitable right is not like a moral right which is not enforced by the State. Equitable right is like a legal right in that it is enforced by the State.
2. A title to an Equitable right need not be created by any one of the recognised modes by which a title to a legal right is created. This is the most important distinction.

Illustration:

(i) A legal mortgage of land must be created by a deed. But an equitable mortgage may be created otherwise than by deed:

(a) The statute of trade required that no action shall be brought upon any contract or sale of lands or any interest therein unless agreement was in writing and signed by the party or his agent.

But if the title-deeds of an estate are, without even verbal communication, deposited by a debtor in the hands of the creditor, the mere fact of such deposit is enough to constitute the creditor a mortgage of the estate.

(b) An agreement that a creditor shall hold land at a fair rent to be retained in satisfaction of the debt, is a mortgage in equity but not in law.

(ii) Assignment—Legal and Equitable.

*Legal:*

(1) Assignment must be in writing under the hand of the assignor—signature of the agent not sufficient.

(2) The writing must contain a direction or order to the debtor by the creditor to pay the assignee.

(3) There must be express notice of assignment to the debtor.

***Equitable:***

(1) The mode or form of assignment is immaterial provided the intention of the parties is clear. Assignment may be verbal.

(iii) Charge—Legal and Equitable.

(iv) Lease—Equitable and Legal.

(v) Servitude—Equitable and Legal.

## Married Women's Property

This illustrates how an equitable right can arise without the legal formalities of conveyance required for the creation of a legal right.

(1) At Common Law, husband and wife were one person, and the status of the wife merged in that of the husband. The result of this merger was that the husband became the absolute owner of her personal property and acquired the sole right of controlling and managing her real estate. On her death he became absolutely entitled to any of her personal property that had not already been sold and to a life estate by *courtesy* in her fee provided a child had been born.

(2) Secondly, a husband could not make a grant to his wife directly or enter into a covenant with her, for to allow either of these things would have been to suppose her separate existence.

(3) The effect of marriage at Common Law was to make a man complete master of his wife's property and to deprive her of contractual capacity.

(4) If property was given to a married woman by words which indicated either expressly or by implication that she was to enjoy it *"for her sole and separate use"*. Equity removed that property from the control of the husband by regarding him as a trustee, and conferred upon the wife full powers of enjoyment and disposition.

But equity went even further than this. Perceiving the danger that a husband might persuade his wife to sell her separate property and hand the proceeds to him, it permitted the insertion in marriage settlements of what is known as *"restraint upon anticipattion"*. The effect of such restraint, which is still usual, was that a woman while possessing full enjoyment of the income was prevented during her coverture from alienating or charging the corpus of the property. She could devise but could not sell or mortgage it. This was in complete contravention of the Common Law. At Common Law, not only marriage became a vestitive fact giving the husband a title to the property of his wife but no agreement either with the wife or any other person could take away his right to hold and to alienate her property.

This is an illustration which shows that an Equitable right arises in a manner very different from that in which a legal right arises.

Second distinction between a legal right and an equitable right may be formulated thus:

1. A legal right vested in one owner destroys either partially or completely the right vested in its previous owner. The destruction may be complete or may be partial. If it is a lease, it is a partial destruction. If it is a sale, it is a complete destruction. But whether complete or partial, it is destruction. This is what is meant when it is said that a *vestitive fact* is also *divestive* fact.
2. This is not true when there is a competition between a legal right and an equitable right. An equitable right does not destroy a legal right even when it prevails as against the owner of a legal right. In a conflict between a legal and an equitable right, the equitable right does not destroy the legal right, as one legal right does another legal right.
3. *Why is this so*? For this it is necessary to know how an equitable right came to be recognised at the very start by the Court of Chancery. The historical setting may be presented briefly as follows:

   (i) It was a common practice in England before the

Norman conquest for one person to do something *ad opus*—on behalf of another. For instance the Sheriff seized lands and held them *ad opus domini Regis* or where a knight went about to go to the crusades, conveyed his property to a friend to hold it on behalf of his wife and children. The word *opus* became gradually transformed into *use* and the land transferred came to be spoken of as land put in use.

(ii) Now if in certain circumstances some persons could deal with land on behalf of or to the use of another, the question that inevitably occurred to men, why one person should not in a general way be allowed to hold land to the use of another. This as a matter of fact was exactly what was done in course of time. The tenant *A* would transfer his land by a Common Law conveyance to *B,* who undertook to hold it on behalf of, or adopting the correct expression, to the use of A.

In such cases B was called *the feoffee to use,* that is, the person to whom the feoffment had on certain conditions been made, while *A* went by the name of the *Astin que use,* which being interpreted, meant the person on whose behalf the land was held.

(iii) Reasons why this practice grew, are many. There were altogether six reasons why people liked to follow this practice of putting land in use. Of these two are of importance:—

(1) It enabled a party to escape the feudal burdens to which was liable at Common Law. At Common Law the following burdens were placed upon the tenant— (i) *Relief—paid* by a new tenant upon the death of an old tenant. (ii) *Aids*—payable in three cases— (a) to ransom the Lord when imprisoned; (b) when the Lord desired to make his Lord a knight; (c) when the Lord was obliged to supply his eldest daughter with a dowry. (iii) *Escheat—*

The commission by a tenant of a crime serious enough to amount to felony caused the land to escheat. (iv) *Wardship.*—If an existing tenant died leaving as his heir a male under 21 or a female under 14, the Lord was entitled to the wardship of the heir and as a consequence was free to make any use he liked of the lands during the minority without any liability to render accounts. (v) *Marriage*:—To find a suitable match for an infant ward was the right of the Lord, and if the infant ward refused, the Lord was entitled to compensation. The feoffor became free by putting his land in use. The burden fell on the person who acquired *Seisin,* namely, the feofee to uses.

(2) The second advantage was avoidance of forfeiture and escheat. Land held by tenure at Common Law was forfeited to the Crown if the tenant committed high treason, and upon his conviction or on slavery for felony, it escheated to the Lord. These unpleasant consequences were avoided, if a tenant, before embarking upon some doubtful enterprise, had the prescience to vest his lands in a few confidential friends. The deliquent might possibly suffer the extreme penalty, but at least his family would not be destitute.

4. Legal effect of putting lands in use:

(i) The legal consequence of this practice of putting lands in use is an important point to note. It was to cut off the *cestui que use* in the eyes of the Common Law from all connection with the land. By a conveyance operative at Common Law, he had conveyed his estate to the feoffee *to uses* and was, therefore, deprived of all Common Law rights over the land. He was nothing, the feoffee was every thing. Instead of keeping scisin, he chooses to rely upon the confidence which he reposed in the feoffee.

(ii) If the feoffee failed or refused to carry out the directions imposed upon him or if he deliberately alienated the land for his own purposes, there was no Common Law action by which he could be rendered liable.

(iii) If a *cestui que use* was let into possession of the land by the feoffee to uses, he was regarded as a mere tenant at will of the *feoffee to uses* and could be turned out any moment, and in the event of contumacy could be sued in trespass by the feoffee.

5. The nature of the remedy provided by the Court of Chancery to protect the feoffor must be clearly understood:

(i) The Chancellor could not interfere with the jurisdiction of the Common Law Courts by proceeding directly against the land itself because the absolute title to the land was vested in the feoffee by the conveyance. The Chancellor could not disregard the fact that a feoffee was absolute owner at Common Law by virtue of the Common Law conveyance called feoffment whereby the land had been transferred to him.

(ii) The Chancellor distinctly recognised the fact that the feoffee was the owner of the land and had a legal right but what he said to the feoffee was this: "You have the legal right, I do not take it away from you but I will not permit you to exercise that legal right in such a way as to infringe the understanding on which the feoffor made the feoffment."

(iii) The Chancery in assuming jurisdiction over the *use* left untouched and inviolate the legal right of owner at Common Law. It exercised no direct control over the land. It only regulated the mode and manner of the legal right by imposing upon the owner of the legal right an obligation to observe the condition. The legal owner retained his legal right to own and to possess the land. The Chancellor gave the feoffor an equitable right to demand observance of the conditions of feoffment.

6. This is the explanation of that difference between a legal light and an equitable right according to which while one legal right destroys another legal, either partially or wholly, an equitable right does not destroy a legal right.

7. This is also the explanation of the proposition enunciated by Strahanin *Article 11,* namely, that a legal right or interest issues *outflows out* of the property itself while equitable right or interest issues or flows out of the legal interest and not out of the property. This is so because the Chancellor did not recognise the right of the equitable owner to obtain possession of property. That right he retained in the legal owner. What he gave to the equitable owner was the right to impose a duty upon the conduct of the legal owner and he did not give him the right to claim the property itself.

   ***Illustration*:** (1918). *2K.B.* (Ir.)353—Graham vs. Mellwaine.

8. The consequences that follow from this fact may be noted:

   (1) Because an equitable right issues out of a legal right and not out of the property:

      (i) It cannot be greater than the legal estate out of which it issues. *Illustration:* Land conveyed to *A* for the use of *B* and his heirs. *A* is the legal owner of the land. *B* is the equitable owner.

      But land is conveyed to A and not to A and his heirs. Consequently the legal right of *A* vanishes at his death. As *A's* legal right vanishes so does *B's* equitable right An equitable interest cannot survive the legal interest out of which it flows, *(1914) i Ch. 300*

      (ii) Equitable right will be affected by all the infirmities attaching to the legal right

> *A* died intestate leaving B and C as his sons, B being the eldest.
>
> *B* being away C takes possession and transfers it to *D* for the use of his wife *E*.
>
> *B* returns and claims the property. The legal title of *D* comes to an end by reason of the flaw in C's title.
>
> The equitable estate of *E*, the wife of C, also comes to an end.

The third difference between a Legal Right and an Equitable Right is that, a legal right may be a right in *rem* or may be a right in *personam.* But an equitable right is always a right in *personam.* Who is bound to respect the right of an Equitable owner? Not the world but the legal owner and no one else.

It is true, the legal owner, who is bound, is not the legal owner against whom the equitable right first arose but includes also every legal owner to whom the right is transferred.

All the same the proposition stands that an Equitable Right is a right in *personam* which binds only the legal owner.

Explain, "Equitable rights have a resemblance to rights in rem."

(i) It is true that Equitable Rights have a resemblance to rights *in rem.*

(ii) How does this resemblance arise?

An equitable right will be enforced not only against the owner of legal right but it will be enforced against:

(a) his representatives and volunteers claiming through or under him,

(b) persons who acquire the legal right

  (i) with the knowledge of the legal right,

  (ii) against those who could have had knowledge.

  (iii) The standard of knowledge set up by the Court of Chancery was so high that no one could escape and every purchaser was bound.

## Equitable Priorities

1. An equitable right is a right *in personam*—operating against the owner of a legal right out of which it flows.
2. There may be two equitable rights flowing out of one legal right. Both would be rights in *personam* against the owner of the legal right out of which they flow.
3. An equitable right being a right in *personam* arising out of the legal and not out of the property which is the object of the legal right, could be defeated by transferring the legal right to a new owner. Or another equitable right may arise by this transfer which may defeat the prior equitable right.
4. The question to be considered is, in what cases can such a transfer defeat an equitable right?
5. The subject is discussed generally under the heading of *Equitable Priorities.* It is so designated because the test applied for the determination of the issue is the priority in time. But the real subject matter is the possible cases where an equitable right can be defeated by transfer of a legal right out of which it arises or by the creation of another equitable right out of the same legal right?
6. Cases to be considered fall under two classes:
   (i) Cases where there is a conflict between Legal Right and an Equitable Right
   (ii) Cases where there is a conflict between two equitable rights.
7. Under the first class of cases there are two contingencies which must be distinguished:
   (a) Where the 'Equitable Right is prior in existence to the legal right (b) Where an equitable right arises subsequently to the legal right.

   Mrs. Thorndike was the beneficiary of a certain Trust Fund of which C was a trustee. In a suit by Mrs. Thomdike, the Court directed the Trustee to transfer of the fund into the Court for the purposes of the Thorndike Trust and was held by the Administrator. It appeared that the Trustees against whom the order was made had provided themselves improperly with the means of discharging themselves from their personal liability to bring the fund into Court and that there are third persons whom they had injured. The third party so injured filed a suit praying that the fund held in the name of Thorndyke should be transferred to them. *Contention:* Legal title not in Mrs. Thorndyke and therefore, her right could not prevail. Contention disallowed. Held, not necessary to acquire legal title personally. Also no notice.

8. Altogether we shall have three questions to consider which may be formulated thus:
   (i) Whether a person who acquires a legal right will be subject to a prior equitable right?
   (ii) Whether a person who has acquired a legal right will be postponed to an equitable right arising subsequently.
   (iii) Where neither party has a legal right and both have only equitable rights, which of them will have priority?

Whether a person who has acquired a legal right will be subject to a prior equitable right?

1. The answer to this question is this: A purchaser obtaining a legal estate for valuable consideration and without notice of a prior equitable right will not be bound by the equitable right.
2. There are three important elements in this proposition: (1) *Purchaser must have acquired a legal Estate.*— There is not much to be said about this. But the following points may be noted:
   (a) It is not necessary that he should acquire the legal estate personally. It is enough if somebody does it on his behalf. Thorndike vs. Hunt, (1859) 3 De.g. 1. 563 =44 ER. 1386.

(b) The purchaser's title need not be *a perfect title.*

*Illus.:* If a trustee's title to property is defective, he may never the less convey to a *bonafide* purchaser an interest which will be effective against the beneficiary who is the owner of a prior equitable right.

Jones vs. Powles (1834) 3 My & K.581.

### *Facts*

1. *John Jones* Owner—Mortgaged his house to Holbrook, redeemed it, obtained acknowledgement of payment—-but did not obtain reconveyance. The legal estate remained outstanding in Holbrook.
2. On the death of Jones Meredith, his shop assistant forged a will of Jones and on its vests obtained possession of the house.
3. Meredith mortgaged it to Hall by a conveyance.
4. Meredith died leaving his wife to whom he left the equity of redemption by a will and thereafter to James Jones.
5. James Jones conveyed it to Watkins.
6. James Jones & Watkins became partners and mortgaged the property to *Powles* who acquired possession as mortgagee.
7. Powles died leaving his wife *Sarah.*
8. Sara Powles secured surrender of the estate and full ownership.
9. Sara Jones sued Sara Powles alleging that the will was a forgery and that Sara Powles had notice and that she could not defeat her right to redeem. (c) The purchaser should obtain a legal right. But this may be:
   (i) at the time of his purchase, or
   (ii) he may get it subsequently.

The purchaser must have given valuable consideration for his right.

A volunteer is always subject to an equitable right. The reason is that he does not suffer by being made liable to the prior equitable right not having paid any consideration.

An existing debt is, however, sufficient consideration.

***Illus. Thorndike vs. Hunt.***

T had paid no consideration. His right was a sort of an existing debt against the trustee.

The purchaser must have acquired the right without notice of the existence of the prior equitable right.

This is the most (important) element in the proposition and the question that arises for consideration is: (further portion not found—ed.)

## *What is Notice?*

1. Notice may be *Direct* or *Imputed,* Direct notice is notice to the purchaser himself. Imputed notice is notice to the agent of the purchaser.
2. Direct Notice may be *actual* or *constructive:*
   (1) Actual notice is where the matter is *within* the knowledge of the purchaser or his agent.
   (2) Constructive notice (is) where it would have come to his own knowledge or to the knowledge of his agent if proper inquiries had been made.

## *Actual Notice*

1. If reliance is placed upon actual notice to defeat a legal right it must be proved that:
   (i) It was given by a person interested in the property;
   (ii) it was given in the course of negotiations;
   (iii) it was clear and distinct.

## *Constructive Notice*

1. Constructive Notice arises where there is notice of a fact or facts from which notice of the existence of an equitable right could be presumed. It is not notice but evidence of notice.

2. There are three varieties of constructive notice:

   (i) Where there is actual notice of a fact which would have led to the notice of the existence of the right, *Bisco vs. Earl of Banbury (1676) 6) 7 Ch. Ca. 287.*

The purchaser had actual notice of a specific mortgage but did not inspect the mortgage-deed which referred to other rights and encumbrances.

He was held to be bound by other encumbrances for he would have discovered their existence if he had inspected the deed as any prudent man would have done. *Davis vs. llutchings, 1907 I Ch. 356..*

A trustee transferred a share of the beneficiary to the Solicitor relying upon the statement made by him that it was assigned. They did not call for the assignment. The assignment was subject to a charge in favour of another. *Held* they had constructive notice of the charge.

***Occupation of tenant as Constructive Notice***

Where land is in the occupation of some one other than the vendor, the fact of the occupation gives the purchaser constructive notice of any right of the occupying tenant.

It will not amount to notice of a third person's right—9. Moo. *P. C.* 18.

We now come to the parole evidence of notice. Upon this subject the rule is settled, that a purchaser is not bound to attend to vague rumours about purchaser—to statements by mere strangers, but that a notice in order to be binding must proceed from some person interested in the property:

R. 3 Ch. App. 488 *LIoyd* vs. *Banks* Carries j—1868

If he attempts to prove knowledge of the trustee *Aliunde,* the difficulty which this Court always feel in attending to what are called casual conversations or in attending to any kind of intimation which will put the trustee in a less favourable position as regards his mode of action than he would have been in if he had got a distinct and clear notice from the encumbrances. At the same time I am bound to say that I do not think it would be consistent with the principles upon which this Court has always proceeded, or with the authorities which have been referred to, if I were to hold that under no circumstances could a trustee without express notice from the encumbrancer be fixed with knowledge of the encumbrance. — *Illus..-9 Moo. P. C. 18 Barnhart vs. Greenshields.*

Where it was held that vague reports from persons not interested in the property will not affect the purchaser's conscience.

Should notice be directly from the Encumbrancer?

A purchaser cannot safely disregard information, from whatever source it may come. It is of such a nature that a reasonable man of business would act upon that information even if it came from a newspaper report.

S.*R. 3 Ch. App. 488* 1868.

## *Registration*

The registration of any instrument or matter required or authorised to be registered by law is to be deemed to constitute actual notice of such *instrument* or *matter* but not necessarily of its contents.

(ii) Where inquiry is purposely avoided to escape being bound by notice.

1. John Towsey contracted for the purchase of certain property in 1776.
2. He borrowed the amount of purchase money from one Dr. P, and placed the title-deeds in his hands as a security for repayment.
3. In 1790, T was very much indebted to one Ellames in a considerable sum of money and executed a mortgage of the same property to Ellames.
4. Dr. P did not give any information of his claim to Ellames.
5. Ellames said that he made no inquiries after the title-deeds before he took the security,

and admitted that upon executing the mortgage he inquired for them, and was informed of their being in the hands of Dr. P. but that he understood them to be so for safe custody only.

6. He received this information from one J. who was his brother-in-law, who had prepared the mortgage and appeared as his agent at the time of the execution of it.
7. Dr. P claimed priority over Ellames. It was granted as Ellames was held to have had notice.

(iii) Where there is gross negligence in not making usual and proper inquiries:

1899. 2 Ch. 264

1921. I Ch. 98.

## *Imputed Notice*

I. The underlying theory of agency is that a man can do a thing by an agent which he can do himself. Conversely, what is done by the agent is done by him. This being so, it is open to argument that what is known to the agent must be taken to be known to the Principal. This is the theory on which the doctrine of imputed notice is founded.

## *The Essentials of Imputed Notice*

1. *The knowledge must have come to him as an agent* and not in any other capacity. In other words, agency must be strictly proved.

   Dyllie vs. Pollen—32 L. J. Ch. 782 (N. S.)
2. Agent must be distinguished from a person employed to do merely ministerial act—*e.g.* a person employed to procure a deed is an agent.

   Knowledge to such a person cannot be the basis of imputed notice.
3. In this connection, the position (of) a person who is in the service of two Principals as their agent has to be

considered. Suppose, there are two companies, A and B, and C is an officer employed in both A & B. Suppose that A company transferred their legal right to B company which was subject to an equitable right in favour of D of which C had knowledge.

Can D say that B company had notice of his equitable right because C, their agent, had notice of it in his capacity as the agent of A?

The answer is that, his knowledge which had acquired as agent of A company, will not be imputed to B company unless he owes a duty to the A company to communicate his knowledge and also a duty to the B company to receive the notice.

(1896) 2 Ch. 743—In *Re Hampshire Land Company. Facts:*

1. Hampshire Land Company was registered under the Companies Act, 1870.
2. The Company was closely interconnected with the Port Sea Island Building Society. Four Directors and a Secretary by name Wills were common to both.
3. On the 19th February 1881, a general meeting of the Company was held at which a resolution was passed authorising the Directors to borrow 30,000 £.
4. The Directors borrowed this amount from the Port Sea Society.
5. The Society went into liquidation in 1892. The Liquidator of the Society sought to claim the sum of £ 30,000 lent to the company.
6. It was contended that the resolution of the company authorising borrowing was *ultra vires* and that because William, the Secretary was a common officer notice to him was notice to Society and therefore Society could not recover.
7. *Held* that the Society could *recover* for reasons at p. 749.

The notice to the agent must have been obtained by him *in the same* transaction and not *in a previous* transaction.

There is a further qualification. Even if the notice was acquired by the agent in the *same* transaction, it will not be imputed to the purchaser, unless it is so material to the transaction as to make it the duty of the agent to communicate it to the principal.

(1886)—31 Ch. D. 671—In Re Cousins.

***Facts:***

1. In 1871, one William's cousins made a will of his property and left it in trust to his trustees.
2. One William Banks was a solicitor for the trustees.
3. Mathew, a cousin was to receive a share in the proceeds of real and personal property left by William's cousins under the will.
4. Mathew mortgaged his share to William Banks, the Solicitor as security for a loan of £ 35.
5. In 1873, Mathew mortgaged his share to William Richardson through Banks and Banks was paid off.
6. In 1874' Richardson transferred his mortgage to William Drake. No Notice was given to the Trustees.
7. In 1875 Mathew mortgaged his share to Dennis Pepper to secure a payment of £ 500. Banks acted as the Solicitor. The mortgage to Dennis Pepper did not mention the previous mortgage to William Drake. Subsequently a notice of this transaction was given to the Trustee.
8. Drake took out a summons for payment of his mortgage debt due from Mathew out of the funds in the hands of the Trustee in *priority* to Pepper's claim. *1884. 26 Ch. D. 482*
9. Pepper's contention was that, he had no notice of Drake's claim—Mathew not having mentioned it in his deed of mortgage.
10. It was replied by Drake that Pepper had notice because Banks, the Solicitor who acted as his agent knew of Mathews mortgage to Drake.

11. That Banks had notice, it was not denied. That Banks was the agent of Pepper was not denied. But the question was whether notice to Banks can be held to be notice to Pepper.

12. *Held:* No—p. 677.

    *Reasons.* The knowledge of Banks did not arise in the course of the transaction with Pepper in 1875. Pepper could not be said to have any notice.

13. Pepper's claim was allowed.

Notice to agent will not be imputed to the purchaser when the agent is shown to have intended a fraud on the principal which would require the suppression of his knowledge and not communicate it to the Principal.

(1880) 15 Ch. D. 629 Cane vs. Cave.

(1428) ACI—Houghton & Co vs. Nolhard)

*Where an equitable right has come into being subsequently to the acquisition of a legal right.*

1. Leading case on the question is *Northern countries of England Fire Insurance Co.* vs. *Whip?.*

   1884 26 Ch. D. 482

### *Facts*

C, the Manager of a company, executed a legal mortgage to his company, delivered title-deeds. They were kept in a safe of the company, the key to which was in C's possession. C— some time after took out the title-deeds and created another mortgage on the same property in favour of Mrs. Whipp. Mrs. Whipp has no notice of the first mortgage to the Company. *Held:* Company entitled to priority.

2. The proposition laid down in the case is this— Where the owner of a legal estate has assisted in or connived at the fraud which has laid to the creation of a subsequent equitable estate and the owner of equitable estate had no notice of the prior legal right, the Court will postpone the legal estate to the equitable estate although it is subsequent in its origin.

3. What is the evidence of assistance in or connivance at fraud:
   (i) Omission to use ordinary care in inquiry after title-deeds.
   (ii) Failing to take delivery in title-deeds are treated as evidence of assistance in or connivance at fraud where such conduct cannot otherwise be explained.
4. The same authority lays down another case in which also a legal estate will be postponed to a subsequent equitable estate.

   Where the mortgagee, the owner of the legal estate has constituted the mortgagor, his agent with authority to raise money on the property mortgaged and the estate created has by the fraud or misconduct of the agent been represented as being the first estate.
5. For the operation of this rule, mere carelessness or want of prudence on the part of the legal owner will not be a sufficient ground. There must be fraud and connivance at or assistance therein. Nothing but fraud I will postpone.

   *(1913)* 2 *Ch. 18.*

Where the competition is between two equitable **rights.**

1. In the two former cases the competition was between a legal right and an equitable right. In the third case the competition is between two equitable rights.

   *Cave vs. Cave.* (1880) 15 Ch.D. 639.

***Facts:***

*A* Trustee & *B* a beneficiary.

*A* purchased land from trust-monies in breach of trust and executed a legal mortgage thereof to *C*.

*C* had no notice of the trust.

Later by an equitable mortgage transferred the same land to There are three persons who have acquired rights. C, who has a legal right, is mortgagee, being a legal mortgage.

*B* has an equitable right flowing out of A's right which has been transferred.

*D* has an equitable right flowing out of A's right.

What is the position of the parties?

1. As between *C* and B, although B's Equitable right is prior to C's legal right as C had no notice, C takes priority.
2. As between *C* and D, C takes priority, because C is not party to a fraud in creating the rights of D.
3. As between *B* and *D,* their rights are equitable rights: whose right prevails? B's right. The rule is that where there is a competition between two equitable rights, the right earlier in origin prevails over the subsequent right.
4. This rule applies only where the equitable rights have equal equities on their side. If the equities are unequal, the better of the two prevails.

   *Rice* vs. *Rice.* 2. Drewry, 73 (76-78).

   *A* sells land to *B* and without receiving purchase money (1) conveys land to B, (2) signs a receipt for moneys and (3) delivers title-deeds to B. *B* subsequently mortgages the property to *C* who has no notice *of A's* claim. Between *A* and *C* although *A's* equitable right is earlier than that of C, yet the equities are unequal. *A* is guilty of negligence, therefore, *C's* Equity is better and will prevail although later in time.
5. In some cases conflict as to priority between two equitable interests by the respective times at which the interest was transferred. In other cases, it is determined by the respective times at which written notice is given to the proper person or persons of the interest transferred (*e.g.* in the case of the assignment of chose in action).

*Sum up.* Three maxims of Equity.

1. Where equities are equal, the law prevails.
2. Where equities are equal, the first in time prevails.
3. Where equities are unequal, the better equity prevails.

### *Explanation*

1. The first proposition has reference to cases where there is conflict between an equitable right and a legal right and applies to both classes of cases: (1) where the equitable right is prior to the legal right as well as to cases (2) where the equitable right is subsequent to the legal right.
2. Law prevails means that legal right prevails over an equitable right where no inequity can be attributed to the owner of a legal right. — Such as notice or fraud.
3. Propositions two & three have reference to cases where there is a conflict between two *equitable rights.*

## *Equitable Assignment*

### *I. General*

1. Although the subject is called Equitable Assignment, it is an abbreviation. The subject is equitable assignment of a chose in action.
2. There are three matters of a preliminary character which must be dealt with at the outset:

### *What is an Assignment*

1. Under the English Law of Property, property is classified as *Realty and Personality.*
2. In connection with the transfer of rights over Realty, the word used is *Conveyance.* In connection with the transfer of rights over Personality, the word used is either *Transfer* or *Assignment.*
3. Assignment, therefore, means the transfer by a person of his rights over personal property and particularly one form of it, namely, *chose in action.*

### *What is a Chose in Act on*

1. Under the English Nomenclature, Personality is divisible into two classes:
   (i) Moveable goods of which one can take physical possession.

(ii) Personal rights of property which car only be claimed or enforced by action and not by taking physical possession.

2. The former are called: (i) Chooses in Possession—Things in Possession. (ii) Choses in Action—-Things in Action.
3. The definition of a chose in action— *(1902) 2 K.B. 427 (430) ChannellJ.* It is really speaking a debt.
4. The word assignment is used in respect of chose in action. It is something which you can only sign it away if you want to transfer it. You cannot deliver possession of it.

## *Necessity of Studying Equitable Assignment*

1. An assignment is a transfer of a right by its owner, subsisting against another, to a third person to whom the person against whom it was subsisting, becomes bound.

   *Illustration.* *A* is creditor. *B* is debtor. *A* assigns his right to debt against *B* to *C:B* becomes bound to *C* and *C* gets a right to recover it from *B*.
2. Three persons are involved in an assignment: (i) The original owner. (ii) The person bound to the original owner. (iii) The person to whom the original owner has transferred the right.
3. The right, *i.e.*, the chose in action may be legal or equitable such as a legacy or an interest in a trust fund.
4. Assignment of a chose in action was differently treated by Equity and by the Common Law.

## *Common Law and Chose in Action*

1. There could be no assignment in Common Law of a Chose in action. Not only there could be no assignment of an equitable chose, there could be no assignment even of a legal chose.
2. The reason was the fear of multiplicity of suits.
3. Statute law and Special law made certain kinds of Choses of action assignable:

(i) Negotiable Instruments became assignable by the law merchant

(ii) Policies of Life Insurance and Marine Insurance were made assignable by Statute.

(iii) Section 25(6) of the Judicature Act: all legal Choses in Action have been made assignable.

## *Equity and Chose in Action*

1. In Equity, a chose in action was always assignable. Not only an equitable Chose was assignable in Equity but a legal Chose was also assignable in Equity.
2. If the Chose was equitable, the assignee could bring his proceedings to recover it in a Court of Chancery in his own name.
3. If it was a legal Chose, the proceedings had to be taken in the name of the assignor and the way the Court of Chancery interfered, was to restrain the assignor from objecting to this use of his name on the assignee giving him a proper indemnity against costs.
4. There were, however, some Choses in action to the assignment of which equity did not give effect on the ground of public policy:

   (i) Assignment of pay and half pay of public officers paid out of the National Exchequer.

   (ii) Assignment of alimony to a wife.

   (iii) Assignment affected by maintenance of property.

## *Conclusion*

1. There are thus two ways of making an assignment— (i) Legal, (ii) Equitable.
2. Although the Judicature Act has laid down the form and procedure for the legal Assignment of a legal Chose, it has not abrogated the rules of Chancery relating to Equitable assignment of a legal Chose. So that if an assignment is ineffective in law by reason of some defect, it will be good if it conforms with the rules of

equity. Secondly, the Judicature does not touch the assignment of an Equitable Chose in action.

***Categories of Cases to be Considered:*** There are three categories of cases to be considered in connection with the assignment of a Chose in action:

(i) Legal assignment of a legal Chose in action.

(ii) Equitable assignment of a legal Chose in action.

(iii) Equitable assignment of an Equitable Chose in action.

***Requisites of a Legal Assignment of a Legal Chose***

1. Assignment must be absolute, *i.e.,* it must amount to a *complete* divesting of his right by the assignor. The debt must be certain and must be of the whole amount.
2. The assignment must be in writing signed by the assignor. It need not be by deed. It need not be for value.
3. Express notice must be given to the debtors of the assignment.

The Section does not say:

(i) By whom is notice to be given—by the assignor or assignee.

(iii) At what time notice is to be given so that it may be given by the assignee after the death of the assignor.

## *Effect of Want of Notice*

1. Absence of notice does not disentitle an assignee of suing on the assignment. It only imposes certain disabilities and results in certain disadvantages.

(i) The assignee cannot sue the debtor in his own name without making the original creditor a party to the action.

(ii) The assignee will be subject to equities arising between the debtor and his original creditor before the date of the assignment and will lose his right against the debtor altogether if the debtor pays the original creditor. On the other hand, if the debtor pays the original *creditor* after receiving notice of assignment, the *assignee* could still recover the debt from him.

(iii) The assignee, who fails to give notice to the debtor of his assignment, will be postponed to a subsequent assignee for value who has no notice of the previous assignment, and gives notice of his assignment to the debtor.

## *Requisites of an Equitable Assignment of a Legal Chose in Action*

An Assignment which does not comply with the statutory requirements is not necessarily ineffectual, for it may operate as an Equitable Assignment.

Two things are necessary:

(1) There must be value given by the assignor.

(2) A charge created by agreement between the debtor and the creditor upon specific funds or by an order given to the creditor upon a person holding money belonging to the debtor, will amount to an assignment.

1839. *Burn vs. Carvallo 4 Hylve & Craigs Reports. 690*

***Facts:***

*F* was in the habit of sending consignments of goods to *R*, who was trading in a different town and used to draw Bills of Exchange upon *R*. It was arranged by *F* with *B & Co.* that they should endorse and negotiate his Bills drawn upon *R* against consignment and they were to credit him with the amount and he was to draw upon it and *B & Co.* was reimburse itself by recovering the amount from *R*. *F* drew for certain amounts on *B & Co.* But *R* failed to meet the Bills on maturity.

*F*, who was the debtor of the *B & Co.* by a letter to *B & Co.* promised that he would direct and by a subsequent letter did direct to deliver the goods to *V* as the agent *of B & Co.*

*F* wrote to *R* to transfer the goods in his possession to *V*, the agent of B & Co. in the town. *R* accordingly delivered the goods to *V* on the 30th of June 1829.

On the 23rd of June 1829, F was adjudged insolvent for an act done on the 23rd of May 1829. His trustee in bankruptcy sued for the recovery of the value of the goods from *B & Co. B & Co.* contended that there was an equitable assignment of the value of the goods by *F. Held* the order of the debtor was a good assignment in Equity.

***Rodick* vs. *Gandell.***

(1851-2) I Degex.763. 42.E.R.749

Gandell was an Engineer and was indebted to a certain Bank for a large amount and the Bank was pressing for payment.

Gandell was a creditor of a Railway Co. To induce the Bank not to press for payment and also to pay other drafts outstanding against him, it was arranged that Gandell should instruct his Solicitor to recover the amount due to Gandell from the Railway Co. and pay it to the Bank. G, by a letter to the Solicitors of the Company, authorised them to receive the money due to him from the Railway Co. and requested them to pay it to the Bankers. The Solicitors by letter promised the Bankers to pay such money on receiving it.

Why—no agreement between debtor and creditor. The Solicitor recovered the amount from the Railway Co. but instead of paying it to the Bank, paid it to Gandell. Gandell became insolvent and his property was taken possession of by the official assignee. The Bank sued for a declaration that there was an equitable assignment by Gandell of his funds claimable from the Railway in favour of the Bank and collected by the Solicitor and the Bank was therefore entitled to recover the amount from the official assignee. *Held* this was not an equitable assignment. It was not an order given by the debtor to his creditor upon a person owning money or holding funds belonging to the debtor directing the *person* to pay such funds to the Creditor.

There must be *privity* between the *assignor* and *assignee* in order to constitute an equitable assignment. If there is no privity then there is no assignment even in equity.

Consequently, if the Principal directs his agent to collect

money owing to the principal and pay it to a third person, such third person is not an assignee in equity if the mandate is not communicated to him. It may be revoked by the principal.

Similarly a Power of attorney or authority to collect money and to pay it to the creditor of the party granting the power does not amount to an equitable assignment. A cheque is not an equitable assignment or appropriation of money in the drawer's Bank.

***Hopkinson* vs. *Forster, (1874) L. R.19 Eq.74.***

There can be no valid appropriation or assignment if no specific fund is specified out of which the payment is to be made.

***Percival* vs. *Dunn. (1885) 29 Ch. D. 128***

Whether notice is necessary in the case of an equitable assignment?

1. An equitable assignment is complete between the assignor and assignee although no notice is given to the debtor.
2. Notice of the assignment should, however, be given to the debtor for two reasons.
   (i) If there is no notice, the debtor will be free to pay to the assignor, the original creditor and will not be liable to the assignee. On the other hand, if he pays to the assignor in disregard of the notice, he will be liable to pay over again to the assignee.

***Stocks* vs. *Dobson (1853) 4 De. G. M & G. II***

   (ii) If there is no notice, then the assignee will not be allowed to have priority over subsequent assignee of the same chose in action by the same assignor.

This is called the rule in Dearl vs. Hall (1823) 1 Rsess 1=S. F. C. p. 57.

***Facts:***

Peter Brown died and left a Will whereby he made a trust of his personal estate and of the monies to arise from the sale of his real estate and directed his executors to invest the same and pay interest to his son Zachariah Brown during his life. The income came to about £ 93 a year,

On 19th December 1808, Brown, in consideration of £204 paid to him by William Dearle, assigned a part of his annuity of £ 37. On 26th September 1809, Brown, in consideration of £ 150, assigned another part of his annuity of £27 to Sherring, subject to the assignment in favour of Dearle.

Neither Dearle nor Sherring had given notice of assignment to the executor.

In 1812 Brown advertised the life interest of 93 pounds p. a. in trust funds for sale as an unencumbered fund.

Joseph Hall proposed to purchase it and through his Solicitor investigated Brown's title. He also made inquiries of the executors, who knew of no encumbrance affecting Brown's interest. Thereupon Hall purchased Brown's interest for £711-3-6 and had it assigned to him.

On the 25th April 1812, Hall gave the executors written notice of the assignment to him.

On the 27th October 1812, Dearle and Sherring gave notice of their assignment to the executors.

The executors refused to pay any one of the three until their rights were decided.

Dearle and Sherring brought a Bill in chancery against Hall praying that the income of £ 93 should be applied in satisfying their's before that of Joseph Hall.

Dearle contended that the doctrine *first in time is first in law* should be applied and as he was first he should be preferred to Hall.

Held No. Hall should be preferred.

***Judgement of Plumer M. R. S. & C. p. 55***

The rule was based on carelessness and negligence to perfect one's claim. But the rule is now absolute and independent of conduct. The assignee who gives proper notice first will be paid first, whether the other assignee has been guilty of carelessness nor not.

***Re Dallas. (1904). 2Ch. 385.***

The rule in Dearle *vs.* Hall has always applied to assignment of all equitable interests in personality.

To whom notice should be given under the rule in Dearle vs. Hall

1. It must be given to the debtor, trustee or other person whose duty it is to pay the money to the assignor. *Stephens* vs. *Green, (1895) 2 Ch. 148*
2. Notice to the Solicitor will be effectual only if Solicitor was expressly or impliedly authorised to receive it. *(1880) 14 Ch. D. 406.*
3. If there are several debtors or trustees, notice to one is notice to all.
4. Fresh notice to new trustees is not necessary, if notice is given to old trustees.

***What should be the Form of Notice***

1. Formerly, notice need not be a formal notice and might have been by word of mouth.
2. But since 1925, it must be in writing.

What title is acquired by the assignee by an Equitable assignment.

1. It has always been the rule of equity that the assignee of a thing in action cannot acquire a better right than the assignor had.
2. In other words, the assignee takes it subject to all the equities affecting it in the hands of the assignor.

*Roxburghe* vs. *Cox, (1881) 17 Ch. D.* 520. So that:

(1) If the Contract between the assignor and the debtor was violable, the debtor can set up the violable character of the contract against the assignee, even if the assignment was for valuable consideration.

(2) If the debtor had a right of set-off against the assignor, the same would be available to him against the assignee.

(3) The assignee is, however, free from equities arising after notice.

A debtor cannot diminish the rights of the assignee such as they are, on the date of notice, by any act done after date of notice.

### *Assignment of Rights to be Acquired in Future*

1. So far, we have dealt with assignments of rights which had accrued when the assignment had taken place.
2. We must consider the assignment of rights to be acquired in future.
3. Example of such rights: (i) The expectancy of an heir-at-law to succeed to the Estate. (ii) The expectancy of a next of kin to succeed to personality. (iii) Freight not yet earned. (iv) Future Book-debts.
4. At Common Law, they were all void. A man could not assign what he had not got. In equity, they were assignable, if for valuable consideration.
5. Equity treated them not as assignments but as *contracts to assign,* and when the assignee became possessed of it, he was compelled to perform *his* contract.
6. When the right was acquired by the assignor, the beneficial interest passed immediately to the assignee. But the legal interest remained with the assignor. So that, if the assignor transferred it to a subsequent assignee who gave value and had no-notice of the previous assignment, the title of the subsequent assignee would prevail.

### *Conversion*

#### *Necessity for the Doctrine of Conversion*

1. The English Law had prescribed a different mode of devolution of the *Realty* and *Personality* of the owner, if he died *intestate.* His Realty went to his heir and *Personality* went to his *next-of-kin.*
2. That being so, whether the property will go to the heir or to the next of kin must depend upon the state of the property on the date on which the succession opens.

3. Ordinarily there is no difficulty. The actual state in which the property will be found on the material date will determine its devolution. But suppose, circumstances are such that on the date on which the succession opens, land *is to be sold* for money *but is not sold*, or money is *to be invested* in the purchase of land *but is not so invested,* how is the devolution of the property to be determined? If the land is to be treated as land, until it is actually sold, then it will go to the heir. On the other hand, if it is to be treated as money, because it was intended to be sold for money, then although it is land, it will go to the next-of-kin. In other words, the question was whether property was to devolve according to the actual state in which it is found to exist or according to the form in which it was intended to be converted. The answer given by equity was, that property was to devolve, not according to the actual state in which it exists, but according to the form in which it was intended to be converted.
4. This is what is called the **doctrine of conversion.** There would have been no necessity for the doctrine had there been no difference in the rules of inheritance for Real and Personal Property. This difference is now abolished by Sections 33,45 and therefore, conversion has lost all its importance.
5. In India there is no such distinction in the inheritance of property—Realty to heir and Personality to next-of-kin.

There are four cases which give rise to conversion.

(1) By operation of the law.

(2) By operation of the order of the Court.

(3) By operation of a Contract.

(4) By operation of a direction in a deed or a will.

### *Conversion by Operation of the Law*

1. There is only one case in which conversion takes place by operation of the Law. That case is the case of Partners. Under the Partnership Act of 1890, Section

39, every partner has a right to require, that the property belonging to the Partnership shall be sold and the proceeds, after the discharge of all debts and liabilities, shall be divided among the partners according to their shares in the capital. As a result, land which is partnership property is treated as Personality and not as Realty.

2. It is treated as Personality, not only as between Partners themselves and their representatives after death, for the purposes of distribution of the partnership assets, but it is also treated as personality for purposes of inheritance as between the persons entitled to the property of a deceased partner.
3. The conversion of Realty into Personality under the Partnership Act takes place not on the date of the dissolution of the Partnership or the death of a partner but at the moment when it became Partnership Property.
4. The doctrine of conversion applies to Partnership Realty unless the contrary intention appears. The reason why partnership agreements convert Realty into Personality is, because a partner ordinarily is not entitled on dissolution to any specific part of the partnership property. But there may be a proviso in the partnership agreement permitting a partner to have specific property, in which case conversion will not apply, there being intention to the contrary.

### *Conversion by Order of the Court*

1. Where an order is made by the Court for the sale of Realty, the Realty is treated as being converted into Personality for purposes of succession to the estate of the person whose property was ordered to be sold.

   *Illus.* A B C have equal shares in a Realty. The Court orders the sale of the Realty. This order has the effect of converting their shares in Realty into Personality, so that the persons entitled to succeed would be the next of kin and not the heir.

2. The following points must be noted:
   (i) The order for sale must be within the jurisdiction of the Court
   (ii) It is immaterial whether the purpose for which it is sold will or will not exhaust the sale proceeds. The sale may be merely to pay cost. All the same, if the order is for sale, within the jurisdiction, it will effect conversion
   (iii) It is immaterial whether it is actually sold or is merely ordered to be sold. Order for sale is enough to effect conversion.
   (iv) Conversion takes place from the dale of the order and not from the date of the sale.
3. There are two cases in which the order of the Court will not effect conversion for the purpose of inheritance.
   (i) Where the Court itself makes an order that such change in the nature of the property shall not affect its devolution on death, in which case the sale proceeds will go to the heir and not to the next-of-kin.
   (ii) Where the provision of some statute prohibits a change in the nature of the property from affecting its devolution *e.g.* Section 123 of the Lunacy Act, 1890, which provides that if the property of a lunatic is sold, the proceeds will go to persons entitled to them as though it was not sold.

### *Conversion by Operation of a Contract*

1. When there is a binding contract to sell Realty, the Realty is treated as part of vendors Personality. Conversely, the interest of the purchaser is treated as Realty, even if he dies before completion.
2. This is, however, subject to one condition. That is, the contract must be one of which specific performance would be ordered by the Court—*34 Ch. D. 166.*

   Mere notice to treat does not suffice to bring into operation the doctrine of conversion. There will be no conversion if the contract is abortive or unenforceable.

***Conversion under a Contract to Lease with an Option to Purchase***

*A* leases certain property *to B* for seven years, giving him by the lease an option to purchase the property at a certain price during the term. *B* exercises his option.

Three questions arise:

***Does the Exercise of the Option Effect a Conversion?***

In law, the option given is an offer to sell. The exercise of the option is an acceptance of the offer and when there is an acceptance of the offer, there is a contract. The exercise of the option by respiting in a contract effects a conversion. The answer to the first question is therefore in the affirmative.

***Exercise of the Option before the Death of the Lessee and After the Death of the Lessor***

1. If the Lessee exercises his option *before* the death of the Lessor, *i.e.*, while he is alive, then there is conversion, because the offer conveyed by the option can be legally accepted and a binding contract can arise.
2. If the lessee exercises the option *after* the death, then, on principle, there ought not to be conversion, because there cannot be a contract. An offer cannot be accepted after the person, who make the offer, is dead. But in *Lawes* vs. *Benett* (1785) 1 Cax 167, it was held that the exercise of the option, even *after the* lessor's death, is good for the purposes of conversion.
3. The rule in *Lawes vs. Benett* being anomalous, is confined in its operation. It is applied as between persons claiming under the lessor. But it is not made applicable as between lessor and lessee.

***Illus.*** A leased certain property to B with an option to purchase. The premises were insured. They are destroyed by fire *before* the option is exercised by B. B, on exercising the option, cannot claim the insurance money as part of his purchase. That is claim as between A and B (1878)7Ch.D.858, 10 Ch. D. App. 386.

From what date does conversion by contract begin to operate.

1. Conversion becomes operative from the moment when the contract is made.
2. In the case of option to purchase, conversion takes place as from the execution of the lease.
3. For the purposes of profits etc., the property remains real estate until the option is exercised, so that the rents and profits are taken by the heir entitled to Realty.
4. For the purposes of devolution it is personality.

***Conversion by Direction of the Owner:*** Whether contained in a deed or a will.

1. Two things are necessary for conversion by deed or will: (i) There must be a direction to sell or purchase Realty. (ii) There must be some person in existence who can be said to have the right to insist upon the direction being carried out. Conversion is always for the benefit of some person. If there is no person to claim the benefit, then there need be no conversion.
2. In order to effect a conversion, the direction must be imperative. If direction is only *optional*, there will be no conversion and property will be treated as real or personal, according as to the actual condition in which it is found.

   ***Note:*** For a difference between a direction which is *really* optional and a direction which is *apparently* optional but really *imperative See Earlom vs. Saunders—(1754) Ambler's Reports 241.*

   Direction, if it is optional, must be *express.* Otherwise it will always be held to be imperative.
3. Distinction must be made between direction to sell or purchase Realty and discretion as to the time at which sale or purchase shall be made:
   (a) If the direction is imperative, mere fact that it is accompanied by discretion, will not prevent conversion having its effect.

(b) If the direction is imperative, the fact that those to whom the direction was given have failed to carry it out, will not prevent conversion having its effect.

4. Distinction must be made between a simple direction to sell or purchase and a direction, the execution of which, is made dependent *on the request* or *consent* of some other person.

   In such a case, whether there will be conversion or not, rests upon the construction of the document: (a) If the intention of the clause is to enable the person named to *enforce the obligation to convert,* then there will be conversion. (b) If the intention of the clause is *to control the operation of the direction* by making it subject to application, then there will be no conversion until such application is made.

5. Distinction must be made between the *power to convert* and *direction to convert:*

   (1892) I Ch. 279.

   (1910) I Ch. 750.

A mere power to convert is not imperative direction and therefore, there will be no conversion, where there is mere power.

***Illus.:***

*A* borrowed £ 300 from *B* on a mortgage *of A's* property and gave B power of sale by the terms of which the surplus proceeds of sale were to be paid to A, his executors and administrators.

*A* died intestate, and after *A's* death *B* sold the estate and there were surplus sale proceeds. *To whom would the surplus go?*

As this was not a direction to sell, the property would devolve according to its *actual* state at the death of A. At the death of A it was Realty, therefore, the heir was entitled to it. If the sale had taken place during the lifetime of A, at the death of A it would be personality and would have, therefore, gone to the next-of-kin.

Time from which conversion by direction takes.

1. This varies according as the direction is contained in a will or in a deed.
2. If the direction is contained in a will, conversion will take place as from the death of the testator.
3. If the direction is contained in a deed, conversion will take place as from the date of the execution of the deed—not withstanding that the trust to sell or purchase is not to arise until after the, settlor's death.

Effect of the failure of objects for which conversion was directed in a will or deed.

Two cases must be distinguished:

### *Cases of Total Failure*

1. Where there is a *total* failure of the objects *before* or *at the time* when the deed or will came into operation, or before the time at which the duty to convert is to arise, no conversion will take place at all and the property will remain as it was. The reason is that, there is no one who can insist upon the character of the property being altered.
2. The failure must *beprior* failure and not *subsequent* failure.
3. The rule regarding conversion is uniform in the case of total failure and there is no difference between the effects of a direction in a deed and a direction in a will.

### *Cases of Partial Failure*

1. Where the purposes have only partially failed, then conversion is necessary to carry out such purposes as have not failed. Consequently the doctrine of conversion would operate and the representative entitled to take the property in the form in which it is directed to be converted.
2. It will be carried out to the extent necessary.

***Illus.:*** A devises Realty to trustees upon trust to sell and divide the sale proceeds between *B* and C. *B* predeceases A and C survives him. Here, sale is necessary in order that *C* may have what A intended to give him, *i.e.*, money. C will take his share in money.

What would happen to the share of *B*?

It is money *in fact* and *ought* to go to the next-of-kin. But it will go to the heir because conversion to that extent was unnecessary. Heir takes it but as money.

***Illus.:*** A bequeaths personality to trustees to invest in the purchase of land for B and C. B predeceases A and C survives him. Here, purchase is necessary in order that C may have what A intended to give him, *i.e.*, land. C will take his share in land.

What would happen to share of B? It will go to the next-of-kin, because, conversion to that extent was unnecessary. But the next-of-kin will take it as land.

### *Reconversion*

1. Reconversion means annulment or cancellation of prior conversion. It is a reversion or restoration of the notional state of the property to its actual state.
2. Reconversion can take place in two ways:

#### *By Act of Parties*

1. This occurs where a person has the right to choose between taking the property in its converted State or in its actual state.
2. Persons who have a right to make such an election and thereby reconvert property are:—
   (1) An absolute owner.
   (2) A owner of an undivided share—-without the concurrence of the co-owner in the case of money to be converted into land but not in the case of land to be converted into money. This is because money is capable of apportionment while land is not.

***Illus.:***

(1) Where money is to be invested into land in the interest

of *A* and *B* as joint tenants. A can elect to reconvert without the concurrence of B.

(2) Ques:— Can a remainder man effect a reconversion by electing to take it in its actual state? This is not clearly settled.

(3) This rule of reconversion by act of parties applies where the owner who has aright to elect and thereby to effect reconversion is subject to the limitation that he must not be under any disability.

***Infants*** **and** ***Lunatics*** are persons under disability and cannot, therefore, reconvert. But the Court may direct reconversion on their behalf if it is beneficial to them. Married woman can reconvert if the property belongs to her for her separate use. If it is not her separate property, then she can do so only with the consent of her husband. (4) Evidence of election to reconvert—

(i) express declaration of intention in that behalf;

(ii) conduct amounting to election.

***Reconversion by Law:*** Where a person, who is under an obligation to convert property, is in possession of and absolutely entitled to the property after the obligation has ceased/the property is at home and reconverted without any act on his part. Thus—*A* converts within 3 years after his marriage with B to invest £ 1,000 in the purchase of lands and settle them upon his wife *B*. B dies within a year of the marriage. Since the obligation to invest money in land and the right to require its investment are both vested in A, the obligation is discharged by operation of law and the money which was converted into land by the covenant is reconverted and passes to the next-of-kin.

### *Election*

Distinction between election in law and election in equity.

(a) *Election in law* is connected with the choice of a party to repudiate a liability arising out of an unauthorised act or to ratify the act and accept the liability.

(b) *Election in Equity* is connected with the choice of a person to accept a gift which is subject to a burden or to reject the gift.

***Necessity for the Equitable Doctrine of Election.***

What is the problem which the doctrine deals with:

***Nature of the Problem:*** A gives his property to B by an instrument-deed or a will—and by the same instrument gives to *C* a property belonging to *B*.

What can *B* take under such an instrument?

Here there are two gifts—

(i) by A to B of A's property

(ii) by A to C of B's property

The gift *to B* of *A's* property is a valid gift, because A is the owner of the property gifted away. The gift to C of ***B's*** property by *A* is invalid, because it is not authorised by *B*.

Question is, can *B* take the gift from *A of A's* property and repudiate the gift of his property by A to C? It is this problem with which the doctrine of Election deals.

*The doctrine of Election* says that the gift to B shall take effect only if B elects to permit the gift to *C* also to take effect.

***The Principle of the Rule:*** When a person makes a gift of this sort, equity presumes that in such a gift there is an implied condition that he who accepts a benefit under an instrument must adopt the whole of it, conforming to all its provisions, and renouncing every right inconsistent with it.

Courses open to a person called upon to elect.

(A) Two courses are open to a person who is called upon to make an election.

(1) *B* may allow C to take his (B's) property and himself take A's property.

(2) *B* may take A's property and not allow C to take his (B's) property but give him compensation to the extent required to satisfy C.

***Illus.:*** *A* gives to *B* a family estate belonging to *C* worth £ 20,000 and by the same instrument gives to *C* a legacy of £ 30,000 of his *(A's)* property. *C* can do either of the two things.

(i) allow B to take the family estate *or*

(ii) keep the family estate and give B £20,000.

(B) The former course is called *taking under the instrument.* The latter is called *taking against the instrument.* The following points must be noted in connection with these two modes of Election:

(i) Election against the instrument is allowed in Equity only where the gift is made upon an *implied* condition that the donee shall part with his own property. Where the gift is made upon an *express* condition that the donee shall part with his own property. Equity will not allow Election against the instrument. The donee would take nothing if he refused to comply with the condition.

(ii) No question of compensation arises when a person elects under the instrument.

(iii) Election against the instrument where it is permitted—does not involve a forfeiture of the whole of the legacy but only of a part sufficient for compensation.

Conditions for the application of the doctrine:

(1) The donor must have given the property of the donee to a third person.

(2) The donor must have by the same instrument given his own property to the donee. To this the following must be added.

(3) The property *given to* the donee must be such that it can be used to compensate the third person.

(4) The property of the donee must be alienable.

***Note:*** The donor will be deemed to be disposing of such interest as he may have in the property and no more.

Some cases which must be distinguished from cases of election:

***Cases of Two Gifts to one Person:*** In such cases the

doctrine of election does not apply. They are cases of gifts of his own property. Here the donee may accept the one that is beneficial and reject the one that *is onerous*—unless the intention of the donor was that the acceptance of the *onerous* was a condition for the grant of the beneficial.

***Case of Two Properties in one Gift:*** One beneficial, the other onerous.

The beneficiary must take both or neither unless an intention appears to allow him to take the one without the other.

### *Conclusion*

(1) Conversion and election are doctrines which illustrate the maxim of Equity—Equity looks to intention.

(2) That being so there would be no election if there was no intention on the part of the donor to put the donee to election.

### *Performance*

1. *The problem:* A covenants with B to do a certain act. A does an act which can wholly or partly effects the same purpose *i.e.* available for the discharge of the obligation arising under the covenant but does not relate the act to the covenant. The question is *how is this act to be construed?* Is it to be construed that it is an independent *act* quite unconnected with the covenant or is it to be construed that the intention of A in doing this *act* was to perform the obligation. The answer of equity is that the *act* must be treated as being intended to perform the obligation under the covenant.
2. *Principle:* The principle underlying the doctrine of Performance is that, equity presumes that every man has an *intention* to perform his obligation and when he does an *act* which is similar to the one he promised to do, then equity gives effect to that intention.
3. *The difficulties that would occur if this principle was not recognised.*

***Illus:*** A convenanted on his marriage to purchase lands of the value of £ 200 a year and to settle them for the jointure of his wife and to the first and other sons of the marriage in fail.

A purchased lands of that value but made no settlement, so that, on his death the lands descended to his eldest son.

The eldest son brought a bill in equity founded on his father's marriage-articles to have land purchased out of the personal estate of the father of the value of £ 200 a year and settled to the uses in the marriage-articles. But for the doctrine of *performance* the man would get both.

The cases in which the questions of Performance arise fall into classes:

(i) Where there is a covenant to purchase and settle lands, and a purchase is in fact made.

(ii) Where there is a covenant to leave personality to an individual arid the covenanter dies intestate and the property thereby comes in fact to that individual.

***Cases Arising under the First Class:*** Points to be Noted.

(i) Where the lands purchased are of less value than, the lands covenanted for, they will be considered as purchased in part performance of the contract.,

(ii) Where the covenant points to a future purchase of lands, lands of which the covenantor is already ceased at the time of the covenant, are not to be taken in part performance:

(iii) Property of a different nature from that covenanted to be purchased by the covenantor, is not subject to the doctrine of Performance.

***Cases that fall under the Second Class :*** Covenant is to leave certain money.

A covenanted previously to his marriage to leave to his wife £620. He married and died intestate. His wife's share under the intestacy was less than £620.

The wife sued for the performance of the covenant. The

question was, having received £ 620 on intestacy, was it not a performance of the covenant. It was *held* that it was, so that the widow could not claim her share on intestacy and £ 620 over and above as a debt under the covenant.

In this case, the covenant was wholly performed. But even if the amount received was less than the amount due under the covenant, the doctrine of performance would apply and the convenant would have been held to be performed *pro tanto.*

Two points to be noted:

(i) Where the covenantor's death occurs at or before the time when the obligation accrues, there is performance.

(ii) Where the covenantor's death occurs after the obligation has *accrued due,* there is no performance.

***Satisfaction***

I. *Problem:* A is under an obligation to B. A makes a gift to B. The Question is: Is the gift to B to be taken as a gift or is the gift to B to be taken as satisfaction of A's obligation to B?

II. There is a similarity between satisfaction and performance. There are fundamental distinctions between the two.

(1) In performance, the act done is available for the discharge of the obligation, but is not related in specific terms to the obligee. In satisfaction, it is related to the obligee but not in discharge of the obligation.

(2) In performance, whether the covenant has been performed depends, not upon the intention but, upon whether that has been done which was agreed to be done. The question, whether a gift satisfies an obligation, depends upon the intention of the donor.

(3) If an obligation has been performed according to its terms, the obligor is discharged. If an obligor makes a gift by will in satisfaction of his liability, it rests with the obligee either to accept the gift or decline

it. If he accepts it, he looses the right to enforce his obligation, if he declines it, he retains his original rights.

Intention is that, the gift is in satisfaction of the prior obligation.

Cases in which the question of satisfaction arises fall into two classes:—

(i) Cases in which the prior obligation arises from an act of bounty.

(ii) Cases in which the prior obligation is of the nature of a debt.

Class of cases in which the prior obligation arises from an act of bounty.

In this class fall two kinds of cases— (A) Satisfaction of legacies by portion. (B) Satisfaction of portions by legacies.

### *Satisfaction of Legacies by Portion*

***Portion:*** That part of a person's estate which is given or left to a child.

***Illus.:*** A has three sons B, C, D. He makes a will and in that will gives a legacy to each of his sons. Subsequently to the making of his will, A makes an advancement of a certain sum of money. Here, there is a legacy and afterwards a portion. Are they cumulative or are they alternative. Is the child which has got a portion also entitled to get the portion? Or is the claim for legacy satisfied by the subsequent portion given by the father? The answer of equity is that, a child cannot get both, legacy and a portion. The claim for legacy shall be held to be satisfied by the subsequent grant of the portion. This is called the rule against *double portions.*

### *Satisfaction of Portion by Legacies*

1. This is the converse of the first. In the first class of cases, there is first legacy then a portion. In the second, there is a portion first and then there is a legacy.
2. In the former case, the question was whether a legacy

by will was satisfied by a subsequent portion, In this, the question is whether the obligation to give a portion is satisfied by a subsequent legacy.

3. The answer here is the same as in the former case. The same rule against double portion applies. So that a portion will be satisfied by a legacy.
4. When the will precedes the settlement, it is only necessary to read the settlement as if the person making the provision had said, "I mean this to be in lien of what I have given by my will". But if the settlement precedes the will, the testator must be understood as saying," I give this in lien of what I am already bound to give, if those to whom I am so bound, will accept it ".
5. The same rule applies in the case of a portion followed by a portion.

## *Limitations on the Rule of Double Portions*

The rule does not apply:

(1) In the case of legacy and a portion—where the legacy is *expressed* to be given for a particular purpose and the portion subsequently advanced is for the same purpose.

(2) In the case of portion and legacy, and in the case of portion and portion—where the property is actually transferred to the child and then a provision is made either by way of a legacy or portion—in short it applies only where the first portion is only a debt.

(3) Where the person, who makes the provision is the parent or a person *in loco parentis*— If, therefore, a person gives a legacy to a stranger and then makes a settlement on the stranger or *vice versa,* the stranger can take both, the rule against double portion does not apply to him:

(i) An illegitimate child is a stranger;

(ii) A grand child is also a stranger:

(iii) a stranger cannot take advantage of the satisfaction of a child's share.

Cases of two Legacies given by the same will or by a will and Codial.

1. Question is whether the second Legacy is intended to be additional to the first or to be merely repetition.
2. The leading case is *Hooby vs. Hatton, 1 Bro. C. C. 390 N.* 3'. Two class of cases to be considered separately—
   (1) Where the subject-matter of the legacy is a thing.
   (2) Where the subject-matter of legacy is money.

***Where the Subject-matter of the Legacy is a thing,***
***Rule: Where*** the same thing is given twice—not additional but repetition.

### *Where the Legacies are Pecuniary Legacies*

(1) The rule varies according as the gifts are contained in the same instrument or in different instruments.

(2) Two pecuniary legacies in the *same* instrument.

***Rule:***

(i) If equal— repetition.

(ii) If unequal—cumulative.

3. Two pecuniary legacies in *different* instrument. *Rule.*— They are cumulative.

***Exception:*** If same motive is expressed for both gifts and the *same* sums are given—then repetition.

### *Cases in which the Prior Obligation is of the Nature of a Debt*

Cases may be divided into two classes— (i) Satisfaction of debt by a Legacy, (ii) Satisfaction of debt by a portion.

***Satisfaction of debt by a Legacy***

(1) This case arises where a debtor, without taking notice of the debt be queathes a sum by way of legacy to his creditor. Question is: Is the legacy to be taken as satisfying the debt or is the creditor entitled to the legacy and also the debt?

(2) *Rule*—That the legacy shall be taken as satisfying the debt.

(3) *Limitation on the Rule*—The rule does not apply in the following cases—

(i) Where the legacy is of lesser amount than the debt—no satisfaction, even *protanto.*

(iii) Where the legacy is given upon a contingency.

(iii) Where the legacy is of an uncertain amount— *e.g.* residue.

(iv) Where the time fixed for payment of the legacy is different from that at which the debt becomes due—so as to be equally advantageous to the creditor.

(v) Where the subject-matter of the legacy differs from the debt, *e.g.* land.

### *Satisfaction of Debt by Portion*

(1) Such a case arises where the father becomes indebted to his child and then advances a portion to him in his lifetime. The Question is: Can the child claim both—the debt as well as the portion? Or Is the debt satisfied by the portion?

(2) *Rule*—Debt is satisfied by the portion.

(3) This rule is subject to the same limitations.

### *The Dominion Status*

The Statute of Westminster to some extent lays down and codifies the law which regulates the constitutional relationship of these parts of the British Empire which is known as the British Common wealth of Nations. The Statute of Westminster applies to the Dominions and establishes for them what is called Dominion Status. Our inquiry will be directed to understand the meaning of Dominion Status. Before approaching the subject we must ask.

1. What is a Dominion? A Dominion is a colony which is declared to be a Dominion by the Statute of Westminster.
2. What is a Colony? A Colony is a British Possession other than U. K. and India.
3. What is a British Possession? A British Possession is any part of the British Empire exclusive of the

United Kingdom over which the King exercises sovereignty.

4. What is British Empire? (British Empire) denotes the whole of the territories over which the King possesses sovereignty or exercise control akin to sovereignty. It includes therefore all the King's Dominions, over which he is sovereign, and the protectorates and Protected States whose foreign relations are controlled by the Crown.

It also includes the mandated territories.

### *What is Dominion Status?*

1. The subject could be better under (stood) if we compare the system of Government inaugurated by the Statute of Westminster with the system of Government which was in operation before it came into force.
2. The system which was in operation was known as Responsible Government. We must therefore grasp as a first step the characteristics of Responsible Government.
3. Why Responsible Government came in some colonies and why it did not come in others?
4. The Government of a colony differed according to the nature of the colony.
5. Colonies fall into two classes:

#### *Colony by Settlement*

1. Thus in a colony by settlement there came up the inevitable conflict between an irresponsible executive and representative legislature, a conflict of mandates.
2. Responsible Government had to be introduced in these colonies by settlement in order to solve this conflict.
3. The nature of the responsible government.

The position of the King in relation to settled colonies differs from his position in relation to conquered colonies.

The King stands to possession acquired by settlement in a position analogous to his status in the United Kingdom. *10*

*App. Calls 6921(744).* He is possessed of the executive power and has authority to establish Courts of law, but not celesiastical Courts *[3 Moo. P. C. 115, 1865: I Moo P.I.C.C 411, 1863].* But he cannot legislate, and if laws are to be passed this must be done:

(1) by a legislative body of representative character on the analogy of the U.K.

(2) where this form of legislation would be difficult to carry out, parliamentary authority must be obtained authorising the establishment of a different form of Constitution.

***Colonies by Conquest:*** In these, the King possesses absolute power to establish such executive, legislative and judicial arrangements as he thinks fit, subject only to the condition that they do not contravene any Act of Parliament extending to all British Possession.

But this right is lost by the grant of a representative legislature unless it is expressly retained in whole or in part. If not so retained, power to legislature as to the Constitution or generally can only be recovered under the authority of an Act of Parliament. 1835 2 Kuapp. 130 (152) Jehson v/s Pura; 1932 A. C. 260.

1. The Statute of Westminister applies to:
   (1) The Dominion of Canada,
   (2) The Commonwealth of Australia,
   (3) The Dominion of New Zealand,
   (4) The Union of South Africa,
   (5) The Irish Free State,
   (6) New Foundland.
2. This statute calls these colonies as Dominions and confers on them what is called Dominion Status.
3. These Colonies had Responsible Government before the Statute of Westminister.

What is the difference between Responsible Government and Dominion Status?

Mechanism of Responsible Government.—

(1) the claim by the colony to colonial autonomy in matters which affected them.

(2) the claim to unlimited sovereignty by the imperial parliament.

These two claims are contradictory. A self-governing colony is a contradiction in terms.

The solution of this question involved two questions:

(1) How was the division of authority to take place between the Colonial and Imperial Governments.

(2) How were the powers given to each were to be exercised by each.

The division proposed was not along the lines of imperial and colonial legislative competence.

All legislation was to be within colonial competence except what was barred by the colonial laws, but some of it would be liable to veto by the Imperial Government not on the ground that it was beyond the competence of the colonial legislature, but it affected some Imperial interest.

The matters of Imperial concern were not reduced to writing by enumeration. The Imperial Government was free to decide whether any particular matter was or was not of Imperial concern.

The following provisions were a feature of the Constitution of these colonies:

(1) The appointment of the G. and G. G. by the Crown on the advise of the Imperial cabinet

(2) The Right of the G. G. to act otherwise than the advice of his ministers.

(3) The power of the Governor to Reserve Bill for the pleasure of the King on the advice of the Imperial Government.

(4) The Power of Disallowance by the King on the advice of the Imperial Government.

### *The terms of the Statute of Westminister*

I. It frees the Dominion Legislature from the overriding effect of the laws made by the British Parliament:

(1) It abrogates the Colonial Laws Validity Act.

(2) It gives the Dominion Legislature to repeal any U. K. Act in so far as the same is the part of the Dominion.

II. It puts limitations upon the legislative sovereignty of the British Parliament:

(1) No Act of Parliament passed after December 11,1931 shall extend, or be deemed to extend to a Dominion as part of the law of that dominion unless it is expressly declared in the Act that the Dominion has requested and consented to the enactment thereof.

(2) Any alteration in the law touching the succession to the throne or the Royal Style and Titles requires the assent of the Parliaments of the Dominion as well as of the United Kingdom.

III. The Statute does not alter the other provisions:

(1) The appointment of Governor General.

(2) The Reservation of Bills.

(3) The Disallowance of Bills.

But a great change has taken place in the exercise of these powers.

Right of advice to the Crown.

## *Dominions*

1. The Dominion Office was established in 1925 to take over Dominions' business from the colonial office.
2. At first the Secretaryships for the Dominions and for the colonies were held by the same minister, but in 1930 a separate S of S for the Dominions was appointed.
3. The Dominion Office deals with business connected with the Dominions, Southern Rhodesia, the South African High Commission [*i.e.* Basutoland,

Bechunaland, Protectorate Swaziland], Overseas settlement, and business relating to

Imperial Conferences. See Sir G. V. Fiddes—*The Dominions and Colonial Offices.*

***Old Halsbury, 1. p. 303.*** 662. The dominions of the Crown include—

(a) The U. K. and any Colony, plantation, island, territory or settlement within H M's dominions and not within the U. K. (Naturalization Act, 1870,33 Ne. c 14 s. 17)

(b) Places situated within the territory of a Prince, who is subject to the Crown of England in respect of such territory. [Crow and Ramsay (1670) Vaugh. 281]

(c) British ships of war and other public vessels *(Parliament V/s. Belge. (1880) 5 P.D. 197.)*

(d) British Merchantmen on the high seas [1870 S. R. 6 Q. B. 31. *Marshall v/s Murgatroyd]* and probably even in the territorial waters of a foreign country [*Compare R v/s Carr and Wilson (1882) 1.0 Q.B.D.* 76].

***Halsbury X. p. 503 para 856***

1. "British Possession "means any part of H M's dominions exclusive of the U.K.; and where parts of such dominions are under both a central and a local legislature, all parts under the central legislature are deemed to be one British Possession. [Interpretation Act 1889 (52 & *53 Vict.* c. *63) S. 18 (2)].*
2. A Colony is any part of H M's dominions exclusive of the British Islands and British India; and where, parts of such dominions are under both a central and a local legislature, all parts under the central legislature are deemed one colony [*Ibid.* S.18(3)].
3. A British settlement means any British Possession which has not been acquired by cession or conquest and is not for the time being within the jurisdiction of the legislature of any British possession. [British Settlements Act, 1887 *(50-51 Vic. C.54)* S. 6].
4. The expression ' Dependencies ' is used to signify places

which have not been formally annexed to the British dominions, and are therefore, strictly speaking foreign territories, but which are practically governed by Great Britain, and by her represented in any relations that may arise towards other foreign countries. Most of them are" Protectorates "that is territories placed under the protection of the British sovereign, generally by treaty with the native rulers or chiefs. Cyprus and Weihaiwei arc foreign territories held by Great Britain under special agreements with their respective sovereigns, but administered under the Foreign Jurisdiction Act, 1890 [53-54 Vic. C. 37 ], on the same general lines as protectorates. India including both the Native States and the strictly British territory of that Empire, is frequently spoken of as our great dependency.

5. Crown colonies are those in which the Crown retains complete control of the public officers carrying on the Government, and the legislative power is either delegated to the officer administrating the Government [S. S. Gibralter, Ashanti, Virgin Islands, St. Helena and Basutoland] or is exercised by a Legislative Council which is nominated by the Crown either entirely or partly the other part being elected. In these colonies, with seven exception, the Crown has reserved to itself the power of legislating by Order in Council.

*Protectorates* although not parts of H M's Dominions are administered in much the same manner as Crown colonies.

*Dominions* are those colonies which possess elective legislatures to which the executive is responsible, as in the U. K. the only officer appointed and controlled by the Crown being the Governor or G. G. Halsbury X, p. 521

885. There is no statutory or authoritative definition of the term "protectorate "although it appears in two recent Statutes. Protectorates are not British territory in the strict sense; but it is understood that no other civilised power will interfere in their affairs. They are administered under the provisions of orders in Council issued by virtue of powers conferred upon H. M. by the Foreign Jurisdiction Act, 1890 "or otherwise vested

in His Majesty "which latter phrase may be taken to be intended to bring in aid any exercise of the Royal prerogative that may be necessary to supplement H. M's statutory powers.

***Halsbury XIV, p. 420***

For a recent treatment of the meaning of "dominions" see *R v/sCrewe 1910 S.K.B.576,607',622.*

***Halsbury IX, p. 16***

The authority of the King extends over all his subjects wherever they may be, and also over all foreigners who are within the realm. The jurisdiction of English Courts of Law, however, is limited, first, by the stipulations contained in the enactments by which the kingdoms of Scotland and Ireland were incorporated in the United Kingdom; Secondly by the Charter of Justice, letters patent and statutes affecting particular colonies; and thirdly, by the consideration that no English Court will decide any question where it has not the power to enforce its decree.

The jurisdiction of each particular Court is that which the King has delegated to it, and this delegation has been complete, for the King has distributed his whole power of prosecution to diverse Courts of Justice.

## Development of Dominion Status

1. There is first the claim to unlimited sovereignty by the Imperial Parliament and Government stated in its logical perfection by Lord John Russell.
2. There is second the claim to colonial autonomy an effective demand that, in matters which interested them, the colonies should manage their own affairs.
3. There is third, the contradiction between the two. A self-governing dependency is a contradiction in terms.

***Solution***

On the one hand, the Imperial Parliament granted to a colony a sphere of activity in which the colonial legislature, executive and judiciary had authority to exercise governmental power. In this sphere the colony was sovereign. On the other hand, the Imperial Parliament had the authority and full legal power, as and when it saw fit, to withdraw or limit the rights of the Colony to exercise power within a prescribed sphere, either by repealing or amending the Constituent Act of the Colony or by passing an Imperial Act explicitly applying to some subject within the jurisdiction of the Colony.

*Two Questions:* (1) How was the division of authority to take place between the Colonial and Imperial authority? (2) The method of exercising the powers given to each.

(1) The division proposed was not along the lines of Imperial and Colonial legislative competence. All legislation was to be within colonial competence, but some of it would be liable to veto by the Imperial authority, not on the ground that it was beyond the competence of the colonial legislature, but because it affected some specified Imperial interest.

(2) It was advocated that the possible matters of Imperial concern should be reduced to writing by enumeration of those matters which were deemed of Imperial concern. The British Government refused to bind itself specifically in this way [and the provisions were not allowed to stand in the Australian Bills].

(3) How were the activities of the Colonial and Imperial authorities to be adjusted and coordinated so that confusion and overlapping and conflict might be avoided? The solution was found in the following:

    (1) The Powers of Reservations.
    (2) The Powers of Disallowance.
    (3) The appointment of the Governor General.
    (4) The nature of responsible Government in the colonies.
    (5) Right of the British Government to tender advice to the Crown.
    (6) Colonial Laws Validity Act of 1865.

(4) The nature of responsible Government in the Colonies.

The executive Government was vested in the Governor, who was empowered to appoint to his executive council those persons whom he thought fit, in addition to those, if any, who by law were members of it. While in one or two cases it was stipulated in the Constituent statute that ministers were to be members of the executive council or that members of the executive council were to be, or were within a given period, to become members of one or other house of the legislature. In no case is the executive council required bylaw to be composed of ministers and ministers alone.

The executive council includes but does not necessarily consist only of ministers. In certain cases there is no legal necessity for members of the executive council to be members of either house of legislature.

The Act prescribed a sphere of activity within which the colonial legislature had power to make laws for the peace, order and good Government of the colony. Thus far the statute.

The instructions to the Governor empowered him to govern with an executive council whose advice he might disregard if he thought fit.

Responsible Government was based, not upon a statutory basis, but on the faith of the Crown.

## Character of Inter Imperial Relations

In the Commonwealth Merchant Shipping Agreement, the Dominions appear in a position of complete equality, comparable with that of contracting states, and differences arising out of the agreement would seem suitable for reference to the inter-Imperial tribunal contemplated by the Imperial Conference 1930. [Cmd. 3994, Part VII].

But the relations are not governed by International Law. This was asserted clearly in 1924, when the Irish Free State registered with the Secretariat of the Leagus of Nations, the Articles of agreement for a Treaty of December 6, 1921 on the score that it was a treaty within the meaning of Article 18 of the covenant of the League of Nations, and the British Government insisted that neither the covenant nor the conventions concluded under League auspices were intended to govern relations *inter se* of parts of the Commonwealth [Keeth. R. G. II. 884, 885.]

The Imperial Conference 1926, took this view, holding that it had been determined in this sense by the Legal Committee of the Arms Traffic Conference of 1925 [Cmd. 2768 p. 23.]

The Dominions save the Irish Free State as well as the United Kingdom, excluded inter-imperial disputes from those to be submitted to the Permanent Court of International Justice when accepting the optional clauses of the Statute of the Court in 1929 [Cmd. 3452 p. 415] and similarly when accepting the General Act of 1928 for the Pacific Settlement of International disputes [Cmd. 3930 pp. 14, 15]. The inter-imperial preferences are a domestic issue, on which most favoured nation clauses of treaties with foreign states do not operate.

## *Allegiance*

The bond of a common allegiance involving a common status as British subjects, and this bond is one which cannot be severed by the unilateral action of any part as follows from the formal declaration in the Preamble to the Statute of Westminster that inasmuch as the Crown is the symbol of the free association of the members of the British Commonwealth of Nations and as they are united by a Common allegiance, any alteration in the law touching the succession to the throne or the Royal style and titles, requires the assent of the Parliaments of the Dominions as well as of the United Kingdom.

While the Preamble does not make law, it expresses a convention of the constitution which would render it very difficult for the Crown or its representative to assent to a bill passed by any single part which violated this principle of the unity of the British Commonwealth of Nations on a basis of equality of its status.

***Note:*** In approving the report of the Conference of 1929, the Union Parliament recorded that the proposed Preamble "shall not be taken as abrogating from the right of any member of the British Commonwealth of Nations to withdraw therefrom".

***Journal of Parliament of Empire XI. 797 800***

But this view has never been formally adopted by the Imperial Conference.

The equality of status of the Dominions and the U. K. necessitates the consideration of a mode of deciding inter-imperial disputes [cmd.3479 p. 41].

For this purpose, the imperial conference 1930 decided that such disputes should be dealt with along the line of *ad hoc* arbitration, on a voluntary basis. The procedure is to be limited to differences between Government and only such as are justifiable.

The Tribunal is to be constituted *ad hoc* for each dispute; there are to be five members, none drawn from outside the British Commonwealth of Nations.

Each party shall select one from the States members of the Commonwealth of Nations, not parties to the dispute, being persons who have held or hold high judicial office or are distinguished jurists and one with complete freedom of choice. The chairman shall be chosen by these four assessors may be employed if the parties desire-expenses to be borne equally. Each party shall bear those of presenting its case.

### *External Sovereignty of the Dominions*

They have autonomy. But not status. (They Have) ceremonial status, but not *legal, de facto* but *not de jure*

For many purposes the Dominions are endowed with a considerable amount of international personality independent of the United Kingdom. But the Common allegiance and the Common Crown interfere with the idea of each Dominion being a distinct sovereign state connected merely in a personal union.

The issue as to the possibility of neutrality in war has been discussed, but only claimed by the Nationalist Government in South Africa. [Kerth DGII 867 868 71, 72, *Sovereignty of Dominions of D. 300-304 463-471].*

It is open to serious doubt if the King could declare war without automatically involving the Dominions in the war.

### *The Implications of Dominion Status*

1. Does it imply sovereign status?

They have the functions of a sovereign state. But they have not the status of sovereign states.

2. Does it imply the right to secede?

### *Webster*

"The distinction between citizens proper, that is, the constituent members of the political sovereignty, and subjects of that sovereignty who are not, therefore, citizens is recognised in the best authorities of the public law". This distinction is true. The further question of who are and who are not citizens has its difficulties. Accept the definition of citizenship to be the enjoyment of equal rights and privileges at home and equal protection abroad, and consider the question from this standpoint, from which alone it should be treated, for we have no law in the U.S. A. which divides our citizens into classes or makes any difference whatever between them. We then discover the importance that the equal rights of citizens when at home should maintain when abroad, because questions as to citizenship are determined by municipal law in subordination to the law of Nations. Therefore, the value of citizenship should not be underestimated."

## View of Roman Law

1. It was by man that the body politic was organised, and in entering the Organisation with his fellow men, man followed the exercise of his natural rights and became an ingredient of the society of which he, with others, became members.
2. By the Organisation formed as of man and by man, man was so incorporated into the body politic that he could not depart.
3. Although in the early days of Rome, they alone could call themselves Roman citizens who were freeborn and born in Rome, yet very soon thereafter, foreigners were

admitted to citizenship by authority of the legislative body. Later, as Rome advanced in her conquest of the neighbouring states, to these states the legislative authorities conferred charters by which the citizens of such states were admitted to Roman citizenship and their former citizenship was abolished.

4. Cicero lays down the rule, "that every man ought to be able to retain or renounce his rights of membership of a society, "and further adds, "that this is the firmest foundation of liberty. "Under this the Romans received all who came and forced none to remain with them.
5. This view of the Roman Law was based upon natural law.

## *Effect of Invasion*

6. After the downfall of Rome this principle of natural law gave way to the principles of feudalism as introduced by the invaders.
7. The invaders having conquered both the people and their lands, organised their Government, as being in a prince who was all powerful over his subjects. The relation as between man and man and his relation to the Government was forced and involuntary. The natural rights of man as being in man were disavowed.
   (i) Nature that the law permits its Specific Performance
   (ii) Where the Plaintiff is a person in whose favour Specific Performance can be granted.
   (iii) Where the Defendant is a person against whom Specific Performance might be granted.

*The question is:* Is the Court bound to grant Specific Relief in such cases?

The answer to this question is contained in Sec. 22.

(A) Section 22 lays down general rules—(1) It says that Specific Relief is discretionary. The Court may grant it or may refuse it. The Court is not bound to grant it merely because it is lawful. (2) The discretion of the

Court is not arbitrary, sound and reasonable, guided by judicial principles.

(B) Section 22 also specifies cases in which Court may exercise discretion not to grant Specific Performance and cases in which Court may exercise discretion to grant Specific Performance.

Cases in which Court may exercise discretion not to grant Specific Performance

(i) Where Specific Performance would give unfair advantage over the Defendant.

(ii) Where Specific Performance would involve some hardship on the Defendant which he did not foresee and non-performance would not involve such hardship on the Plaintiff.

***Cases in which Court may Exercise Discretion to Grant Specific Performance***

Where the Plaintiff has done substantial acts or suffered losses in consequence of a contract capable of Specific Performance.

***Damages and Specific Performance***

Sections 19,20,29.

Two remedies for breach. Are the mutually exclusive or are they complimentary? Does one bar the other?

These are question which are considered in Sections 19, 20, 29. The rules contained in these three may be summarised as below:

(i) In the same suit, a Plaintiff can ask for both in addition or in substitution.

(ii) In a suit where Court decides not to grant Specific Performance Court can grant Compensation to Plaintiff if entitled.

(iii) If one suit Court may grant compensation in addition to Specific Performance if it comes to the conclusion to Specific Performance is not enough.

(iv) The fact that liquidated damages have been agreed upon is no bar to Specific Performance.

(v) If suit for Specific Performance is decreed, it will be a bar to a suit for damages.

## The Law of Specific Relief

### *Introductory*

#### *I. The enactment which defines Specific Relief.*

1. The law as to specific relief is contained in the Specific Relief Act I of 1877.
2. Before the passing of the Specific Relief Act the law as to Specific Relief was contained in Sections 15 and 192 of the Civil Procedure Code (Act VIII) of 1859.
3. The law was fragmentary. Section 15 dealt with declaratory decrees and Section 192 dealt with Specific performance of contracts.
4. The Act aims to *define* and *amend* the law relating to Specific Relief obtainable in Civil Court.

#### *II. The nature of the Law of Specific Relief*

1. Laws fall into *three* categories.— (a) Those which define Rights. (b) Those which define Remedies. (c) Those which define Procedure.
2. *Illustrations.*
3. The Law of Specific Relief belongs to the second category. It is a law which deals with Remedies.
4. The term *'relief* is only another word for remedy which a Court is allowed by law to grant to suitors.

#### *III. What is meant by Specific Relief?*

1. Specific Relief is one kind of remedy recognised by law. Its nature can be best understood by distinguishing the different remedies which the law allows to a person whose right has been invaded.
2. A right to be real must have a remedy. No right can give protection if there is no remedy provided for its

vindication. Law therefore invariably provides a remedy for a breach of a right.

3. The general remedy provided by law for a breach of a right is *monetary reparation* called compensation or damages.
4. This remedy of money compensation is not an adequate remedy in *all* cases. The loss of some things can be compensated by payment of money. The loss of others cannot be compensated by money. Their loss can be made good by the *return* of the very *same* article. Similarly, the refusal to perform an obligation may be compensated by money. In other cases, the only adequate remedy is to compel the performance of the very *same* obligation.
5. Thus there are two kinds of remedies provided by law: (a) those under which the suitor is granted the *very same* things to which he is entitled, by virtue of the right he has acquired against his opponent; and (b) those under which the suitor is granted not the very same thing to which he was entitled, but money compensation or damages in lieu thereof.
6. Specific Relief is the name given to the first kind of remedy.
7. The relief is called specific because it is relief in *specie, i.e.* in terms of the very thing to which a suitor is entitled.

### *IV. What Specific Reliefs are provided for in the Specific Relief Act.*

1. The forms of Specific Reliefs provided for in the Specific Relief Act form under four divisions: (1) Taking possession of property and delivering it to the claimant who is out of possession. (2) Requiring Performance of Contract. (3) Compelling the Performance of a Statutory Duty. (4) Preventing the doing of a wrong.
2. The subdivisions of the 4th category are: (i) Rectification of an instrument. (ii) Rescission of an instrument. (iii) Cancellation of an instrument. (iv) Declaration of status. (v) Receivers—appointment of— (vi) Injunctions.

### *V. Other Laws defining Specific Reliefs.*

1. These are not the only specific remedies administered by courts in India. There are other specific remedies recognised by the Indian Law and which are enforced by courts in India.
2. These specific remedies outside the Specific Relief Act are: (i) Taking an account of the property of a deceased person and administering the same. (ii) Taking accounts of a trust and administering the trust property. (iii) The foreclosure of the right to redeem or sale of the mortgaged property. (iv) Redemption and reconveyance of mortgaged property. (v) Dissolution of partnership, taking partnership accounts, realising assets; discharging debts of partnership, etc.
3. We are not concerned with these. Consideration of the Different Kinds of Specific Reliefs Recognised by the Act.

## *Division I*

Recovery of possession of Property Sections 8, 9, 10 and 11

Recovery of Possession of immovable property—Sections 8,9.

Recovery of Possession of movable property—Sections 10, II.

Recovery of Possession of Immovable Property.

1. The Question is—When can a person, who has lost possession of immovable property and sues to recovery possession thereof—be granted possession thereof instead of damages or compensation for the loss of possession.
2. The emphasis is on the nature of the relief—*i.e.* the recovery of the specific piece of property of which possession is lost. The relief by way of damages or compensation is always open under the general law. Question is when can an injured person insist upon specific relief for the recovery of property.

3. The cases in which a person has lost possession of immovable property fall under two classes—(i) The case of a person who is entitled to possession but who has lost possession. (ii) The case of a person who had possession but who has lost possession.
4. The difference consists in *being entitled to possession* and *being in possession.*
5. These two cases are dealt with in Sections 8 and 9. Both provide that in either case the Plaintiff shall be entitled to Specific Relief by way of recovery of property.
6. Requirements of Section 8. (i) Prove that you have a title to possession and you will succeed in recovering possession by way of specific relief.
7. Requirements of Section 9. 1. Prove that you were in possession with in six months prior to the date of suit. 2. Prove that you were dispossessed *without your consent or otherwise* than in due course of law.

   A *in possession is dispossessed by* B

   I. a with title "is" without title

   II. a without title "is" with title

   III. a without title "is" without title

   1. In *all* three cases A can recover possession if he brings suit under Section 9 *i.e.* within six months—irrespective of the question of title.
   2. If he brings a suit after six months, he must rely on title so that A can recover possession in (i) because he has a title. (ii) because he has a possessory title.

But cannot recover in (ii) because B has title and A has not.

Who can maintain a suit under Section 10

1. According to Section 10, only a person *entitled to* the possession of the suit property can sue.
2. Meaning of "entitled to possession"
3. Title to possession may arise

   (i) as a result of ownership or

(ii) independently of ownership, as a temporary or special right to present possession

4. Title to possession as a result of ownership.

(i) Ownership may be bare legal ownership or it may be legal ownership coupled with beneficial interest.

(ii) It is not necessary that a legal owner must have also a beneficial interest in the properly to have a right to maintain a suit under Section 10.

(iii) This is made explicit in Explanation I, where a trustee is permitted to sue for the possession of the trust properly although he has no beneficial interest in it.

5. Title to possession independently of ownership

1. Title to possession independently of ownership may arise in two ways: (i) By the act of owner. (ii) Otherwise than by the act of the owner.

Title to Possession by the Act of the Owner:

(i) The owner may by his own act create in another person a right to the possession of the thing which belongs to him as *owner.*

(ii) Illustrations of such a right to possession are to be found in Bailment and lien.

(1) Simple bailment cover the cases of: (i) loan, (ii) custody, (iii) carriage, (iv) agency.

(2) Other Bailments: 1. Pawn, 2. Hire.

2. Difference between Simple Bailment and other Bailments of Pawn or Hire:

(i) In Simple Bailment the owner (Bailer) has a right to possession and the Bailee has legal possession. The Bailee being entitled to possession can maintain a suit to recover possession. The Bailer having a right to possession can also maintain a suit to recover possession against any person other than a Bailee.

(ii) In other Bailments of Pawn or Hire—The

Bailer has no right to possession. The right to possession is vested in the Pawnee or Hirer during the continuance of the Bailment and it is only the Bailee (Pawnee or Hirer) who can maintain a suit for the recovery of possession.

3. Lien is an illustration of a right to possession arising out of the act of the owner.
   (1) Lien is a right to possession of a thing which arises out of debt due by the owner.
   (2) The right to possession of the owner is thus temporarily vested in another.
4. All that is necessary to maintain a suit is a right to present possession.—
   (i) The right of present possession may arise out of ownership or may not. (ii) Right to present possession may be special or temporary.
   (ii) Right to possession otherwise than by the act of the owner. (1) The founder of lost goods has a right to possession. (2) It is not the result of the act of the owner. (3) But it is good against all the world except the true owner.

### *Against whom can such a Suit be Maintained*

1. A suit under Section 10 can be maintained against any one and can be maintained even against the true owner.
2. All that is necessary is that the Plaintiff must be entitled to possession.

### *Section 11. Movable Property*

Q. 1.—Who can maintain a suit under Section 11.

A.—The person entitled to *immediate possession.*

Q. 2.—Against whom can such a suit be maintained?

A.—Against any person if he is not owner.

The Defendant must not be the owner. If he is, then Section 10 would apply.

Q. 3.—In what case will there be specific relief by way of recovery of possession?

A—(i) Where the person who holds the thing is the agent or trustee of the claimant. (ii) Where compensation for money would not be adequate compensation to the claimant for the loss. (iii) Where it is extremely difficult to ascertain actual damage caused by its loss. (iv) Where the possession of the person is the result of a wrongful transfer from the claimant.

Specific Relief regarding Possession of Property

They are dealt with in Sections 8—II.

*Section 8.* Recovery of specific immovable property by a person entitled to the possession thereof.

*Section 9.* Recovery of possession of specific immovable property by a person who is dispossessed.

*Section 10.* Recovery of possession of specific movable property by a person *entitled to its possession.* (1) By reason of ownership (2) By reason of temporary or special rights (Trustee) Bailment Pawn.

*Section II.* Recovery of possession of Specific immovable property by a person who is entitled to its *immediate possession.* This applies when the person having possession is not owner

What is meant by possession in Law?

*Legal possession* is a compound of two ingredients: *Corpus and animus domini.*

***Note:—***

(i) Legal Possession does not involve the element of title or right. Legal Possession is wholly independent of right or title. Legal Possession may be *lawful* or *unlawful.* If a possessor acquired his *de facto* possession by a means of acquisition recognised by the Law *(Justis fitulus)* he has a lawful possession; if he did not so acquire it (as in the case of a thief) he has legal possession, but it is an unlawful one.

(ii) *Legal Possession* confers more than a personal right to be protected against wrong-doers: it confers a qualified *right* to possess, a right in the nature of property, which is valid against every one, who cannot show a prior and-better title.

There are two elements in legal possession. (i) Corpus, *i.e.* the physical relation. (ii) Animus, *i.e.* the mental relation.

*Corpus* or physical relation does not mean physical contact only. It also includes physical contact resumable at pleasure.

The essence of corpus is the power, to exclude others from the use of a thing, *i.e.* an effective occupation or control according to the nature of the thing possessed.

*Animus* is the intention of exercising such power of dealing with a thing at pleasure and excluding others—*animus domini.*

### *Three Forms of Animus*

The mental attitude of the physical possessor in regard to the object of his possession may assume three degrees.—

***First:*** His intention may be merely to protect the thing. There is no assertion of right—Servant's possession of masters goods.

***Second:*** Intention to control for certain limited purposes—*e.g.* tenant—intention to exclude every one except the owner.

***Thirdly:*** Intention amounting to a denial of the right of every other person—This is the real *animus domini.*

***Distinction between Possession and Trespass*** :

1. What the plaintiff is to prove in such cases is possession of the disputed property and not mere isolated acts of trespass over that property. He must prove—
   (i) That he exercised acts which amounted to dominion, the nature of these acts of dominion varies with the nature of the property.
   (ii) That the act of dominion was exclusive.
2. If the occupation of the piff., as indicated by those acts, has been peaceable and uninterrupted and has extended over a sufficient length of time, the inference may properly be drawn that the plaintiff was in possession.

***Objects of Section 8 and 9.***

(i) Section 8 of the Act provides that the person entitled to the possession of specific immovable property may recover it in the manner prescribed by the C. P. C., *i.e.*, by a suit for ejectment on the *basis of title.*

(ii) Section 9 gives a summary remedy to a person, who has, without his consent been dispossessed of immovable property otherwise than *in due course of Law* for recovery of possession without *establishing title.*

***Section 9.***

This Section deals with the subject of unlawful dispossession, and gives to the person dispossessed the alternative of two remedies.—

(i) He may simply prove the fact of his unlawful dispossession, in a suit instituted by him within six months thereof, recover possession of the property. The question of his *title* to the property is quite immaterial.

(ii) He may recover possession by relying on his title in a suit brought by him for that purpose. Here his success depends upon his proof of title.

The former remedy is called remedy by way of a possessory suit and is enacted in Section 9. The latter is the ordinary remedy of a suit based on title and is embodied in Section 8.

***Nature and Object of Section 9.***

(i) To prevent people from taking the law into their own hands, however good their title may be.

(ii) To prevent the shifting of the *burden of proof owing* to dispossession—-Possession being *prima facie* evidence of title.

Anterior possession *per se* constitutes a perfect title to property as between the *dispossessed* and the *dispossessor,* in a suit under Section 9, *i.e.* within six months of the dispossession.

***Question:*** What is the effect of anterior possession in a suit for possession by a person, who is dispossessed after 6 months have elapsed and a suit under Section 9 is barred?

The following propositions have been judicially established:—

(i) Possession for a period of sixty years and upwards is sufficient to create a title in the possessor which no one can question.—8 D.R. 386.

(ii) Adverse possession for 12 years under article 142 is itself title even against the rightful owner himself.

Consequently, where in a suit for possession, a plea of adverse possession during the prescribed period of limitation is set up by the Defat the question of limitation becomes a question of title, and the Plff. must furnish *prima fade* proof of subsisting title at the dale of his suit, before the Defat is required to establish his adverse possession.

(iii) Prior possession, however short, is itself a title against a *mere wrong-doer* and a bare plea of anterior possession, and dispossession, is in fact a good ground for recovery of possession, (1) Where the dispossessor can Drove no title, or (2) Where neither party can prove a title.

### *Statement of the Position*

| *A* in Possession | | *Is* dispossessed by | *B* | |
|---|---|---|---|---|
| (a) with title | (b) without title | | (a) without title | (b) with title |

***Entitled to Possession:*** A right to possession exists either.

(i) as a part of ownership or

(ii) independently of ownership, as a temporary or special right.

These special rights arise either.

(i) by the act of the owner or,

(ii) otherwise than by the act of the owner.

***By Act of the Owner***

(1) Bailment and (2) Lien

*Bailment is* (1) simple and (2) special of *Pawn* and *Hire* (i) *Simple Bailments e.g.* loan, custody, carriage and agency.

In simple Bailments, the Bailor has a *right to Possession* and the Bailee has legal possession.

A is Bailor and B is Bailee. Both can recover possession against C. A can recover possession as against B.

***Special Bailment:*** Pawn and Hire

Bailor has no right to possession during the continuance of the bailment and he only can recover possession.

***Lien:*** Arises out of debt—the Vendor having the right to possession of the thing sold, until the purchaser has paid the purchase money.

II. Right to possession otherwise than by act of owner

Finder of lost goods—entitled to possession as against all the world except the owner.

## *Division II*

## *Performance of Contract*

Specific Performance of a Contract is "its actual execution according to its stipulations and terms; and is contrasted with damages or compensation for the non-execution of the contract.

It is a species of Specific Relief, afforded by ordering a party to *do* the very act which he is under an obligation *ex-contractor* to do.

### *Specific Performance of a Contract*

*Sections 12 and 21* deal with Specific Performance of a Contract.

*Section 21.*—Defines contracts which *cannot* be specifically enforced.

*Section 12.*—Defines contracts which *may* be specifically enforced.

*Section 27.*—There are eight sorts of contracts which *are not* specifically enforceable.

(i) Contracts for the non-performance of which money compensation is an adequate relief.

(ii) Contracts (i) running into minute details. (ii) dependent on personal qualifications or volition of parties. (iii) is such that Court cannot enforce Specific Performance of its material terms.

(iii) Contracts the terms of which the Court cannot find with reasonable certainty—*e.g.* necessary appliances.

(iv) Contracts which in its nature is revocable *e.g.* Partnership without duration.

(v) Contracts by trustees in excess of their powers, or in breach of their trust.

(vi) Contracts by company in excess of its powers.

(vii) Contracts the performance of which involves the performance of a continuous duty extending over a longer period than 3 years from its date.

(viii) Contracts material part of the subject-matter supposed by both to exist has ceased to exist.

(ix) Contracts to refer a controversy to arbitration.

***Note:*** Practically Specific Performance because no right of suit is given.

## *Specific Performance of Contracts*

### *Section 12*

1. There are four cases in which Specific Performance may be enforced.
   (i) Where act promised is in performance of a trust.
   (ii) Where there is no standard to ascertain actual damage.
   (iii) Damages, no adequate relief. (iv) Compensation for non-performance cannot be got.

## *Contract*

The first question to be determined by the Court in a suit for Specific Performance of an agreement is, whether the agreement in question is a contract or not. Section 4 (a)—right to relief unless agreement is a contract.

The following agreements are not contracts because they are not enforceable and are therefore excluded:— (i) Incomplete agreements—Parties not gone beyond the stage of negotiations; (ii) Agreements which are void. (iii) Contingent agreement— until the contingency has applied... should be "arisen".

Voidable contracts are not excluded.

There must always be a contract before the Court which has been unperformed.

***Mutuality:*** The remedy by way of specific performance is *mutual, i.e.*, the vendor may bring his action in all cases where the purchaser can be sure for specific performance.

This principle of mutuality applies both in the case of immovables and movable.

***Doctrine of Mutuality:*** This means, that at the time of making of the contract, there must have been consideration on both sides or promises mutually enforceable by the parties. Hence specific of performance of a gratuitous promise under Seal will not be granted nor can an infant enforce a contract by this remedy. His promise is not enforceable against himself and it is a general principle of Courts of equity to interfere, only where the remedy is mutual.

### *Section 13*

Specific performance of con tract and impossibility of performance. *Section 56* of the Contract Act.

*Section 56 clause 2* enacts a general rule. It lays down when a contract becomes void.

This rule covers every ground of impossibility and is based on the assumption, that there is, in all cases of contract, an implied condition that performance shall be possible.

*Impossibility* in relation to contract.

***Impossibility :*** (1) at the time or (2) subsequently

Physically or legally impossible. Or subject matter of contract not existent.

***Subsequent Impossibility:*** Whether a party can be

relieved upon discovery, subsequent impossibility depends upon—

Whether the contract is conditional or unconditional.

(I) If unconditional— must perform

(II) If conditional— on three circumstances

(i) Continuing legality.

(ii) Conditional by express terms.

(iii) Conditional by implication— continued existence of the subject-matter of the thing in Sec. 56 Contract Act.— subsequent in possibility— the Contract is *void.*

Might on two grounds.

(i) The thing agreed to is physically or legally impossible.

(ii) The subject matter of the contract is nonexistent.

Such Impossibility might be either

***Initial or Subsequent:*** If impossible, the contract is void and no question of Specific Performance arises whether the impossibility is initial or subsequent.

*Section 13* of the Specific Relief Act establishes an exception to Section 56 of the Contract Act in respect of one species of impossibility *i.e. impossibility by reason of nonexistence of the subject-matter.*

*Section 13* says that Specific Performance of a contract may be enforced even though the subject-matter is partly destroyed.

Sale of a house— Destruction by cyclone— purchaser may be compelled to perform.

*Section 13* enacts an exception

It deals with the case where a *portion* of the subject matter ceases to exist.

The rule shortly expressed.

Because A, owing to special inevitable circumstances, is unable to perform his promise, it is no reason why B should not perform his, especially as he might have protected himself by making the performance of his promise conditional upon performance by A. Having made an unqualified promise he must stand by it.

## *Specific Performance of a Part of a Contract*

Can the Court decree the performance of a part of the contract? This question is dealt-with in Section 14-17.

*Section 17* enacts a general rule. It lays that the Court will not, as a general rule, compel specific performance of a Contract, unless it can execute the whole contract. Specific performance must be of the whole or nothing.

Sections 14, 15, 16 form exceptions to the rule.

***Exceptions:*** The promises undertaken— may be divisible or indivisible.

1. *Divisible promises i.e.* promises— one part stands on a separate and independent footing from another part. If the former can and might be specifically performed it will be so enforced, although the latter cannot or ought not to be specifically enforced— Section 16.

II. *Indivisible promisers.*— The part which cannot be performed may— (i) Admit of compensation by money or, (ii) It may not.

(A) Admits of compensation— Two cases.

It may bear— (i) A small proportion to the whole undertaking, (ii) A large proportion to the whole undertaking.

If— (i) it bears *a small proportion,* then a party sue for specific performance of either part and for damages for non-performance of the balance— Section 14.

If—(ii) *itbesrs a large proportion, then* the promise may sue for Specific Performance of the remaining part, if he relinquishes all claim to further performance and all right to damages.

(B) Part which cannot be performed, does not admit of compensation.

Then the promisee may sue for Specific Performance of the remaining part, if he relinquishes all claim to further performance and all right to damages— Section 15.

***Illustration:*** A contracts to sell to B an estate with a house and garden for 1 lakh. The garden is important for the enjoyment of the house. It turns out that A is unable to convey the garden.

Can B obtain specific performance to the contract?—Yes, if B is willing to pay the price agreed upon and to take the estate and house without garden, waiving all rights to compensation either for the deficiency or for loss sustained by him through A's neglect or default.

There are *thus* four exceptions to the rule.

1. Where parts are divisible— Specific Performance can be decreed of one part though not of all parts— Section 16.
2. Where parts being in divisible part which *cannot* be performed admits of compensation and bears a small proportion to the whole, the party may sue for Specific Performance — Section 14.
3. Where parts being indivisible, part which *cannot* be performed admits of compensation and bears a large proportion to the whole undertaking, the promisee may sue for Specific Performance of the remaining *i.e.* of the part which can be performed provided he relinquishes all claim to further performance and all right to damages— Section 15.
4. Where parts being indivisible, the part which cannot be performed does not admit of compensation and bears a large Specific Performance of the part which can be performed may be decreed within the terms mentioned in Section 15.

## *Specific Performance of a Contract*

Where the Vendor or Lessor has an Imperfect Title

1. The rule as to this is contained in Section 18. This Section deals with four clauses: (i) Where Vendor/Lessor has acquired good title after the contract. (ii) Where procuring of the consent of other persons is necessary. (iii) Where encumbered property is sold as though it was unencumbered. (iv) Where

*deposit* has been paid and the suit for Specific Performance has been dismissed.

***Clause ( a):*** Is based on the undeniable proposition that when a person enters into a contract without the power of performing that contract, and subsequently acquires the power of performing that contract, he is bound to do so.

***Illus:*** An heir apparent, who contracts to sell the property to which he is heir, will be compelled to specifically perform such contract if and when he succeeds to the property.

Whatever interest the seller acquires in the property subsequently to the contract, he will be compelled to convey to the purchaser.

***Clause (b):*** Is based upon the proposition that where the validity of a contract is dependent upon the concurrence of a stranger to the contract, and the stranger to the contract is bound to convey at the request of the Vendor or lessor, the Vendee and the lessee can compel him to obtain such concurrence.

***Clause (c):*** Is based upon the proposition that where the property sold or leased is represented as being free from encumbrance but is *encumbered*, the Vendor shall be compelled to free it from encumbrance sale of property which is mortgaged— Provided the price is not above the mortgage money.

***Clause (d):*** Clauses (a), (b) and (c) cover cases where the purchaser or lessee is the plaintiff suing for perfection of title.

Clause (d) covers a case, where the suit is brought by the Vendor or lessor for Specific Performance and it fails because of his not being able to perfect the title.

In such a case the Court cannot only dismiss the suit with costs, but proceeds to award to the defendant purchaser a special relief *viz*—the return of his deposit with interest and his cost and a lien for all these on the property agreed to be sold or let.

***General Rule Regarding Deposit:*** Deposit is paid as a guarantee for the performance of the contract and where the contract fails by reason of the default of the purchaser, the vendor is entitled to retain the deposit. Rights of Parties to a Contract to sue for Specific Performance

Four cases to be considered:—

## *For Whom Contracts may be Specifically Enforced*

*Section 23* deals with the question Who may obtain *Specific Performance?* Clause (a) any party thereto. Clause (b) (i) an assignee from a promisee. (ii) Legal representative of a promisee after his death. (iii) an undisclosed principal of a promisee. Each of these may obtain Specific Performance of a contract in which he is interested, but each is subject to the proviso that the contract must not be a personal one, nor must the contract prohibit the assignment of the interest of the Promisee. (c) Persons entitled to the benefit of a marriage contractor compromise of doubtful rights between members of the same family. (d) Remainder man on a contract made by a tenant for life. (e) Reversioner in possession. (f) Reversioner in remainder. (g) New company on amalgamation. (h) Company on a contract made by the promoters.

Cases where contract cannot be specifically enforced except by varying it—Sec. 76.

(1) By mistake or fraud the contract is in terms different from that which the Deft. supposed it to be.

(2) Deft. entered into contract under a reasonable misapprehension as to its effect between Deft. and Plff.

(3) Enters into a contract relying upon some misrepresentation by the Plff.

(4) Where the object is to produce a certain result which the contract fails to produce,

(5) Where Parties have agreed to vary it. *Comment.*

Sections 91, 92. Evidence Act.—A plff. cannot give oral evidence to make out a variation. It does not debar a deft. from showing that by reason of fraud or misrepresentation, the writing does not contain the whole contract; he can under provision I to S. 92 give oral evidence to prove that there is variation. Plff. in that case cannot have a decree unless he submits to the variation; the Plff. is put on his election either (1) to have his action for Specific Performance dismissed or (2) have it subject to variation. If he elects not to accept the variation, he does not lose his remedy of damages.

Persons for whom contracts *cannot* be specifically enforced. This is dealt with in Sections 24 and 25.

***Section 24:*** (i) Who could not recover compensation for its breach. (ii) Who has become incapable of performing or voilates any essential term of the contract. (iii) Who has already chosen his remedy and obtain satisfaction for the alleged breach. (iv) Who, previously to the contract had notice that a settlement had been made and was in force.

This Section is distinguishable from Section 23 in that the defence to Specific Performance is not founded on anything *in the contract itself* but is based solely upon the *acts* or *conduct* of the Plff.

Section 24 is a general Section. While Section 25 is a Section which is a particular one and is limited in its application to two kinds of contracts only:—(i) Contract to sale and (ii) Contract to let property whether movable and immovable,

Sec. 25 says that such a contract cannot be specifically enforced in favour a Vendor or Lessor, *i.e.* in the following cases:—

(i) Knowing not to have any title to the property, has contracted to sell or let the same.

(ii) Who cannot give a title free from reasonable doubt at the date fixed by parties or Court.

(iii) Who, previous to entering into the Contract has made a settlement of the subject-matter of the contract.

Settlement is defined in Section 3 and means any instrument— where by the destination or devolution. Successive interests in movable and immovable property is disposed of or is agreed to be disposed of.

Persons against whom contract may be enforced *Section 27.*

(i) Either party.

(ii) Any other person claiming under a party by a title arising subsequently to the Contract, [except a transferee for value without notice].

(iii) Any person claiming under a title which prior to the contract voidable and known to the plantiff, and might have been displaced by the defendant.

(iv) New company after amalgamation.

(v) Company in respect of the contract made by promoters.

Against whom contract cannot be enforced *Section 28.*

(i) Where consideration is grossly inadequate as to be evidence of fraud.

(ii) Where assent is obtained through misrepresentation; unfair practice or other promise not fulfilled.

(iii) Where assent is given under the influence of mistake of fact, misapprehension or surprise.

***Specific Performance and Discretion of the Court:*** In granting Specific Relief, the important point is—When is the Court bound to grant Specific Performance Relief? Obviously the Court cannot grant Specific Performance Relief in cases where the law provides that no Specific Performance Relief shall be granted. Such cases fall under three classes:

(i) Where the nature of the contract is such that law does not allow it to be specifically enforced.

(ii) Where the Plff. is a person in whose favour a contract cannot be specifically enforced.

(iii) Where the Deft. is a person against whom a contract cannot be specifically enforced.

## Liabilities of the Parties

### *Liabilities of the Seller*

#### *Before Conveyance*

***1. Aection 55 (1) (A)—To Disclose Material Defects.***

(1) A contract for the sale of land is not a contract uberrimal

fidei: The duty of disclosure is not absolute. The duty to disclose is an obligation to disclose latent defects.

(2) A latent defect is a defect which the buyer could not with ordinary care discover for himself. There is no duty to disclose defects of which the buyer has actual or constructive notice.

(3) As to patent defects of which the seller is unaware, the maxim *caevat emptor* applies. But a mutual mistake as to a matter of fact essential to the agreement will render the agreement void.

(4) A latent defect whether of property or of title must be material. A defect to be material must be of such a nature that it might be reasonably supposed that if the buyer had been aware of it, he might not have entered into the contract at all, for he would be getting something different from what he contracted to buy.

(5) Whether a defect is material or not must depend upon the circumstances of each case. When land was sold for building purposes, an underground drain was held to be a material defect, but not when a house or land were sold mainly for residence.

(6) Defects may be Defects in property or Defects in title.

### *2. Section 55(1)—(B)—Production of Title Deeds*

(1) The obligation is to produce title-deeds for inspection and not for delivery.

(2) The documents of title required to be produced for inspection are not only documents which are in the possession of the seller, but also includes documents which are in his power to produce.

(3) There is no obligation *to produce* title deeds unless the buyer makes a requisition.

(4) The Buyer however must not omit to take inspection, otherwise he will be held to have constructive notice of matters which he would have discovered if he had investigated the title.

### *3. Section 55(1)(C)—Sellers Duty to Answer Questions*

(1) When the documents of title are produced, the buyer examines them and if he is not satisfied makes requisitions. These requisitions are.— (i) Requisitions relating to title. (ii) Requisitions relating to Conveyance. (iii) Other enquiries.

(2) Requisitions on title are objections that the documents do not show the agreed title or that the documents are not efficacious *i.e.* not duly attested.

(3) Requisitions on matters relating to conveyance refer to such matters as the joinder or concurrence of parties to the conveyance.

(4) Inquiries are for the protection of the buyer, and call attention to possible omissions of disclosure by the seller, and seek information on such points as easements, party walls and insurance.

(5) The Seller is bound to answer all requisitions which are relevant to the title and which are specific.

(6) The duty to answer requisitions is altogether distinct from the duty of disclosure under Section 55 (1) (a) of a defect, for, the omission of the buyer to make a requisition will not absolve the seller if he has not made a full disclosure.

(7) A buyer may waive requisitions. Waiver may be express or may be implied.

(8) Waiver is implied from conduct. (i) When a buyer does not press a requisition that has been made. (ii) When a buyer asks for time to pay the price. (iii) When a buyer enters into possession. (iv) When a buyer pays the whole or part of the price.

### *4. Section 55(1) (D)—Execution of Conveyance*

(1) The execution may be to the purchaser or to such person as the purchaser shall direct. Consequently, on a resale by the buyer before conveyance, the conveyance may be direct to the sub-purchaser. The seller may require the original buyer to be a party to the

Conveyance if there is a difference of price but not otherwise.

(2) It is the duty of the buyer to tender to the seller a proper draft—*31 Cal.L.J. 87.*

(3) This duty of the buyer is subject to a contract to the contrary.

(4) The execution of the conveyance and the payment of price are reciprocal duties to be performed simultaneously. They are concurrent promises. If either party sues for specific performance, he must show that he was ready and willing to perform his part.

(5) Proper time for execution:— (i) The section is silent as to what is proper time. (ii) The time is usually settled by the contract of sale. (iii) If time is fixed, and an unreasonable delay occurs, the proper course is to give notice making time the essence of the contract (iv) If time is not settled, the proper time is the date when the seller makes out his title.

(6) Proper place for execution:— (i) The Section is silent. (ii) Since it is the buyer who has to tender the draft conveyance to the seller, the proper place for execution would be the Seller's residence or his Solicitor's office.

(7) Cost of Conveyance:— (i) The Section is silent. (ii) This is usually settled by the terms of the contract. (iii) In the absence of any express term, the buyer has to pay the cost of the Stamp—Section 29 (c) Indian Stamp Act.

### *5. Section 55 (1) (e)—Care of Property*

(1) The contract of sale does not give to the buyer any interest in property. But it imposes upon the seller a personal obligation to take care of the property.

(2) The seller must also take care of the title deeds. The loss of title deeds depreciates the value of the property and damage done to the estate.

(3) To take care means to do what a prudent owner ought to and keep the property in reasonable repair and protect it from injury by trespassers.

(4) The obligation to take care is one collateral to the contract and does not merge in the conveyance. The duty to take care continues even after completion of the sale and the buyer is not responsible for any loss caused by the seller. If the seller neglects his duty, the buyer is entitled to compensation to be deducted from the purchase money; after the completion the buyer may recover damages.

### *6. Section 55(1) (G)—Meet Outgoings*

(1) It is the duty of the seller to pay what are called under England Law outgoings. In India they include—(i) Public Charges, (ii) Rent, (iii) Interest, (iv) Encumbrances.

(A) *Public charges over:* (i) Government Revenue. (ii) Municipal Taxes. (iii) Payment charged upon land by Statute either expressly or implied by reason of their being recoverable by distress or other process against the land.

(B) *Rent:* The payment of rent is a question which arises when the property sold is leasehold property. The seller of the leasehold property is bound to pay rents accruing due up to the date of the sale.

(C) *Interest:* (i) Encumbrance means—a claim, lien, or liability attached to the property. (ii) The seller's duty is to discharge all Encumbrances. It is immaterial that the buyer was aware of the Encumbrances when he contracted to buy. (iii) The sale is not subject to Encumbrances, unless there is an express provision to that effect. (iv) If the Encumbrance is a common charge on the property sold and other properties of the seller, the buyer may insist on its being discharged out of the other property.

(6) This liability imposed upon the seller is collateral to the contract and may be enforced even after conveyance.

## *Seller's Liabilities*

### *After Conveyance*

### *1. Section 55(1)(b)—To give Possession*

1. It is the duty of the seller to give possession after conveyance and not to leave the buyer to get possession for himself.
2. This liability may be enforced by a suit for Specific Performance.
3. Time for giving possession— (i) The Section does not say when the seller should give possession. (ii) Reference to Section 55 (4) (a) shows that possession be given when ownership passes to the buyer. This would be at the time of the execution of the sale-deed—*6 Lah. 308.* (iii) The seller cannot refuse possession because price has not been paid unless there was intention to the contrary. (iv) The buyer's right to possession and the seller's right to unpaid price may be enforced in the same suit.
4. Nature of Possession— (i) Possession does not mean actual occupation. (ii) Physical possession in the case of tangible and symbolical possession in the case of intangible properly is enough. (iii) Symbolical possession is enough in the case of property which is in the possession of tenants or mortgagees.

### 2. *Section 55 (2)—To Assure that the Interest Subsists.*

1. There are two views as to whether this liability of the seller is one which arises before conveyance or after conveyance.
   (i) *Calcutta View:* This clause contemplates a completed contract and corresponds to covenant for title in an English conveyance. 57 Cal. 1189.
   (ii) *Madras View:* This clause contemplates cases, where the transaction has not progressed beyond the stage of contract. 40 Mad. 338 (350):
   38 Mad. 1171.

(iii) Lahore view. Follows Madras.
6 Lah. 308.

(iv) *Bombay View:* It pertains to liability after conveyance
18 Bom. S. R. 292: 52 Bom. 883: 31 Bom. LR. 658.

(a) The provisions of Section 55(1) enable the buyer before completion, to ascertain if the title offered is free from reasonable doubt. Once he has accepted the conveyance and the sale is completed, he has no remedy on the contract except for fraud.

(b) The covenant for title implied by Section 55 (2) gives the buyer a further remedy in case of defects discovered after conveyance.

(v) Another view which probably is the correct view. (a) In the matter of Title, the liability of the seller is twofold. (i) He must pass to the buyer a title free from reasonable doubt. (ii) He must pass to the buyer a title which he professes to pass and nothing less. He must make good his representation.

Under (i) he must prove that he has acquired his title in any one of the recognised ways: such as prescription, possession, inheritance, purchase, etc.

Under (ii) if he professes to transfer a full proprietary interest, then interest transferred must be full proprietary interest and not merely occupancy interest: Sale of free from Encumbrances land which is subject to Encumbrance: Sale of non-transferable land as transferable.

(c) Section 55(1) relates to liability for a title free from reasonable doubt: Section 55 (2) relates to liability for passing title which he professed to pass.

2. Section 55 (2) relates to misrepresentation or misdescription as to title. A distinction must be made between misdescription of title and misdescription of property.

(i) Misdescriplion of title is a breach of the covenant for title under Section 55 (2) and gives right to damages.

(ii) Covenant for title does not extend to misdescription of property *i.e.* as to the extent of the land sold.

(iii) A covenant for title is not a covenant that the land purported to be conveyed is of the extent stated in the sale-deed. It is merely a contract with the purchaser of the validity of the sellers' title. Consequently if the purchaser finds a deficiency in area his, suit must be based not on the covenant for title, but for part failure of consideration.

3. Express covenant for title. Every conveyancer has an implied covenant for title. But parties may enter into an express covenant relating to title. The points to be noted in regard to an express covenant are:

(a) If overrides and does away with the effect of all implied covenants.

(b) Although an express covenant alone can govern the rights of the parties, yet an implied covenant cannot be got rid of except by *clear* and *unambiguous* expression.

4. *Who can Claim the Benefit of the Covenant:* The benefit of a covenant for title can be enjoyed not only by the purchaser and his representatives, but also subsequent alienees, who claim under the purchaser, can enforce it as against the seller.

5. Under this clause the vendor is presumed to guarantee his title absolutely to the property. If he wishes to contact himself out of the covenant he must do so expressly or by necessary implication.

6. The implied covenant for title has nothing to do with the question, whether the buyer has or has not notice of the defect of title and the buyer's knowledge of the defect does not deprive him of the right to sue for damages and can claim a return of the purchase-money if he is dispossessed by reason of a defect in title.

7. *Covenant for Title—what does it Include:* The covenants for title implied in an English conveyance, include:
   (i) Right to convey,
   (ii) Right to quiet enjoyment,
   (iii) Right to hold free from Encumbrances,
   (iv) Right to further assurance.

   Under the covenant for further assurance, the seller is bound to do such further acts for perfecting the buyer's title as the latter may reasonably require. Thus, if a seller has, after the sale perfected an imperfect title by the purchase of an outstanding interest, he can under this covenant, be compelled to convey it to the buyer.

   The English covenants are more extensive as they include the covenant for quiet enjoyment, for freedom from Encumbrances and for further assurance. Under Indian Law they are not included.

8. Covenant for title is a covenant for a title free from reasonable doubt. It has been held by the Privy Council that an absolute warranty of title cannot be insisted upon by the purchaser. *9 I.A. 700 (713).*

9. The implied covenant for title does not apply in the case of a trustee:
   (i) A trustee is only deemed to covenant that he has done no act whereby the property is encumbered, or that whereby he is hindered from transferring.
   (ii) If a trustee conveys without disclosing his fiduciary character, he could no doubt be required to convey "as beneficial owner" so as to become subject to the usual covenants for title.

10. The implied covenant for title does not apply in the case of a guardian selling on behalf of the minor.

## The Law of Trusts Outline

### *What is a Trust and to what the Act applies?*

To what kinds of trusts the act applies?

I. ***Section I says in what cases the Act shall not apply.*** They are:

(i) Wakfs created by a Mohammedan.

(ii) Mutual relations of the members of an undivided family as determined by any customary or personal law.

(iii) Trusts to distribute prises taken in war among the captors.

(iv) Public or Private religious or Charitable Endowments.

***I. Explanations.***

1. *Wakf:* Permanent dedication by a person professing the Musalman faith of any property for any purpose recognised by the Musalman Law as religious, pious or charitable.

   Two classes of Wakfs:

   (i) Where benefit is reserved to the settlor and his family— Act VI of 1913 applies.

   (ii) Where no benefit is reserved—Act 42 of 1923 applies.

***II. Mutual Relations of Members of an Undivided Family***

***Illus:***

1. The manager of a joint Hindu family and other members of the family.
2. A Hindu widow and a reversioner.

Their relations are not governed by the Trust Act. They are governed by customary law or personal law.

***III. Distribution of Prises taken in War.***

1. *Prise,*—A term applied to a ship or goods captured *jure belli* by the maritime force of a belligerent at sea or seized in port.
2. All prises taken in war vest in the sovereign, and are commonly by the royal warrant granted to trustees upon trust to distribute in a prescribed manner amongst the captors.

3. To such a trust created for the purpose of distributing prises the Trust Act does not apply.

***IV. Public Trusts and Private, Religious or Charitable Endowments.***

Trusts are either *Public* or *Private Trusts.*

I. *Public Trusts:* A trust is a Public Trust when it is constituted for the benefit either of the public at large or some considerable portion of it answering a particular description. A Public Trust is for an unascertained body of people though capable of ascertainment.

II. *Private Trust:* A Private Trust is a trust created only for the benefit of certain individuals who must be ascertained or ascertainable within a limited time.

III. *The Purposes of a Public Trust:* They fall under three heads:— (i) Public purposes. (ii) Charitable purposes. (iii) Religious purposes.

(1) The phrase public purposes is used in two senses: (a) In its ordinary sense—it includes purposes. Such as mending or repairing of roads, a parish supplying water for the inhabitants of a parish, making or repairing of bridges over any stream or culvert that may be required in a parish.

(2) The Phrase Charitable Purposes—includes alms-giving, building alms-houses, founding hospitals and the like.

(3) The Phrase Religious Purpose—includes relating to religious teaching or worship—purchase or distribution of religious books, upkeep of Churches, Temples, etc.

If a Trust is a Public Trust—The Trust Act does not apply. If a Trust is a Private Trust—Does the Trust Act apply?

The Act applies only if the Private Trust is a trust which is not a Charitable or Religious Trust.

What is the Law that applies to a Public Trust or a Private Trust which is Charitable and Religious? There are various enactments which apply.

1. Section 92, C. P. C.
2. The Religious Endowments Act, 1863.
3. The Religious Society's Act I of 1880.
4. The Official Trustee Act II of 1913.
5. The Charitable Endowments Act VI of 1890.
6. The Charitable and Religious Trusts Act XIV of 1920.

## Different Kinds of Trusts

1. Trusts fall into different classes. The class into which a trust falls depends upon the point of view a trust is looked at—
2. A trust can be looked at from three points of view— (i) From the point of view of the mode in which a trust is created. (ii) From the point of view of the constitution of the trust. (iii) From the point of view of the nature of the duty imposed on the trustee.
3. From the point of view of the mode in which a trust is created trusts fall into two divisions (i) Express and (ii) Constructive.
4. From the point of the constitution of a trust, trusts fall into two divisions (i) completely constituted trusts and (ii) incompletely constituted trust.
5. From the point of view of the nature of the duty imposed on the trustee trusts fall into two divisions (i) Simple Trusts and (ii) Special Trusts.

### *Express and Constructive Trust*

1. A trust can arise in two ways— (i) It is the result of a voluntary declaration made by an individual. (ii) It may be the result of a rule of law.
2. When a trust is the result of a voluntary declaration it is called an Express Trust or Declared Trust. When a trust is the result of a rule of law it is called a Constructive Trust.
3. The term Constructive Trust is used in another sense. In this sense it is used to signify a trust which is the

result of a construction put upon the deed. A trust is a matter of intention. Intention may be declared in specific terms or it may be found by the Court to have been indicated by the party on a proper construction of the deed. In the latter case the trust is sometime called a Constructive Trust.

4. Two things have to be remembered in connection with a constructive trust used in this sense.
   (i) Such a Constructive Trust is some times contrasted with an Express Trust. This is quite wrong. Such a Constructive Trust is really an Express Trust and is not to be contrasted with it. A trust is none the less an Express Trust because the language used by the settlor is ambiguous or clumsy, if, on the true construction of that language the Court comes to the conclusion that a trust must have been intended.
   (ii) A trust which is constructive in the sense that the intention is deduced by constructing the document must not be confused with a Constructive Trust which is the result of the operation of the law. In the former there is an intention to create a trust and in that sense it is the result of the voluntary act of the party. In the latter there is no intention to create a trust. It is the creation of law and not of an act of the party.

*Constructive Trusts* fall into two sub-divisions:— (i) Resulting Trusts. (ii) Non-Resulting Trusts.

The difference between the two will be considered later when dealing with Constructive Trusts. They have one thing in common— they are both the result of the operation of law and not the result of an act of party.

***Completely Constituted Trusts and Incompletely Constituted Trusts***

1. A trust is said to be completely constituted when the trust property is *vested* in the Trustees for the benefit of the beneficiaries. When there is a mere declaration

of a trust but the property is not vested in the Trustee the trust is incompletely constituted.

2. The question whether a trust is completely constituted or not is of the *utmost* importance where no valuable consideration is given for its creation.
3. If value is given it is immaterial whether the trust is perfect or not, for as equity looks on that as done which has been agreed to be done an imperfect conveyance for value will be treated a contract to convey and the Court will see that it is perfected.
4. If no value is given there is no equity and the Court will not grant any assistance to a person seeking to enforce.
5. If there is a complete transfer of property although it is voluntary yet the legal conveyance being effectually made the trust will be enforced by the Court.
6. There are two ways in which a trust may be completely constituted:
   (i) The settlor may convey the property to the trustees.
   (ii) The settlor may declare himself to be a trustee of it.
7. Distinction between complete and incomplete trust—
   (i) A completely constituted trust is one in which the trust property has been finally and completely vested in the trustees.
   (ii) A trust is incompletely constituted when the trust property has not been finally and completely vested in the trustees.

   ***Note:*** All trusts arising underwills are completely constituted, though may be either executed or executory—

   (iii) A seller must take all due steps to do all that it is his duty to vest the property in the trustee, and the instrument of conveyance must also contain a declaration of trust, if the settlor's intention is to escape defeat.

8. Consequences arising from this difference—
   (i) An incomplete trust will be enforced if it is for valuable consideration. It will not be enforced if it is voluntary, *i.e.*, without valuable consideration.
   (ii) Valuable consideration in the law of trust, as in the law of contract, is some valuable thing assessable in terms of money, with the proviso that marriage, and also forbearance to sue is so considered.
   (iii) A distinction exists between valuable consideration and good consideration. The phrase good consideration is applied to natural love and affection. Such a consideration though good is not valuable.
   (iv) A good consideration does not make an incompletely constituted trust enforceable at the instance of a volunteer. It serves to rebut a resulting trust
   (v) *How far marriage is a consideration:* (i) If the settlement is made *before* and in consideration of marriage, it is made for valuable consideration. So it is also, if made after marriage, but in fulfilment of an ante-nuptial agreement to settle. (ii) But if the settlement is made after marriage, and not in pursuance of an ante-nuptial agreement, it is voluntary.
   (vi) *Who are within the marriage consideration:* (i) The only persons within the marriage consideration are the actual parties, the husband and the wife, and the issue of that marriage. (ii) All other persons are volunteers and cannot enforce the provisions of a settlement *as against the settlor* so far as the transfer of property is still incomplete, *e.g.*, an agreement to settle after—acquired property.
9. Does the Indian Trust Act recognise this distinction between complete trust and incomplete trust.

### *Simple and Special Trusts*

1. A Simple Trust is a trust in which a trustee is a mere passive custodian of the trust property, with no active duties to perform..

2. A Special Trust is a trust in which a trustee is appointed to carry out some scheme particularly pointed out by the settlor and is called upon to exert himself actively in the execution of the settlor's intention.
3. A Simple Trust is spoken of as a passive trust and Special Trust is spoken of as an active trust.
4. Where a Simple Trust exists, the beneficiary, provided that he is *sue juris* and absolutely entitled, has a right to be put into actual possession of the property and he enjoys the further right of compelling the trustees to dispose of the legal estate in accordance with the beneficiary's instruction.
5. Special Trusts are divided into—(i) Ministerial and (ii) Discretionary.
6. In both, the trustees have positive duties to perform.
7. The point of distinction is that in a Ministerial Trust the duties are such that the trustee is not called upon to exercise *prudence* while in a discretionary trust a trustee is required to *exercise prudence.*

## Express or Declared Trust

Two kinds of Declared Trusts:

### *Executed and Executory*

An Express Trust is either an *Executed Trust* or is an *Executory Trust.*

### *Executed and Executory Trusts*

1. The expressions Executed and Executory as used in relation to contract have not the same meaning which they have when used in relation to trust.
2. When used in relation to a contract they refer to the carrying out of the contract. When used in relation to a trust they refer to the creation of a trust as distinguished from its carrying out.
3. In the sense in which the term is used in contract every

trust is executory until it is over. But that is not the meaning in which the word is used in relation to trust.

4. When the words *Executed* and *Executory* are used in connection with a trust they have different meaning.
   (1) A trust is an Executed Trust when the author of the trust has not only designated the persons who are to benefit by the trust but has also indicated the *interests* which they are to take in the trust property.
   (2) A trust is said to be an Executory Trust when the author of the trust has only designated the persons who are to benefit by the trust but has not indicated the interests which they are to take in the trust property but has left it to be defined by another person by another instrument.

***Illus:*** On the marriage *of A* and B it is agreed between them that certain property shall be settled on trust for them and for their children.

***Note:*** Here the parties who are to benefit by the trust are defined—They are *A* and *B* and their children:

(1) But what benefits *A* and *B* their children are to take is not defined.

(2) Therefore, it is an Executory Trust.

(3) The line of cleavage between an Executed Trust and an Executory Trust is different from the line of cleavage between a completely constituted trust and an incompletely constituted trust.

(4) The line of cleavage between a completely constituted trust and an incompletely constituted trust is:-in the former the property is vested in the Trustees upon trust; in the latter the property is not so vested.

(5) The line of cleavage between an Executed Trust and an Executory Trust is that in the former the interests of the beneficiaries are defined when in the latter they are not so defined.

(6) That being so an Executory Trust may be a completely constituted Trust.

***Parties to a Trust:***

1. Apparently there are three parties to the transaction of a trust:
   (i) The party who makes the trust.
   (ii) The party who accepts the trust.
   (iii) The party for whose benefit the trust is made.
2. The party who makes the trust is called "the author of the trust". The party who accepts the trust is called the trustee. The party for whose benefit the *trust* is made by the author and accepted by the trustee is called the beneficiary.
3. Is it necessary that the three parties *should* be distinct and separate and that one of three cannot occupy the role of any two of them? The answer to this question is *some* of them can play the role of two.
   (i) The author of the trust and the beneficiary of the trust must be distinct and separate.
   (ii) The trustee and the beneficiary must be distinct and separate.
   (iii) The author of the trust need not be distinct and separate from the Trustee.
4. The reasons why some parties can occupy the role of two in one and some cannot are important. (i) The making of a trust results in the creation of two different estates in the property which is the subject-matter of the trust— the legal and the equitable. A trust lasts as long as these two interests remain separate, (ii) If the legal and equitable estates happen to meet in the same person, the equitable is forever extinguished by being absorbed in the legal. In other words, where the legal and the equitable interests are coextensive and vested in the same person the equitable merges in the legal interests which means that the trust comes to an end.

There are two principles to be borne in mind (i) There is no trust if it does not create a separate equitable interest. (ii) There is no trust if the separate legal and equitable interest become merged.

5. Applying these two principles we reach the following conclusion—
   (i) There is no merger when the author of the Trust and the trustee are the same. Therefore, they need not be distinct.
   (ii) There is no creation of a separate equitable estate when the author of the Trust and the beneficiary are the same. Therefore, they must be distinct.
   (iii) There is merger when the trustee and the beneficiary are the same. Therefore, they must be distinct.

   *To sum up.* The author of the trust and the trustee may be one and the same person. But the beneficiary must always be a distinct person separate from the author of the trust as well as from the trustee.

6. So far we have taken simple cases where the parties are single individuals. What happens when the parties are multiple parties, and where some of them play double role.

   ***Illus.*** (i) A and B are the beneficiaries of a trust Of them A is also a trustee. Is such a trust valid? (ii) A and B are beneficiaries of a trust Of them A is the author of the trust Is such trust valid?

7. The answer to the first question is in the affirmative. It is found in Section 6 which defines a trust. The definition does not give an answer to the Second question. Yet such a trust is invalid.

## *The Creation of an Express Trust*

***Conditions for the Creation of a Valid Trust:*** For the validity of a declared Trust the following *four* conditions prescribed by law must be satisfied.

*(i) Section 6.*

(1) There must be necessary parties to the trust.

(A) The language of the settlor must be such that the Court can find from it, as a fact,

(a) An intention to create a trust;

(b) of ascertainable property;

(c) in favour of ascertainable beneficiaries and

(d) for an ascertainable purpose.

*(ii) Sections 7-8.*

The trust property must be of such a nature as to be capable of being transferred and settled in trust.

*(iii) Section 4.*

The object of the trust must be lawful.

The English Law of Trust differs from the Indian Law in regard to the creation of a trust. According to Snell the creation of a trust requires three certainties, (i) Certainty as to intention. (ii) Certainty as to trust property. (iii) Certainty as to beneficiary. According to Underhill the creation of a trust requires *four* certainties, those mentioned by Snell and one more namely. (iv) The purpose of the trust.

The English Law does not require the transfer of the trust property to the trustee. But the Indian Law does.

***Certainty as to Intention***

(i) The intendor to create a trust may be by words or acts.

(ii) These are illustrations which show how a trust could be created by the acts of the author of the trust.

***Illus.***: (i) A father opening an account in his book in the name of his son in which money is credited in the name of his son. 9 Bom. 125 (ii) A buying shares in 5 Bom. 268 17 Col. 620 (628)

Examples of trust created by words are unnecessary. The question is what kind of language is necessary to show there is a certainty to show that there was intention to create a trust— (i) No technical expressions are needed for the creation of a trust. The matter is one of construction. The question, therefore, which has to be determined is whether upon construction of the will or deed as a whole, the testator intended that the person to whom property was given should take as a mere trustee or should take beneficially, subject to a mere superadded expression of a wish or desire, which the testator may have thought would be sufficient to influence the donee, but which was not intended to and does not impose upon him any obligation. Question is did the author of the trust merely express a wish that the trustee should do a particular thing or did he impose an obligation upon him to do a certain thing. If an obligation was in fact intended then obviously he had the intention to create a trust.

(iii) The language used may be *either precatory* or *imperative.*

(i) The words request, recommend, desire, hope, etc., are precatory words.

(ii) Such words cannot be said to indicate an intention to create a trust, because they do not show an intention to impose an obligation upon the trustee.

(iii) Under the English Law such precatory words were held to constitute a, trust and the trusts were called precatory trust. But the modem tendency is against.

***Certainty as to Beneficiary***

1. The beneficiary must be specified or described sufficiently as to be capable of identification.
2. Illustrations of uncertainty.
   (i) Estate given to A with the direction that he would continue it in the family—family uncertain.
   (ii) To the settlor's relations—relations uncertain.
3. Illustrations of sufficient description
   (i) Descendants-held to be sufficient description and therefore not uncertain

***Certainty of Purpose***

1. How the property is to be applied must be specified.
2. Illustrations of uncertainty of purpose. (i) To consider certain persons. (ii) To be kind to them. (iii) To make

ample provision for them. (iv) To remember them. (v) To do justice to them. (vi) To take care of his nephew as might seem best in future. (vii) To use property for herself and her children and to remember the Church of God and the poor.

3. The purpose of the trust means the way in which the beneficiaries are to be benefited the way in which the property is to be applied.

***Certainty as to Trust Property:*** The property which is to be the subject-matter of the trust must be indicated with reasonable certainty. It must be specified or sufficiently described so as to be capable of identification.

***Illus.***

(i) A bequeathes certain property to B—directing him to divide the *bulk* of it among the children of C. There is no creation of a trust because the property is not indicated with reasonable certainty.

(ii) A gives property in trust for his wife and directs that such part of it as may not be required by her shall, after her death, be held in trust for his children.

(iii) A gives property in trust for his servants with a direction to reward them according to their deserts out of such parts of my estate as may not have been sold or disposed of by her.

## *Conclusion*

1. Thus, it must be clear that the settlor intended to create a *definite* trust over *definite* property for *definite* persons. No trust can arise in the absence of an intent to create a definite equitable obligation giving definite equitable rights to definite beneficiaries.
2. It will, however, be noticed that the failure to nominate a definite person as a trustee does not invalidate the trust. Where a trust is clearly intended, then (subject to the rules as to voluntary trust); the mere omission to appoint a trustee will not invalidate the trust: for equity never allows a trust to fail for want of a trustee.

So, if no trustee is appointed or if the trustee appointed fails, either by death, or disclaimed or incapacity or otherwise the mist does not fail, but fastens upon the conscience of any person (other than a purchaser for value without notice) into whose hands the property comes and such person holds it as a passive trustee, whose only duty is to convey it to new trustees when properly appointed.

3. The effect of uncertainty as to property or as to beneficiary or purpose of the trust is different:
   (i) Where the trust is affected by uncertainty as to property the trust is void. As there is no property capable of identification there is nothing to litigate about.
   (ii) Where the trust is affected by uncertainty as to the beneficiary or the purpose the trust is void. As there is no person named as a beneficiary no one can come forward to enforce it
   (iii) Where the property is described with sufficient certainty, and the words actually used, or the surrounding circumstances make it clear that although the donor has not sufficiently specified. The objects of his bounty or the way in which the property was intended to be dealt with yet he never meant the trustee to take the entire beneficial interest, the Law implies a resulting trust in favour of the donor or his representative.

## *Trust Property ust be Capable of Transfer*

1. What property is capable of transfer?
2. The answer to this question is to be found in section 6 of the Transfer of Property Act.
3. Property which can be transferred may be subject-matter of a trust.
4. But there can be no trust of a beneficial interest under a subsisting trust. A Beneficiary cannot create a trust of his interest in trust. His interest is transferable but he cannot create a trust of it.

5. This marks an important distinction between the English Law and Indian Law of Trust.
6. Under the English Law a beneficiary can create a trust of his equitable estate.
7. The reason is that the Indian Law does not recognise the distinction between legal and equitable estates in a trust.

***Sec. II.—A Trust may be properly created and yet enforceable.***

1. A trust may have been properly created but may not be enforceable. To be enforceable a trust must satisfy two other conditions:— I. The object of the Trust must not be unlawful. II. The formalities prescribed for the creation of a trust must be satisfied.

***Object of the trust Sec. 4.***

1. The object of a trust must be lawful.
2. What are lawful objects?
   (1) The purpose must not have been forbidden by Law.
   (2) Purpose must not be such which if permitted would defeat the provisions of any law.

***What are Unlawful Objects?***

(1) Purpose which is fraudulent
(2) Purpose which involves or implies injury to the person or property of another.
(3) Purpose which is immoral or opposed to public policy.

***Illus.***

(1) Trust for the care of female founding to be trained as prostitutes.
(2) Trust to carry on smuggling business and to maintain it out of the profits.
(3) Trust by a person in insolvent circumstances—defeating creditors.
(4) Trusts for illegitimate children.

(5) Trust for the creation of a perpetuity.

(6) Trust to take effect upon future separation of husband and wife.

3. Whether the trust is lawful or unlawful is to be determined in the case of immovable property by the law where the property is situated.
4. A trust which is unlawful is *void.*
5. Where a trust has two purposes of which one is lawful and the other unlawful, the validity of the trust depends upon the severability of the two. If they can be severed, the one with a lawful purpose is valid and the one with an unlawful purpose will be void. If they cannot be separated the whole will be void.
6. Consequences of settlor creating an unlawful trust—(i) Court will not enforce it in favour of the person intended to be benefited thereby. (ii) Court will not help the settler to recover the estate.

## Formalities for a Valid Trust

***Sec. 5.***

1. A trust may be a trust of immovable property or it may be a trust of movable property. The formalities prescribed by law for the validity of a trust differ according as the property is immovable property or movable property.
2. Formalities in case the property is immovable. Such a trust may be made in two ways— (i) Either by a non-testamentary instrument signed by the author of the trust or by the trustee, or (ii) By the will of the author of the Trust,
3. Formalities in the case of a trust of movable property. There are three ways by which it could be done.

   (1) By a non-testamentary instrument signed by the author of the trust or the trustee.

   (2) By a testamentary instrument signed by the author or the trustee.

(3) By transfer of the ownership of property to the trustee.

4. Difference between declaration and creation of Trust. (Not explained in ms.)
5. Transfer of Trust Property: 1. No trust is created until the author of the trust has divested him of the trust property. That means he must have transferred the property to the Trustee. 2. This does not apply where the author of the trust is himself the trustee. All that is necessary to show is that he has changed the character in which he holds it. 3. This does not apply when the trust is created by a will. The will operates after his death and the trustees then take possession.

***Section II.—A trust may be valid and yet impeachable.***

1. A valid trust may be impeached on the following grounds by the following persons:—
   (a) By the settlor or his successors in title on the ground: (i) of the incapacity of Parties. (ii) of some mistake made by, or fraud practised on, the settlor at its creation.
   (b) By the settlor's creditors, by reason of its having been made with a fraudulent intention to defeat or delay them or because it infringes the provisions of the Insolvency Act.
   (c) By future purchasers of the property from the settlor without notice of the trust, where the trust property is land, and though was intended by the settlor to defeat the claims of future purchasers.

***Incapacity of Parties to a Trust Capacity of the author of the Trust.***

1. The author of a trust must be a person who is *competent* to contract, *i.e.*, (i) He must be major and (ii) He must be of sound mind.
2. Although this prevents a minor from making a trust yet the law provides for a minor making a trust, if the conditions prescribed are observed under the Law, a trust may be made by or on behalf of the minor, provided

it is done with the permission of the Principal Court of original jurisdiction. The Principal Civil Court of original jurisdiction is according to the Civil Procedure Code the District Court.

3. This competency of the Author of the Trust to make a trust is limited in two ways— (i) The property which is to be the subject-matter of the trust must be transferable. (ii) He can transfer it only to the extent permitted by Law for the time being in force. A trust is not valid if the author had no power to dispose of property.
4. What property is transferable and what is not is defined in section 6 of the T. P. Act.
5. The authority to dispose of property and the extent of such power depends upon law.

***Illus.***

(i) A Hindu father cannot dispose of the ancestral property and therefore, he cannot create a trust thereof.

(ii) A Hindu widow cannot dispose of the estate inherited by her from her husband. She having only a life-estate in it— therefore, she cannot dispose of it by way of Trust.

(iii) A Mohammedan cannot dispose of more than 1/3 of his property after the payment of debts and funeral expenses— therefore, cannot dispose of more than 1/3 by way of a Trust.

***Capacity to be a Trustee— Sec. 10.***

1. Every person capable of holding property is competent to be a trustee.
2. Who is capable of holding property? Every *living person* is capable of holding and taking property. Therefore, every living person whether a minor or a lunatic is capable of being a trustee.
3. There is a difference between capacity to contract and capacity to hold and take property. Every living person does not have the capacity to contract; but every living person has the capacity to hold and take property.

4. This distinction is necessary to make and important to bear in mind because a person may not have capacity to contract yet he may be competent to be a trustee provided he has capacity to hold and take property; be not dead physically he must not be dead civilly: (1) A person who is sentenced to transportation is not civilly dead.
7. There is one further distinction which is to be noted. Ordinarily a person who is competent to be a trustee is also competent to execute a trust. But in the case where a trust involves the use of discretion the person who is competent to be a trustee is not necessarily competent to execute a trust.
8. Where the trust is such that it does not involve the use of discretion the requirement for competency to execute a trust is the same for being a trustee, namely, capacity to hold and take property.
9. Where the trust is such that its execution does involve the use of discretion, then the trustee must have capacity to contract.

***Capacity to be a Beneficiary— Sec. 9.***

1. Every person capable of holding property may be a beneficiary.
2. The requirement for being a beneficiary is the same as for being a trustee.
3. That is every living person can be a beneficiary. That is a trust can be created in the interest of every living person. It is not necessary that a beneficiary should have contractual capacity. In this respect his position is regulated by the same provisions as that of the trustee.

## The Revocation of an Express Trust Declared

***Sec. 78.***

1. Whether a trust can be revoked depends upon how the trust is created. (i) If the trust is created by a will then it can be revoked by the testator *at his pleasure.* This

is because will does not take effect till death. There is can be revoked before it takes effect

2. If the trust is created otherwise than be a will—*i.e.*, by a non-testamentary instrument or by word of mouth then it can be revoked in the following circumstances only— (i) If the power of revocation is expressly reserved to the author of the trust. (ii) If the beneficiaries consent, provided all of them are competent to contract

## The Extinction of an Express Trust

### *Sec. 77.*

1. A trust comes to end in the following cases— (i) When the purpose is completely carried out. (ii) When its purpose becomes unlawful. (iii) When the fulfilment becomes impossible. (iv) When the trust being revocable is expressly revoked. (v) If there is only one beneficiary or if there are several (whether entitled concurrently or successively) and they are or they are not under any disability (such as infant, lunatic) the trust may be extinguished by them without reference to the wishes of the setter or the trustees.
2. The terms for the extinction of a trust are the same as those for the extinction of a contract. 1. Two questions remain to be considered. (i) When does a trust becomes administrable? (ii) What estate does the Trustee and Beneficiary have in the trust? 2. These questions are preliminary to the question of the administration of the trust.

***When does a Trust begin to Function?:*** A trust becomes administrable when it has been accepted by the Trustee and the beneficiary:

## *Disclaimer and Acceptance of a Trust*

### *Acceptance Art. 34=Sect. 10.*

1. Although the author of the trust may appoint a person as a trustee, the person so appointed is not bound to accept such appointment.

2. A person appointed to the office of a trustee may accept the office or he may disclaim it.

3. The acceptance of the office may be indicated expressly or by conduct. If it is by conduct it must indicate with reasonable certainty such acceptance.

   ***Illus:*** *A* by his will bequeaths certain properties *to B* and *C* as Trustees for *D*. *B* and C prove A's will. On a question being raised whether *B* and *C* had accepted the office of Trustee, held that their conduct in proving the will was tantamount to acceptance of office.

4. Other illustrations of acceptance by conduct are:—

   (i) Acceptance by acquiescence—Permitting an action regarding trust property being brought in his name.

   (ii) Acceptance by exercising dominion over the trust property—such as advertising for sell—giving notice to tenants.

   (iii) Acceptance by dealing with property—unless the dealing is plainly referable to some other ground.

   (iv) Acceptance by long silence with notice of the trust and in the absence of any satisfactory explanation of the silence.

   (v) Acceptance of a part of the trust is acceptance of the whole, notwithstanding any attempted disclaimer of part.

5. The law does not say how a disclaimer is to be made by a trustee who does not wish to accept the office. It only says that a trustee must do so within reasonable time.

6. Although the law is silent on the point, the following points with respect to disclaimer have been settled by judicial decisions:

   (i) The disclaimer should be before acceptance. Once a trustee has accepted the office he can renounce it only under circumstances mentioned in section 46.

   (ii) A person can disclaim a trust although he may have consented to act as a trustee during the lifetime of the settlor.

(iii) A person cannot disclaim the office as to a part of the trust and accept as to the rest.

(iv) A disclaimer may be by words or by conduct.

7. Effect of disclaimer.

   (i) If there is only one trustee a disclaimer prevents the trust property from vesting in him.

   (ii) If there are two more trustees and if one of them disclaims, such a disclaimer vests the trust property in the other or others or makes him or them the sole trustee or trustees from the date of the creation of the trust.

8. What happens when there is only one trustee and he disclaims. Two things can happen:—

   (i) A new trustee may be appointed under section 73—(a) By one mentioned in the trust (b) If there be none such, by the settlor if alive and competent to contract

   (ii) If no trustee is appointed in place of the one who has disclaimed the property reverts to the settlor or his representatives if he is dead.

9. What happens to the property? Is it freed from the trust? Does it remain subject to the trust?

The answer is that the trust is not extinguished. The settlor or his representatives, if the settlor is dead, holds it on trust for the beneficiary. In other words the setter or his representative becomes the trustee in place of the trustee who has disclaimed.

The rule is that a trust will never fail for want of a trustee. Wherever a trust exists, and there is no trustee to execute it, the person in whom the legal estate vests holds the property as trustee. This rule is intended to protect the beneficiary.

***Mallott* vs. *Wilson (1903) 2 Ch. 494.***

***II. Disclaimer and acceptance by beneficiary:***

***Section 9***

1. A beneficiary is not bound to accept the trust. He may accept it or he may disclaim it.

2. His disclaimer amounts to a renunciation of his interest under the trust.
3. If he wishes to disclaim he can do so in two ways: (i) By a disclaimer addressed to the trustee or (ii) By setting up a claim inconsistent with the trust with the knowledge of the trust.
4. A claim inconsistent with the trust would be a claim such as ownership of the trust property.
5. What happens to the trust when the beneficiary disclaims?

## The Administration of a Trust

In connection with the Administration of a Trust, the Trustee has certain—

(i) Duties—Sections 12—20.

(ii) Liabilities—Sections 23—30.

(iii) Rights—Sections 31—36.

(iv) Powers—Sections 37—45.

(v) Disabilities—Sections 46—54.

Similarly the beneficiary has certain—

(i) Rights—Sections 55—67.

(ii) Liabilities—Section 68.

***1. Duties of a Trustee Sections 12—20***

V (2) Duty to obey directions contained in the Trust.

IV (3) Duty to act impartially between the beneficiaries.

IV (4) Duty to sell Wasting and Reversionary property.

IV (5) Duty in relation to payment of outgoing of Crops and income.

IV (6) Duty to exercise reasonable care.

IV (7) Duty in relation to the Investment of Trust Funds.

IV (8) Duty to pay Trust moneys to the Right Persons.

IV (9) Duty in relation to delegation of Duties and Powers.

IV (10) Duty to act jointly when there are more than one Trustees.

IV (11) Duty not to set up *Jus Tertii*

IV (12) Duty to act gratuitously.

IV (13) Duty not to traffic in Trust Property.

IV (14) Duty to be ready with Accounts.

***V. Powers of a Trustee Sections 37—45.***

***V. The powers of a Trustee***

V (1) General Powers of a Trustee.

V (2) Power of Trustees to sell or mortgage the Trust Property.

V (3) Power in relation to conduct of sales.

V (4) Power to give receipts.

V (5) Power to compound and settle disputes.

V (6) Power to allow Maintenance to Infants.

V (7) Power of Trustees to pay Cost of Beneficiary.

V (8) Suspension of the Trustee's Powers by Administrative Action.

***VI. Powers of the Beneficiaries***

VI (1) Power of a sole beneficiary.

VI (2) Power of one of several beneficiaries.

25. Is a trustee liable for breach of trust by his predecessor? He is not.

26. Is a trustee liable for the breach of trust committed by a Co-trustee?

*He is not* except in the following cases:—

(i) Where he has delivered trust-property to his Co-trustee without seeing to its proper application.

(ii) Where he allows his Co-trustee to receive trust property and fails to *make* due inquiry as to the Co-trustee's dealings therewith or allows him to retain it longer than the circumstances of the case reasonably require.

(iii) Where he becomes aware of a breach by a Co-trustee and conceals it or does not take proper steps to protect the property.

27. Breach of Trust jointly committed by Co-trustees.

What is the liability for each? Is it for the whole? Each is liable for the whole to the beneficiary. There will be a right of contribution from the rest.

28. Liability for Payment by a Trustee to a person who is not the person in whom the beneficiary's interest is not vested.

Trustee is not liable, provided:

(i) He had no notice that the interest had vested in another person.

(ii) That the person to whom payment is made was a person who was entitled to payment.

***XIII. Protection to Trustees***

(1) General Protection.

XIII (2) Statute of Limitation. Each page contains only the heading and not the details—ed.

XIII (3) Concurrence of or waiver or Release by the Beneficiary.

XIII (4) Protection against acts of Co-Trustees.

XIII (5) Right of contribution and indemnity as between Co-trustees.

XIV. Liability of Third Parties and Beneficiaries.

XIV (1) Liability of Third Parties and Beneficiaries who are parties to a Breach of Trust.

XIV (2) Following Trust Property into the hands of Third Parties.

## Constructive Trusts

1. There are *fourteen* cases of constructive trusts which are enumerated in the Trust Act.
2. They fall *under five* heads:—

(1) Constructive trusts arising out of transfers—Sections 81, 82,84,85.

(2) Constructive trusts arising out of unfair advantage gained by one person as against another person—Secs. 85, 88, 89, 90, 93.

(3) Constructive trusts arising out of contracts made-Secs. 86, 91,92.

(4) Constructive trusts arising out of a merger of two personalities in one individual—Section 87.

(5) Constructive trusts arising out of a past trust—Section 83.

### *(1) Transfer or Bequest of Property*

#### *(i) Section 81.*

1. In certain cases the transfer or bequest of property imposes an obligation upon the transferee or legatee in the nature of a trust in favour of the owner or his legal representative. Ordinarily the transferee or legatee would take the property absolutely without any such obligation.
2. When can it be held that the transferee or legatee takes it subject to an obligation? He takes it subject to an obligation when there is no intention on the part of the owner to dispose of the beneficial interest in the property to the transferee or legatee.
3. How is intention to be determined?—In the light of the circumstances of the case. It is the circumstances which must be referred to in order to find out the intention of the owner.

#### *(ii) Section 82.*

1. The second case where the transfer of property imposes an obligation upon the transferee in the nature of a trust is the case where the transferee is made to one and the consideration is paid by another—in such a case the transferee holds it on trust for the person who paid the consideration. Ordinarily the transferee would be the owner in the eye of the law, the property being conveyed to him by the transferror.

2. This rule that a transferee who has not paid consideration holds it on trust for a person who has paid consideration applies generally except in one case—
3. *Exception:* This rule does not apply where there is an intention on the part of the person who paid the consideration to benefit the transferee.
4. Proof of intention.

***(iii) transfer for an illegal purpose. Section 84.***

1. Ordinarily when a transfer is for an unlawful purpose the Court will neither enforce the transaction in favour of the transferee nor will it assist the transferror to recover the estate if he has parted with it.
2. But the rule does not apply under *all* circumstances. The rule does apply under certain circumstances.
3. What are the circumstances in which the rule does not apply?

   The circumstances in which the rule does not apply are—

   (i) If the propose is not carried into execution.

   (ii) If the transferror is not as guilty as the transferee.

   (iii) If the effect of permitting the transferee to retain the property might be to defeat the provisions of any law.
4. In these cases the Court will help the transferror and impose upon the transferee an obligation to hold the property for the benefit of the transferror.

***Bequest upon trust for an illegal purpose. Section 85.***

1. The position in law with regard to transfers for an illegal purpose is on a par with trust for an illegal purpose.
2. That is, a Court will neither enforce the trust in favour of the parties intended to be benefited nor will it assist the settlor to recover the estate if he has parted with it.
3. Section 85 recognises a trust although the purpose is

unlawful. This is in contrast with the general principle enunciated in section 4 of the Trust Act and therefore requires some explanation.

4. The general principles governing the rights of the parties to an unlawful trust and the exceptions to those principles may formulate as follows:—

   I. Where a trust is created for an unlawful and fraudulent purpose, the Court will neither enforce the trust in favour of the parties intended to be benefited nor will it assist the settlor to recover the estate (except in one case).

      Q.—Why is a beneficiary not allowed to enforce it?

      A.—Because it would be giving effect to an unlawful purpose.

      Q.—Why is the author not allowed to recover the estate if he has parted with it?

      A.—Because it would be helping him to take advantage of his own fraud.

   II. The one case in which the settlor allowed to recover the property although the trust is for an illegal purpose is the case where the illegal purpose has failed to take effect.

      Q.—Why is this exception made?

      A.—There are two reasons:—

      (i) The purpose being unlawful no trust arose—it being void *ab initio.*

      (ii) The trustee having paid no consideration has no right to retain the beneficial interest in the property which must, therefore, return to the settlor.

   III. The disabilities attaching to the author of an unlawful trust do not apply to his legal representatives—

      Q.—why?

      A.—Because they are not parties to the transactions.

5. The reason why section 85 recognises a trust in favour

of legal representatives is because they are innocent parties having nothing to do with the creation of an unlawful trust.

***Constructive Trusts arising out of unfair advantage—***

***1. Section 85.***

1. The first case under this head arises where property is bequeathed under a will and the testator during his lifetime wanted to revoke the bequest and he is prevented from revoking it by coercion.
2. Under such circumstances the legatee takes the property not as a beneficial owner thereof but holds it as a trustee for the legal representatives of the testator.
3. The reason is that the legatee has taken unfair advantage by using unfair means. He cannot, therefore, be allowed to retain such an advantage.

***II. Section 88***

1. The second case arises when any person who is bound to protect the interest of another person by reason of his fiduciary relationship with the latter.
2. Persons who fall in this category are—
   - (i) Agent and Principal.
   - (ii) Partners in a firm.
   - (iii) Guardian and ward.
   - (iv) Trustee and beneficiary.
   - (v) Executor and Legatee.
3. The section says—
   - (i) That any such person who gains any pecuniary advantage by availing himself of his fiduciary.
   - (ii) Enters into any dealings under circumstances in which his own interests are adverse to those of the person whom he is bound to protect and thereby gains for himself a pecuniary advantage

     Then,

     He must hold the advantage so gained for the benefit of the person whose interest he was bound to protect.

4. *Illus.*

   (i) A partner buys land in his own name with funds belonging to his firm. He must hold it for the benefit of the partners.

   (ii) A trustee, retires from his trust in consideration of a bribe paid to him by his Co-trustee. The trustee must hold the sum for the benefit of the trustee.

   (iii) An agent is employed by A to secure a lease from B of a certain property. The agent obtained a lease for himself. The agent must hold it for the benefit of B.

   (iv) A guardian buys up the Encumbrances on his ward's property at an undervalue. He can charge the ward only for the value he has actually paid for the Encumbrances.

### *III. Section 89*

1. The third case arises where advantage is gained at the cost of another person by the exercise of undue influence.
2. This is dealt with in section 89. Section 89 says that such a person must hold the advantage for the benefit of the person who is the victim of such undue influence.
3. This is subject to two limitations— (i) The advantage must have been gained without consideration or (ii) The person must have had notice of the advantage having been gained by undue influence.

### *IV. Section 90*

1. The fourth case arises where advantage is gained by a qualified owner availing himself of his position as such in derogation of the rights of other persons interested in the property.
2. This is dealt with in section 90. Section 90 says that such an advantage shall be held for the benefit of all and not merely for the benefit of the one who secured it.
3. Subject to two conditions— (i) The others must repay their due share of expenses properly incurred for

securing such advantage. (ii) The others must bear proportionate part of their liabilities properly contracted for gaining such an advantage.

4. Cases covered are those of cotenants, members of joint family, mortgagee, etc.

### *V. Section 93*

1. The fifth case arises where the advantage is gained by a creditor secretly.
2. Such a case generally arises when the creditors accept a composition from a debtor who is unable to pay his debts in full.
3. If it is found that one of the creditors who is a party to the composition has by arrangement with the debtor unknown to the other creditors gains better terms for himself he shall not be entitled to retain the advantage gained by him by reason of such better terms which have caused prejudice to other creditors.
4. The law will regard him as a trustee for the other creditors in so far as the advantage gained by him is concerned.

## *Constructive Trusts Arising out of Contracts*

### *I. Section 86*

1. The first case dealt with by the Trust Act under this head relates to a contract for the transfer of property.
2. It falls under section 86. Section 86 refers to a contract in pursuance of which property is transferred and where the contract is of such a character that— (i) It is liable to recession or (ii) It is induced by fraud or mistake.
3. The transferee of the property under such a contract shall hold the property for the benefit of the transferror.
4. This obligation arises only under certain circumstances and is not absolute:
   (i) The obligation arises only on receiving notice from the transferror that the contract is liable to recession or that it has been induced by fraud or mistake.

(ii) The obligation will be enforced only on repayment by the transferror of the consideration actually paid by the transferee.

*II. Section 91*

1. Acquiring property with notice that is subject to a contract with another person.
2. In such a case the person who acquires the property must hold it for the person who had contractual rights in it.
3. This obligation is limited in its extent. It is enforced only to the extent necessary to give effect to the contract.
4. This obligation does not arise in the case of every acquisition of property which is subject to a contract. It applies only in the case of a contract which could be specifically enforced.
    1. Property bought for being held on trust for certain persons.
    2. A contracts to buy property from B and represents to B that the purpose of buying it is to hold the property on trust for C. B believing in the representation of A sells the property to A.
    3. A must hold the property for the benefit of C.
    4. This obligation is also limited in its extent—It is enforced only to the extent necessary to give effect to the contract.
    5. The contract may be to hold part of the property in trust for C. In that case the obligation will be enforced only to the extent of the property.

***Constructive Trust Arising out of Merger of Two Personalities in one Individual.***

*1. Section 87*

1. This provides for the case of double personality —one man but two persons.
2. Every contract, debt, obligation or assignment requires two persons.

3. But these two persons may be the same human being.
4. In all such cases, were it not for the recognition of double personality, the obligation or Encumbrance would be destroyed by merger.
5. Because no man can in his own right be under any obligation to himself; or own any Encumbrance over his property.
6. But with the recognition of the double personality this is possible.
7. In fact this is necessary.
8. *Illustration*— Debtor becoming executor. Executor is the owner in the eye of the law. Merger. Extinction of debt.
9. Section says no.

## The Administration of a Constructive Trust

### *The Indian Trust Act*

1. The Law relating to Trust is contained in Act II of 1882.
2. It is an Act which defines and amends—that means that it does not introduce any new principle.
3. The Act does not consolidate the Law—That means that it is not an Exhaustive Code.
4. The object of the Act was to group in one to enact the legal provisions relating to trusts. Before the Act of 1882 the statutory law relating to trust was contained in 29 *Car II. C. 31 sections 7— II.*

   ***Act XXVII of 1866 Act XXVIII of 1866:*** There were also few isolated provisions scattered through the Penal Code, Specific Relief, C. P. Code Stamp Act, Limitation, Government Securities Act, Companies Act, Presidency Banks Act.
5. As originally passed, the Act did not apply to the whole of British India. For instance, it did not apply to Bombay. But provision was made to extend it by notification by local Government.

6. It is unnecessary to discuss here whether the Hindu Law and Mohammedan Law recognised trust as defined in the Trust Act. That may be dealt with by others.

### *The Nature of a Trust*

1. Trust is defined in section 3. A trust involves three things:
   (1) A person who is the *owner* of some property.
   (2) Ownership burden with an obligation.
   (3) Obligation to use the property for the benefit of another or of another and himself.
2. It is ownership without beneficial enjoyment. It involves separation of ownership and beneficial enjoyment.
3. A trust arises out of a confidence reposed in and accepted by the owner.
4. The owner in the eye of the law is the trustee. After the trust is created the author of the trust ceases to be the owner of the property.

#### *What is a Trust*

1. The terms Trust and Trustee are defined in various enactments of the Indian Legislature.

(i) Definition in Specific Relief Act I of 1877. Section 3—
   (1) *Obligation* includes every duty enforceable by law.
   (2) *Trust* includes every species of express, implied or constructive fiduciary ownership.
   (3) *Trustee* includes every person holding expressly, by implication, or constructively a fiduciary ownership.

(ii) *Definition in the Indian Trustees Act XXVII of 1866. Section* 2—"Trust shall not mean the duties incident to an estate conveyed by way of mortgage; but with this exception, the words *trust* and *trustee* shall extend to and include implied and constructive trusts, and shall extend to and include cases where the trustee has some beneficial estate or interest in the subject of the trust, and shall extend to and include the duties incident to the office of executor or administrator of a deceased person.

(iii) *Definition in Limitation Act IX of 1908. Section 2 (ii)— Trustee* does not include a benamidar, a mortgagee remaining in possession after the mortgage has been satisfied or a wrongdoer in possession without title.

(iv) *Indian Trusts Act II of 1872.*

(1) Section 3—"A trust is an obligation annexed to the ownership of property...

(2) Ingredients of a Trust (i) A Trust in an *obligation.* (ii) The obligation must be annexed to the *ownership* of property. (iii) The ownership must arise out of *confidence* reposed in and accepted by the owner. (iv) The ownership must be for the benefit of another (*i.e.*, a person other than the owner) or of another and the owner.

## *Explanation of Terms*

I. There must be obligation.

II. Obligation must be annexed to ownership property.

1. There may be an obligation to which a person is subject although there is no property to which it is annexed.

   *E.g. Torts* assault—

2. There may be property without there being any obligation attached to it. *E.g. Full* and *complete* ownership—sale of property.

III. The ownership of property may befounded in confidence or it may not.

***Illus.***: A person may transfer ownership to another with the intention of conferring upon him the right to enjoy the property.

A person may transfer ownership to another without the intention of conferring upon him the right to enjoy the property. The difference between ownership founded in confidence and ownership not founded in confidence consists in this—

(i) In the latter there is *a jus in re* (a complete and full right to a thing) *or jus ad rem* (an inchoate and imperfect right).

(ii) In the former there is not. *E.g.* Bailment.

3. The nature of a trust can be better understood by contracting it with other transactions resembling a trust.

## *Trust Distinguished from Agency*

1. Where there is a trust, the ownership of the trust property is in the trustee. The trustee is personally liable on all contracts entered into by him in reference to the trust, although he may have a right of recourse against the trust funds or against the beneficiary.
2. An agent has no ownership in law in the goods entrusted to him. If an agent enters into a contract as agent, he is not personally liable. The contract is with the principal.

## *Trust Distinguished from Condition*

1. Cases of condition differ from cases of trust in two respects—

   *First.* A trust of property cannot be created by any one except the owner. But A may dispose of his property to B upon condition express or implied that B shall dispose of his own property in a particular way indicated by A.

   *Second.* The obligation of the person on whom the condition is imposed is not limited by the value of the property he receives, *e.g.*, if A makes a bequest to B, on condition of B paying A's debts, and B accepts the gift, he will be compelled in equity to discharge the debts although the exceed the value of the property.

2. But the words "upon condition" may create a real trust. Thus a gift of an estate to A on condition of paying the rents and profits to B constitutes a trust because it is clear that no beneficial interest was intended to remain in A.

   A may dispose of his property to B upon condition express or implied that B shall dispose of his property to C. There is a condition in favour of C.

## *Is this a Trust? Trust Distinguished from Bailment*

1. Bailment is a deposit of chattel and may in a sense be described as a species of trust. But there is this great difference between a bailment and a trust, that the general property in the case of a trust, is in the trustee, whereas a bailee has only a special property, the general property remaining in the bailor.
2. The result of this difference is that an unauthorised sale by a trustee will confer a good title upon a *bonafide* purchaser who acquires the legal interest without notice of the trust, whereas such a sale by a bailee confers as a rule no title as against the bailor.
3. Bailee does not become the owner of the property as a result of the bailment. But a trustee does in law become the owner of the property as a result of the trust notwithstanding he is under an obligation to deal with the property in a certain specified manner.

## *Trust Distinguished from Gift*

Ordinary contract differs from a trust. Contract which confers a benefit on a third party closely resembles a trust.

1. There is a similarity between a Trust and a Gift inasmuch as in both the transfer results in ownership. The Trustee and the Donee both become owners of the property.
2. But there is a difference between the two. In a gift the donee is free to deal with the property in any way he likes. In a Trust the trustee is under an obligation to

use the property in a particular manner and for a particular purpose.

### *Trust Distinguished from Contract*

1. That there is a distinction between trust and contract is evident from the existence of differing legal consequences attached to a trust and to a contract:
   (i) A trust, if executed, may be enforced by a beneficiary who is not a party to it whilst only the actual parties to a contract can, as a rule, sue upon it
   (ii) An executed voluntary trust is fully enforceable while a contract lacking consideration is not.
2. However, the determination of the question whether a given set of facts gives rise to a trust or a contract is not easy. What is the test?

   Keetan—-pp. 5-6 (1919) A. C. 801 | 38 Bom. S. R. 610.

   (1926) A. C. 108

   It is a question of intention.

### *Trust Distinguished from Power*

1. The term "power" in its widest sense includes every authority given to a person (called the donee of the power) to act on behalf of or exercise rights belonging to the person giving him the authority (called the donor of the power).
2. Powers are of many kinds *e.g.*
   (i) The common law power of an agent to act for his principal, given sometimes by a formal "power of attorney".
   (ii) Statutory power such as the power of sale given to a mortgagee.
   (iii) The various express and implied equitable powers possessed by trustees and executors.
   (iv) Powers to appoint trusts so as to create equitable interests.
3. The power of appointment is a transaction which

resembles a trust and it is this which must be distinguished from a trust.

The word appointment means-pointing out, indicating-the act of declaring the destination of specific property, in exercise of an authority conferred for that purpose-the act of nominating to an office.

The last class *termed, powers of appointment* are made use of where it is desired to make provision for the *creation* of future interests, but to postpone their complete declaration.

Thus in a marriage settlement, property may be given to trustees upon trust for the husband and wife for their lives and, after the death of the survivor upon trust for (i) *Such of the children* of the marriage as the survivor shall appoint, or (ii) *All the children* of the marriage in such shares as the survivors shall appoint. In such a case, upon appointment being made, the child to whom it is made takes exactly as if a limitation to the same effect had been made in the original instrument.

A power of this kind, where there is a restriction as to its objects (*i.e.*, persons in whose favour it may be exercised) is termed a *special power of appointment.* But there may be a *general power* of appointment when there is no such restriction, so that the donee may appoint to himself. In such a case the donee having the same powers of disposition as an owner, is for most purposes treated as the owner of the property:

(i) A power may give a mere discretion and therefore is distinct from a trust, which creates an obligation or

(ii) A power may impose an obligation to exercise the discretion.

In the former case there is no trust. In the latter case there is. The former is called *mere power.* The latter is called power in the nature of a trust *or power coupled with trust.*

(iii) There is also a third category of cases which arc cases of a *trust coupled with a power.*

These are cases where a trustee of a property though under an obligation to apply it for the benefit of certain individuals or purposes, may have a *discretion* as to whether he will or will not do certain specified acts, or as to the amount to be applied for any one individual or purpose or as to the time and manner of its application.

In such cases, the Court will prevent the trustee from exercising the power unreasonably, it will not compel him to do such acts or attempt to control the proper exercise of his discretion.

1. Power resembles a trust and also differs from it.
   - (i) It resembles a trust inasmuch as a power is an authority to dispose of some interest in land, but confers no right to enjoyment of land.
   - (ii) It differs from a trust inasmuch as a power is discretionary, whereas a trust is imperative; the trustee if he accepts must necessarily do as the settlor directs.

***New Trustees:***

(1) Survivorship of the office and estate or trustee on death.

(2) Devolution of the office and estate on Death of the survivor.

(3) Retirement or Removal of a Trustee.

(4) Appointment of New Trustees.

***Appointment of a Judicial Trustee.***

***The Public Trustee.***

(1) Nature and Function.

(2) Appointment of a Public Trustee as an ordinary Trustee.

(3) Appointment and Removal of the Public Trustee.

(4) Duties, Rights and Liability of the Custodian Trustee and Managing Trustee.

(5) Special Rules relating to the Public Trustee.

***The Rights of the Trustee***

(1) Right to Reimbursement and Indemnity.

(2) Right to discharge on completion of Trusteeship.

(3) Right to pay Trust Funds into Court.

Right of trustees and beneficiaries to seek the assistance of public trustee or court.

(1) Right of Official audit.

(2) Right to take direction of Court.

(3) Right to have Trust administered by Court.

(4) Right to take direction of Court.

(5) Right to have Trust administered by Court.

***Consequences of a Breach of Trust.***

***Definition of Breach of Trusts:*** Breach of trust is defined in section 3, a breach of any duty imposed on a trustee, as such, by any law for the time being in force, is called a breach of trust.

***Under the English Law:*** Any act or neglect on the part of a trustee which is not authorised or excused by the terms of the trust instrument, or by law, is called a breach of trust.

***Breach of Duty:*** A trustee has Duties, Right, Powers and disabilities. Only breach of duty is breach of trust.

1. The measure of liability is the loss caused to the trust property.
2. Is he liable to pay interest? Only in the following cases:
    (a) Where he has actually received interest.
    (b) Where the breach consists in unreasonable delay in paying trust-money to the beneficiary.
    (c) Where the trustee ought to have received interest, but has not done so.
    (d) Where he may be fairly presumed to have received interest.
    (e) Where the breach consists in failure to invest trust-money and to accumulate the interest or dividends.
    (f) Where the breach consists in the employment of trust property or the proceeds thereof in trade or business.
3. Is he entitled to set off a gain from breach of trust against a loss from breach of trust.

## *Introductory*

What is the nature of the Law of Limitation?

1. There are various ways in which a time-limit enters into a course of litigation: (1) Cases where the law says action shall be taken within a stated period:

   ***Illus.***—Order 6 Rule 18.—Amendment of a Plaint. Party obtaining leave to amend must amend within the time fixed by the Court for amendment and if no time is fixed then within 14 days. (2) Cases where the law says action shall not be taken before a certain period has elapsed.

   ***Illus.***—Section 80 of the C. P. C.—Suit against Secretary of State. No suit shall be instituted against the Secretary of State for India in Council or against any public officer in respect of any Act purporting to be done by such public officer in his official capacity, until the expiration of two months next after notice in writing has been given. (3) Cases in which the law prescribes that action shall not be taken *after* a certain period has elapsed.
2. It is the *third* class of cases which strictly speaking constitute the subject-matter of the Law of Limitation.

***Distinction between Limitation—Estoppel—Acquiescence and Laches:*** All these have the effect of denying to an aggrieved party a remedy for the wrong done to him. That being so it is necessary to distinguish them from Limitation as such.

## *Limitation and Estoppel*

1. By Limitation a person is prevented from getting relief because of his having brought the action after the time prescribed for bringing his suit.
2. By Estoppel a person fails to get relief because he is prevented by law from adducing evidence to prove his case.

## *Limitation and Acquiescence*

1. Limitation defeats a suitor in the matter of obtaining relief for a wrong because he has *consented* to the doing of the wrong because his suit is beyond time.
2. Acquiescence defeats a suitor in the matter of obtaining relief for a wrong because he has *consented* to the doing of the wrong.

## *Limitation and Laches*

1. Both have one common feature—relief is denied on the sole ground that action is not brought within time.
2. The distinction lies in this—In limitation time within which action shall not be brought is prescribed by Law. In laches there is no time prescribed and the Court, therefore, in granting relief works on the principle of unreasonable delay.
3. In India the doctrine of laches has not much scope because of the Law of Limitation which has prescribed a definite time limit for almost all actions. It does not, therefore, matter whether a man brings his suit on the first day or the last day of the period prescribed by law for his action.

The doctrine of laches applies in India only in the following cases:

(1) Where the relief to be granted by the Court is *discretionary*.

This is so (i) In cases falling under specific relief. (ii) In cases falling under interlocutory relief.

(2) Where the Law of Limitation does not apply *e.g.* Matrimonial suits. Delay would mean that the offence was condoned.

## *The Object of Limitation*

1. Two things are necessary for a well-ordered community (i) Wrongs must be remedied. (ii) Peace must be maintained.

2. To secure peace of the community it is necessary that titles to property and matters of right in general should not be in a state of constant uncertainty, doubt and suspense.
3. Consequently, if persons are to be permitted to claim relief for what they think are wrongs done to them, then they must be compelled to seek relief within a certain time. There is nothing unjust in denying relief to a person who has tolerated the wrong done to him beyond a certain period.
4. The Law of Limitation is based upon this principle.
5. That being the underlying principle, the Law of Limitation is absolute in its operation and is not subject to agreement or conduct of the parties. That is to say it is not subject to (1) Waiver. (2) Custom. (3) Estoppel. (4) Variation in respect of enlargement or abridgement of time by agreement of parties sections 28 and 23 of the Contract Act.
6. In this respect the Law of Limitation differs from the Law of Negotiable Instruments.
7. Limitation and the onus of Proof.
   1. The onus of proof is upon the Plaintiff. He must prove that his suit is within time.

      37. Bom. S. R. 471-A.I.R.. 1935 September.

      A by a registered lease, dated 8th July 1922, gave certain lands to B on a rental for a period of 25 years. Subsequently, A dispossessed B alleging that the lease was taken by undue influence. B brought a suit against A for an injunction restraining A from interfering in any way with his possession and enjoyment and for possession of land.

      It was contended on behalf of B that A was precluded from challenging the validity of the lease, on the ground that if he had sued to have the lease set aside the suit would have been barred by Limitation. In other words, it was contended that the plea of the Defendant was barred of the Limitation.

Question is: Is Defendant bound by the Law of Limitation?

The answer is No. —Section 3 refers to Plaintiff and not to Defendant.

8. Plea of Limitation and the Stage of the Proceedings.
    1. The plea of limitation may be raised at any stage of the proceedings, *i.e.*, it can be raised even in second appeal.
    2. It can be raised for the first time in appeal

        38 Mad. 374

        36 Cal. 920

        38 Cal. 512

        38 Bom. 709 (714).
    3. It can be raised in appeal even though it was abandoned in the trial Court.

        3 All. 846 (848).
    4. It can be raised before the Privy Council although it had been abandoned in the Courts below.

        361 A. 210.
    5. This is subject to the proviso that when it is raised in the appeal stage Court will not allow it if the facts on record are not sufficient for its decision and if it involves a further inquiry into facts.

        57 Cal. 114.

# The Indian Law of Limitation

## *Its Scheme of Arrangement*

Operation of Lapse of time under Indian Statute Law

1. Lapse of a definite period of time produces four results under Indian Statute Law.
    (1) It multiplies the right of the holder to obtain a remedy for the wrong—Section 3 of the Limitation Act.

    (2) It not only bars his remedy but extinguishes his right—Section 28 of the Limitation Act.

(3) It confers a right to light, air, way, watercourse, use of water or easements on a person who has enjoyed it for a prescribed period— Section 26 Limitation Act. (4) It extinguishes right to easements—Section 47 of Act V of 1882. (2), (3), (4) are cases which fall under the Law of Prescription. (1) Only falls under the Law of Limitation. The Limitation Act deals with a mixed body of law and two must be studied separately.

## *Its Applicability*

### *In Respect of Territory*

1. The Act extends to the whole of British India—*Section 1(2).*
2. The Act applies to *every* suit instituted, appeal preferred and application made in Courts functioning in British India.
3. It does not matter where the cause of action, whether in British India or outside British India, it does not matter where the transaction took place, whether in British India or outside British India, if the suit is instituted or appeal is preferred or application is made in a Court in British India, the Law of Limitation that will apply will be the Indian Law of Limitation and not Foreign Law of Limitation.
4. There is one exception to this rule which is enacted in section 11 (2) which says: A Foreign Rule of Limitation shall be a defence to suit in British India on a contract entered into in a foreign country if the rule has extinguished the contract and that the parties were domiciled in such country during the period prescribed by such rule.

### *In Respect of Proceedings*

1. Special Proceedings
   (1) *Arbitration Proceedings:* It was at one time doubted if the Limitation Act applied to proceedings before an Arbitrator on the ground that it applied only to

suits, appeals and applications to the *Court* and that the Arbitrator was not a Court. This doubt has now been resolved by the Privy Council which has held that where persons have referred their disputes to arbitration, the arbitrator must decide the dispute according to the existing law and that he must recognise and give effect to every defence of limitation, unless that defence has been excluded by agreement between the parties. (1929) 561. A. 128.

*Ques.* This decision goes to the length of laying down that parties can vary the Law of Limitation by private agreement. This seems to overlook the provisions of sections 28 and 23 of the Contract Act.

(2) *Proceedings under the Companies Act.:* When a Company is being wound up and a liquidator is appointed to carry on the affairs of such Company, Section 186 of the Company's Act provides that the liquidator may make an *application* to the Court for an order upon a person "to pay any moneys due from him to the Company. "Ordinarily there would have to be a suit. But to avoid multiplicity of suits this special proceedings is permitted by law.

Question is whether Limitation applies to such proceedings. It has been held that "money due" in section 186 means moneys due and recoverable in law, *i.e.*, *moneys not* time-barred. This means that the Law of Limitation applies to such proceedings. *601.A.13(23)*

(3) *Proceedings under the Income Tax Act.:* The Civil Courts in India have no jurisdiction in matters of public revenue.

They can have such jurisdiction only if a particular Revenue Act invests them with such jurisdiction. For example a provision will be found in section 66(3) of the Indian Income Tax Act of 1922. Under the section, a party aggrieved by an order of the Income Tax Officer in the matter of assessment may apply to him for stating a case to the High Court and if he refuses may apply to the High Court for an order compelling the Commissioner to state a case and refer it to the High Court.

There is a time-limit for such an application. But the Law of Limitation does not apply to it. The time-limit is the time-limit prescribed by the Income Tax Act and not by the Law of Limitation.

(4) *Proceedings before the Commissioner of Workmen's Compensation:* The Workmen's Compensation Act, 1923, provides for Compensation to be paid to workmen for injuries caused to them in the course of their employment. The cases are heard by a Commissioner. The Commissioner is a special tribunal and not a Court and therefore the Limitation Act does not apply to proceedings before him.

This does not mean that the claim for compensation for injury can be prosecuted before him at any time. That would be so if the Act had made no provision for a time-limit. As the Act has presented six months as the time-limit, suits have to be brought within that period.

(5) *Proceedings under Registration Act.*

(1) Presentation of Documents—4 months.

(2) Appearance of Parties for admitting Documents-4 months.

### *Criminal Proceedings*

1. Criminal Proceedings are generally instituted in the name of the Crown because they involve a breach of the King's peace.
2. It is a maxim of Constitutional Law that lapse of time does not affect the right of the King.
3. That being so the Law of Limitation does not apply to criminal prosecutions.
4. Two things may be noted:

(1) There are many Acts which prescribe limits of time for institution of prosecution under those Acts. *E.g.* Government of India Act, Section 128: Opium Act, Customs Act, Salt and Excise Acts and Police Act.

(2) Limitation Act, although it does not provide for any time-limits for criminal prosecutions, it does provide for *appeals* under the Cr. P. C.

*Civil Proceedings*

(i) With regard to *suits* different kinds of suits have been specified in different Articles. There is also a general residuary Article No. 120 which is made to apply to any suit for which no period of limitation is provided elsewhere in the Schedule. The Act, therefore, applies to *all* suits.

(ii) With regard to *appeals* there are two Courts to which appeals can lie in India—(i) The Court of a District Judge and (ii) The High Court. The Limitation Act specifies appeals to both these Courts and therefore, it can be said that the Law of Limitation applies to all appeals.

(iii) With regard to applications, different kinds of applications are enumerated in the different articles in the Schedule. As in the case of articles relating to suits there is also an Article 181 for applications for which no period of limitation is prescribed elsewhere in the schedule or by section 48 of the C. P. C. But almost all High Courts have held that the operation of this Act is to be restricted to applications under the C. P. C. only. That being so it is clear that the Limitation Act does not apply to all applications. For instance it does not apply to:

(i) Applications for the grant of probate letters of administrations succession certificates.

(ii) Applications under the Rules of the High Court

32 Bom. I

48 Cal. 817

46 Cal. 249.

(iii) Applications under a Local or Special Act (unless such Act provides for it).

These not being matters dealt with by the C. P. Code.

***In Respect of Persons***

1. The general rule is that the plea of limitation applies to every Plaintiff.
2. Originally, limitation did not apply to the Crown when it sued as a Plaintiff, on the ground that lapse of time did not affect the Crown. This maxim of Constitutional Law although it governs criminal prosecutions has been negatived so far as civil proceedings by the Crown are concerned by Article 149 of the Limitation Act which applies to every kind of suit brought by Government, and prescribes 60 years as the time-limit. Suits against Government must be brought within the ordinary time-limits.

   15 Mad. 315.

   Similarly, suits by private persons claiming through Government are also subject to the ordinary time-limit prescribed by the Act. This was always the rule. It was not always the rule for Government to bring a suit within any prescribed time. This has now been altered. It can, therefore, be said that as a rule the Law of Limitation applies to all persons whether they are private persons or corporate bodies of Governments, and that the plea of limitation is available to every Defendant as against every Plaintiff whether that Plaintiff is a private person or a Government.
3. The plea of limitation is available to every Defendant. To this rule there are certain exceptions.

   37 *Bom.—S. R. 471*

***Section 10.***

The defence of limitation is not available to a person in whom property has become *vested in trust* for any specific purpose nor is it available to his legal representatives or assigns (not being assigns for valuable consideration), in a suit for recovery of the property or the proceeds thereof or for an account of such property. This section is to be applied to an *express trust* as distinguished from an *implied* or *constructive trust.* A trustee of an implied or constructive trust can take the defence of limitation.

Distinction between an Express Trust and Implied or Constructive Trusts. Persons, therefore, who are holding a fiduciary position are not trustees within the meaning of Section 10; *E.g.* Agent, Manager, Factor, Benamidar, Executor or Administrator, Banker, Surviving partner. Director of a Company Liquidator of a Company, *Karta* or Manager of a joint Hindu family. Secondly Section 10 is applicable only in cases of persons "in whom property has become *vested* in trust for a *specific purpose" 44 Mad.* 277 *(281-2).*

*What is Specific Purpose*? A specific purpose is a purpose that is actually and specifically defined in the document by which the trust is created for a purpose which from the specified terms can be certainly affirmed.

49 1.A. 37 (43)

58 I.A.I

That being so even a trustee *de son tort* would fall within this Section.

Meaning of *a trustee de son tort.*

***Explanation:*** Hindu, Mohammedan and Charitable endowments are declared to be express trusts and their managers express trustees.

Thirdly.-Section 10 not only applies to the defaulting trustee himself, but also applies to his legal representatives and assigns except assigns for valuable consideration. Purchasers for value from a defaulting trustee are protected and they can plead limitation.

Whether purchasers from a trustee must in addition to being purchasers for value should also be purchasers without notice of trust is a point on which the Act is silent. Judicial decisions on this point are, however, in conflict.

Section 29 (3) II. The Limitation Act does not apply to parties litigating under the Indian Divorce Act (IV of 1869).

***As against a Special Law***

1. Besides this General Law of Limitation there are other special or local laws which also prescribe time-limits for suits, appeals or applications. In case there is a difference between the time-limits fixed by the general and special law, question is which law is to prevail.
2. The answer to this question is given in Section 29. According to the Section the special law will prevail over the general law.
3. Section 29 also provides for the applicability and non-applicability of the other Sections of the Limitation Act in cases of conflict between the general and special law as to time-limit.
4. According to Section 29, in cases of conflict the provisions of Sections 4, 9 to 18 and 22 of the Limitation Act will apply (unless expressly made inapplicable) and the remaining provisions of the Act shall not apply (unless expressly made applicable by the Special Law).

***The Scheme of the Law of Limitation***

1. The Indian Limitation Act consists of 29 Sections and one Schedule.
2. The Schedule is divided into three Divisions:

   *First Division*—deals with Suits.

   *Second Division*—deals with Appeals.

   *Third Division*—deals with Applications.
3. The Schedule in respect of each of its Divisions is cut up into 3 Columns.

   *Column 1*—Describes the nature of the claim for which suit is brought or of the appeal or if application is made. Provision is made for 154 different classes of suits.

   Provision is made for 9 different classes of appeals. Provision is made for 26 different classes of applications.

Each of these provisions is numbered seriatim and is called article no so and so. There are in all 189 articles in the Schedule though the last article is 183, that is, because some articles have the same number and are distinguished by the addition of A to the same number.

*Column 2.*—Specifies the period *within* which the suit must be filed, appeal or application must be made.

*Column 3.*—Specifics the starting-point of the period of limitation within which *suit* must be filed or appeal or application must be made.

4. The Sections of the Act in so far as they deal with the Law of Limitation as distinguished from the law of prescription deal with various questions arising out of the three columns of the Schedule. The Schedule, therefore, is the most important part of the Law of Limitation.

# 4

# Ambedkar's Quest for Distributive Justice

Bhimrao Ambedkar (1891-1956) who was a dominating figure and active organiser of the dalits during the anti-colonial struggle against the British in India. His concept of distributive justice was based on the idea of a casteless society. This is of course a vast topic, and in order to make it manageable, let us concentrate on certain aspects of his theory, namely, the critique of domination and oppression of dalits, and their exclusion from the rights of citizenship. Ambedkar's main claim is that a society based on the caste system cannot be a 'real' community because it violates the respect and dignity of individuals. His critique of a caste-ridden society raises some interesting questions about the limits of the theory and practice of citizenship and liberal politics in India. Intention here is to analyse his ideas on equality and justice in the way they complement other themes and concepts in his work. Since many arguments were are part of a larger project, the numerous simplifications may be regarded as tentative and provisional.

To develop the setting for the discussion on distributive justice, In section I Ambedkar's critiques of both the rule of the Indian National Congress and Brahmin domination of society place him in an uneasy position within the discourse of nationalism. In Section II, the views of Gandhi and Ambedkar on equality and distributive justice, which reflect the differences in their approach towards the abolition of the caste system. In

Section III, critical examination of three components of Ambedkar's theory of distributive justice. Having done this, a brief work or in the final section to argue that while Ambedkar believed both in the basic tenets of liberal politics and a casteless society, the principles behind the one often contradict those behind the other.

Some of the questions raised in this account are: first why did Ambedkar differ from other nationalist leaders in his analysis of Indian society? What is the concept of Swaraj in Ambedkar's account of Brahmin domination? How did Ambedkar resolve, if he ever did, the idea of separate electorates with a conception of distributive justice in the struggle for the liberation of dalits? But in focusing on Ambedkar, some might object to have ignored many other arguments presented in favour of liberation. Before looking at possible answers to these questions let us give some reasons why it is important to look at Ambedkar from this perspective. There are three contemporary debates to which this essay will make a contribution.

First, consider the claims made by the historians of the freedom movement led by the Indian National Congress. The view that the national movement is a 'popular, multi-class movement' is grounded on the assumption that the entire world of political action can be comprehended through the categories of imperialism, nationalism and communalism. As a corollary to the above, there is the assumption that the concept of nationalism has a deeper significance and therefore it resists multiplicity and retains its indissolubility despite every attempt to resolve it into subdivisions such as region, class, caste and gender.

Of course, recent history writings, represented for example by the historians of the subaltern school, question these assumptions to a large extent. But it is surprising how often one reads about 'subaltern' protests without encountering the name of Ambedkar, and his efforts to improve the condition of the dalits. Moreover, these critiques of colonial discourse valorise indigenous communities; this makes impossible sympathetic evaluations of many movements for women's rights and lower-caste protests which might have utilised aspects of colonial policies and western ideologies. It is argued that the question of the identity and existence of the nation was addressed by Ambedkar in opposing there elite-led nationalist project. What was the nation, what was national oppression and the way to overcome it, was a common question. What is interesting is his answer which focuses on the oppressive character of the Hindu community based on the principles of the caste system. By arguing for the rights and basic needs of the dalits, he challenges the assumptions of both nationalist politics and indigenous communitarian politics. By choosing to discuss Ambedkar, we hope to point towards histories not neatly preoccupied with anti-colonial nationalism; once ensnared within the 'particularism' of national politics, these leaders found it difficult to maintain focus on social disadvantage as the main fulcrum around which politics should be organised.

The second problem which arises in focusing on Ambedkar is of locating him in the debate on modernity and tradition. Of the various streams which responded to colonialism, Ambedkar could be inaccurately placed, in the category of 'modernists'. This response, as described by Bhikhu Parekh, viewed Hindu society as "beyond hope and their salvation lay in radically restructuring it along modern or European lines". The modernist programme for the "regeneration of India consisted in creating and using a strong, interventionist, democratic, secular and centralised state to recreate society". Although they covered a wide spectrum, the proponents of this view were united in their belief that the state stood for modernity and society for tradition.

Ambedkar articulates the theme of modernity by claiming that individualist forms of organisation typically replace communitarian ones like the caste system in modern society. He shares much with his contemporaries in the liberal tradition on this project. However, he goes further because he envisions the reconstruction of our existence embedded in social relations characterised by caste groups. Despite his belief in the project of modernity, he departs from other exponents of this tradition by giving new arguments for certain concepts like equality and distributive justice in the colonial context and by adopting a critical position on the European experience. The prospect of moulding India or its institutions in the image of the British had no appeal for Ambedkar. For how else could he turn to Dhamma?

This point is raised because it is of great importance in the current debate on modernity and tradition in political science. Some scholars question this dichotomy by arguing that "a transformed version of this "traditional" structure had become a vehicle for representative and parliamentary democracy and was functioning as a democratising force". Caste, according to this view, "was anti-caste, in that the horizontal mobilisation of larger lower caste communities was gaining them power, status and wealth which allowed them to challenge and overturn the hierarchy of caste as ritual rank... In this sense, "traditional" structures and communities of sentiment, identity and action seemed to us by no means irrelevant even to competitive democratic politics and the realisation of egalitarian values."

Now this is very different from what Ambedkar wished to achieve by questioning this dichotomy; he saw the caste system as a serious obstacle in the path of democracy. According to him, democracy lies not in the form of government but in terms of association between the people who form that society. Because Indian society is divided and graded on the basis of the caste system, it is not democratic.

The third problem is to explore how questions of caste have entered into formulations of both Indian and Hindu nationalism. According to Gail Omvedt, even before Veer Savarkar developed a coherent Hindu ideology during the 1920s equating 'Hinduism' and 'nationalism', "the dominant elite ideological trend by the end of the 19th century was that of a revitalised Hinduism equated with nationalism". This is the most difficult area to explore. Ambedkar's relationship to the national movement was complicated and problematic. The fundamental error, Ambedkar believed, was to fail to see the danger from the views of, not of the orthodox Hindu, whom he had given up years before as hopeless, but of Gandhi and the Congress. Why could he not isolate the obscurantist and parochial current in this confrontation?

## Indian Society: Ambedkar's Analysis

The first question which arises is: Why did Ambedkar not endorse the nationalist discourse of this period? There are several answers to this. One explanation for this is given by Omvedt when she writes: "It is impossible to conceptualise the Dalit movement in India in the absence of Ambedkar, it is equally difficult to imagine, sociologically, Ambedkar coming of any other region than the Marathi-speaking areas of British presidency". Let us explore this a little bit more.

Omvedt refers to the existence of an important tradition of anti-caste movement in Maharashtra that needs to be seen as part of the response to industrialisation and urbanisation. This was the site of the radical movement of Jotiba Phule's Satyashodhak Samaj, and from the time of Tilak, it had also provided a strong base for Hindu revivalism in the form of a Hindu Mahasabha. In fact, the Indian National Congress held its first session in 1885 in Bombay.

There was another reason for Ambedkar's critical position on nationalist politics. He was a Mahar, the largest untouchable caste in Maharashtra. His actions, then, according to Zelliot, "were moulded not only by his own personal background, and achievements, and the Maharashtrian thinking of his day, but also by his status as an untouchable". This group he came from had begun social and political movements before he assumed a position of leadership. Behind this identification with a non-Brahmin group lay the logic of a movement that was essentially anti-caste and not simply a movement for 'untouchability removal' or 'self-reform'. This is not to say that the Mahar movement in the later 19th century was an isolated movement but only to suggest that all these influences constantly streaming in are employed by Ambedkar in a new sense and directed towards a new solution.

To what extent does his work, in this political scenario, represent more than a resuscitation of known and traditional ideas and to what extent does it deviate from the traditional mode and contain new and original thought? There is no doubt that Ambedkar's writings chiefly captured the political tradition of their time: the philosophical views of that time must be at least in part responsible for his dissatisfaction with the nationalist discourse – the new political mood after the Montague-Chelmsford Reforms; an awakening among the minorities for safeguarding their interests in relation to the Hindu majority which pointed towards wider political participation in the national movement. Yet, his thesis does not fit in with the dominant discourse on nationalism. One of the reasons behind Ambedkar's verdict on the national movement and its leaders, was their general indifference to caste issues. The intelligentsia, as part of the Congress leadership, organised first as social reformers against the British, and also organised as nationalists to challenge many aspects of Indian tradition. But they remained very ambiguous towards removal of the caste system. Linked to the debate on social and political reform was the issue of class. Many communist leaders analysed caste in a mechanical class framework and sought to override traditional identities rather than reinterpret them.

Therefore, a plausible explanation could be found in his own solution for liberating the dalits. Ambedkar realised that the identification of Indian culture with Hinduism is incorrect. Because he believed that absorption into Hinduism meant the acceptance of Hindu leadership in the national movement, he felt it would be wiser to take chances with a religion which has many safeguards. At first, he tried to assert the path of radical autonomy, encouraged the dalits to form their own organisations and to deal independently with some basic issues. It means that the dalits themselves, "would have to redefine and reconstitute their relations with the whole of Hindu society". But if the dalits were not Hindus, what were they? In fact, a non-Hindu choice seems to have led him finally, to identify with Buddhism.

At the theoretical level, Ambedkar's language turned out to be singularly open to misconstruals. It was not easy for many to accept the Indian National Congress, social reform organisations and the Hindu Mahasabha as irreconcilable opponents of the dalits; neither was it easy to accept the praise accorded by Ambedkar to the British state for raising the status of untouchables. Even more open to misunderstanding was Ambedkar's critique of nationalism: whereas Ambedkar attacked the Congress for their failure to recognise caste issues, he was erroneously taken to reject nationalism altogether. He was supposed to be not only anti-national but to advocate a separatist policy which was anti-sectarian as well. Opposed by both traditionalists and Congress leaders, Ambedkar reserved his most bitter attack for Gandhi's reformism.

## Distributive Justice: Debate with Gandhi

The conflict between Gandhi and Ambedkar in terms of their ideological difference on the caste system. Both the thinkers approach the matter from quite different angles. There are real and serious disagreements between them, especially regarding the conclusions that each of them draws from their premises.

Gandhi had two arguments against untouchability: the unity or the political argument and the ethical argument.

As a leader working for a national goal, Gandhi argued for removing injustices faced by 'untouchables' because he felt the need to weave the divergent interests in India into a unified opposition to the British; he argued for pursuing this course of reform without challenging the social fabric of Indian society. He emphasised that a political separation of untouchables from the rest of the Hindu population would reduce Hindu plurality vis-a-vis other minority groups, in part, the Muslims.

The ethical argument is premised on the view that Hindu society must rest on moral consensus, that political conflict can only be kept within bounds if there is a moral consensus on the caste system. Gandhi's ethical argument rested on two claims. First, he claimed that the heart of the caste Hindu could be changed by applying moral pressures within the framework of the Hindu tradition. Second, there was an obligation on the caste Hindu to be individually responsible towards the lower caste groups. In his conception of the moral or perfect society, Gandhi maintained that its enduring basis can only be the moral calibre of the individuals who constitute it. Although Gandhi's views changed over the years, he always believed in the *varnashrama dharma,* the divinely ordained division of society into four defined groups according to duty: Brahmin, Kshatriya, Vaishya, Sudra. In an exchange of views on this problem, he said:

> *I do not believe the caste system even as distinguished from varnashrama to be an 'odious and vicious' dogma. It has its limitations and defects but there is nothing sinful about it, as there is about untouchability, and, if it is a bye-product of the caste system, it is only in the same sense that an ugly growth is of a body or weeds of a crop. It is wrong to destroy caste because of the outcaste, as it would be to destroy a body because of an ugly growth in it, or of a crop because of its weeds...*

Later, he distinguished between caste and varna. In his response to Ambedkar's undelivered speech titled: 'Annihilation of Caste' (1936), he said:

Caste has nothing to do with religion... it is harmful both to spiritual and national growth. Varna and Ashram are institutions which have nothing to do with castes. The law of varna teaches us that we have each one of us to earn our bread by following the ancestral calling. It defines not our rights but our duties... The callings of a Brahmin– spiritual teacher–and a scavenger are equal, and at one time their due performance carries equal merit before god and seems to have carried identical reward before man.

To this Ambedkar replied, questioning the logical conclusions of his doctrine: "When can a calling be deemed to have become an ancestral calling so as to make it binding on a man? Must man follow his ancestral calling even if it does not suit his capacities, even when it has ceased to be profitable? Must a man live by his ancestral calling even if he finds it to be immoral?"

Following arguments from justice, rather than arguments for unity, Ambedkar states that existing inequalities cannot be morally defended: to avoid the morally illegitimate exclusion of untouchables one would have to differentiate conceptually and practically between different levels of citizenship. Ambedkar proposed these arguments when he came into conflict with the Congress, and with Gandhi in particular, on two occasions – the temple entry attempts and separate electorates. Ambedkar put forward arguments based on the principle of liberal equality and distributive justice to sustain his case. Equality meant not the equal status of varnas, but equal social, political and economic opportunity for all.

At first, he made several attempts to gain religious and social rights for the untouchables, by using the Gandhian technique of satyagraha; drinking water from a public tank in Mahad (1927), temple entry to the Parvati temple at Poona (1929), and then the Kala Ram temple at Nasik (1930-35). The failure of temple entry movements demonstrated, according to Ambedkar, that the untouchables were not really a part of Hindu society and would never be accepted as equals by Hindus within that framework. It was quite obvious that this low threshold concept of a legal conception of equality allows for different degrees of political participation. In short, it does not allow for a corresponding conception of political citizenship. Thus, from a position of questioning the brahmanical social order, Ambedkar moved towards its rejection: raising the issue of conversion by the untouchables in 1935.

But there was another reason. The second occasion was the Round Table Conference held in 1930 at London, where both leaders confronted each other on the issue of the political rights of depressed classes.

Earlier, in the 'Evidence before the Southborough Committee on Franchise' (1919), Ambedkar (invited as a delegate of the depressed classes) had argued eloquently for uniform franchise, for securing access for the depressed classes to the public sphere–to public wells, roads, schools, temples, and cremation grounds–and for special provisions for their adequate representation of their interests and opinions.

Untouchability constitutes a definite set of interests which the untouchables alone can speak for. Hence, it is evident that we must find the untouchables to represent their grievances which are their interests, and secondly, we must find them in such members as will constitute a force sufficient to claim redress.

After the Round Table Conference, (where he argued against a general territorial electorate for the untouchables), the communal award of 1932 gave the depressed classes, a double vote, one in a special constituency and one in the general electorate – a decision which appeared to recognise untouchables as a minority group outside of Hinduism. Gandhi's response was to enter fast unto death on September 20, 1932. He expressed his argument on the grounds for unity between the two:

> A heart understanding between the two, the greatest opportunity of repentance and reparation on the part of the suppressors... I would therefore favour widest possible franchise for the suppressed and establish a convention between the two sections for securing proper election of representatives of the suppressed.

Under great pressure from other political leaders, Ambedkar relented. However, the Poona Pact, which followed, recognised untouchables as a political category across British India by providing reservations of seats for the depressed classes in the central legislature and in the provincial legislature. Admittedly, all of these changes had hardly any effect on the economic conditions of the untouchables, but it did set in motion an important process of transformation at the level of ideology.

## Limits of Ambedkar's Quest for Liberation

In a limited sense, Ambedkar's conception of equality and justice derive from the liberal vision and tradition. But given the context of the colonial state, he departs from that tradition and innovates thinking about justice in a remarkably novel way. There are three components of Ambedkar's theory of distributive justice:

(a) equality of opportunity for all citizens

(b) critique of Hindu society based on an autonomous ideology, and

(c) establishment of a casteless society by removing oppression and domination.

Ambedkar accepted a legal and social conception of equality, which call the formal principle of a liberal conception of equality. It entails the elimination of arbitrary advantages in a social and economic system, irrespective of whether the inequality results from one's choice or that of another.

What he also found desirable was the idea of equality of opportunity for all human beings in the social and political sphere. It was further linked to his argument for more abundant political and civil liberty for dalits. On his account this requires that any government treat all those in its charge as equals, that is, as entitled to equal concern and respect. This idea of equality of opportunity as an example of the maximisation of equal liberty. In this view, to demand equality of opportunity is to demand the removal of obstacles that stand in the way of an individual realising his potential.

Ambedkar's initial programmes attempt to integrate the dalits into society and politics through 'modern' political institutions. He put his faith in the constitution and the legislative process, as well as the representative bodies to correct social and economic injustice. Ambedkar's ideal for the low caste groups was to raise their educational standard so that they may overcome the social disadvantages imposed by their birth, and be in a position to use political power in resolving problems of injustice. His adaptation of western concepts is reflected in the way he used to justify political rights of the dalits based on democracy, fraternity and liberty, in Marathi speeches; he conveyed the implication of these concepts in a single word, manuski which means 'humanness'.

While Ambedkar saw the prescriptive uses of the concept of equality in moral and political arguments as quite useful, he was conscious of the inequality of treatment based on caste and tradition. To bring about a more substantial equality must involve treating people differently which is contrary to the formal principle. For such reasons he advocated a separatist policy for the dalits which might accentuate caste distinctions at an initial stage but eventually make these identities unimportant. Therefore, Ambedkar insisted on the right to take into account the special claims of certain communities which had for centuries been excluded from position of equality and respect.

Departing fundamentally from the individualist premise of the equality principle he proposes:

(1) A theory of rights as legal entitlements casting obligations on the members of civil society. The 'untouchables' had a set of rights and the state a duty to eradicate discriminatory practices. Norms of nondiscrimination apply not only to government but also to civil society–corporations, schools, places of worship, etc.

 Where the rights theorists of the 17th and 18th century tended to regard right as a faculty of possession, Ambedkar encourages us to stress the relational aspect of rights. The important point here is that these rights are put forward as important elements or vital ingredients in a fully realised human life. The core argument is that members of the group suffer because they are neither accorded the same respect nor afforded the same opportunities as other persons or groups. They are prevented from realising their capacities, in other words, they are not treated with full respect and dignity.

(2) The basic human needs of the dalits were not only material (wealth, occupational mobility) but non-material; all have the right to be human and the right to live with dignity and self-respect. Although, he stressed the need for reservation in representative institutions, this is only to acquire equality in other goods. For such reasons, he extended his theory to cover such goods as self-respect, power and honour.

Therefore, Ambedkar accepted the premise of equality but advocated group-based politics to achieve that goal. The first is constitutive and the second derivative. Ambedkar eloquently pleaded the case the necessary priority of community claims over individual rights on the grounds that these departures from formal equality could be justified in the following way:

***The Anti-discriminatory Theme:*** The anti-discriminatory principle's main purpose is to prevent private practices and legal procedures from stigmatising the individuals involved. This was viewed as necessary given that structural forms of oppression against the dalits were well entrenched. To remedy this social malaise Ambedkar raises the possibilities for political participation of dalits through reservations. It was his view that a legislature 'mainly composed of high caste men, will not pass a law removing untouchability, sanctioning inter-caste marriages, removing the ban of the use of public streets, public temples, public schools.'

***The Reparation Theme:*** The other idea was that of historic injustice suffered by the dalits. This theme was proposed to offset the systematic and cumulative deprivations suffered by lower castes in the past. Ambedkar argues that some oppressive cultural practices and social institutions result in injustice and accumulated disabilities for untouchables.

He was aware of the conceptual incoherence these themes gave rise to when applied to policy issues. But this is a derivative political position. In fact, he was to warn of the possibility that these special claims might eat the general rule of equality altogether. Unlike anyone else, he pursued the argument that "the constitution should not only declare that we shall have specific rights that every community will have, but that the constitution should provide ways and means by which we shall be protected in the exercise of these rights".

The second component of Ambedkar's theory of distributive justice was the construction of an 'autonomous' ideology opposed in fundamental respects to the traditional ideology of varna. The central problem, for him, in this regard was the formulation of a counter-ideology which can bring about radical social change; he was concerned to fight for a new society based on equal concern for all. This is evident from his critique of the Hindu community on the following basis:

(1) the community as unequal;
(2) the community as based on segregation both territorial and ideological;
(3) the closed nature of the community; and
(4) the distinction between the public and private sphere.

The first aspect of his critique was directed at the theory of 'chaturvarnya' which makes the principle of graded inequality 'the basis for determining the terms of associated life as between the four varnas'. This is not merely notional, but legal and penal: under this system the sudra is subjected to innumerable ignominies and disabilities so as to prevent him from raising above the conditions fixed for him by law.

The second aspect draws attention to the permanent segregation of people in the Hindu community based on the ideological principle of purity and impurity. He rejects the territorial segregation which accompanies this. While distinguishing between the rights of untouchables and the pure he raises some fundamental questions of citizenship: "But the impurity of the 50-60 million of the untouchables of India, quite unlike the impurity arising from birth, death, etc., is permanent: The Hindus who touch them and become polluted thereby can become pure by undergoing purificatory ceremonies. But there is nothing which can make the untouchables purer... It is a case of permanent, hereditary stain which nothing can cleanse".

The third aspect of his critique is directed at the nature of closed religious communities without entry points. In 'Mr. Gandhi and the Emancipation of Untouchables' (1945), he points out that the legislative majorities and minorities are political categories which are fluid subject to the process of party formation and electoral practices. But the Hindu and the untouchable relationship cannot be captured by these categories. Their difference is that 'they are separated by a fundamental and deadly antagonism'. Hindus and untouchables are not fluid categories but they are 'fixed as permanent communities'.

He argues against nationalist attempts to define what it means to have equal opportunities – in terms of having the same distribution of results for major social groups in the public shaper. He revealed the inequality in the social sphere arising out of the nature of closed religious communities, because "most people do not realise that society can practise tyranny and oppression against an individual in far greater degree than a government can... What punishment in the penal code is comparable in its magnitude and its severity to excommunication?"

On the basis of these propositions, Ambedkar's solution for the dalits – the establishment of a casteless society – went beyond the liberal framework he was located in.

From a liberal point of view, Ambedkar was arguing for an individual's freedom to associate; to form communities and to live by their own terms based on equal concern. A corollary of this is that the individuals should be free to dissociate from such communities.

Again, his view placed great weight on the nature of communities as voluntary associations. But, since membership is determined by birth in a Hindu community, rather than by deliberate choice, it is a coercive association. There is no option of entry for those born outside–even though groups might seek to redefine their boundaries. While superficially attractive, the liberal view of the self as a totally unencumbered and radically free subject seemed plagued with difficulties.

This eventually led Ambedkar to locate the distinction between a (voluntary) political community within which an individual exercises his legal rights, and a (coercive) cultural community within which individuals could not even formulate their aims. People who have the same rights to citizenship may not have the same cultural rights. A political community, argued Ambedkar, may not be coextensive with one cultural community, as is envisaged by the nation state. For Ambedkar the two forms of community do not always coincide. This distinction leads him to argue that individuals are free to leave–to renounce– membership and to reconstitute their own community. Here Ambedkar was mistaken in his assertions about liberalism's implications: there was no good reason for any liberal to support him in this. But, it is this very justification that inspired him to seek conversion to Buddhism.

In Ambedkar's opinion the transition from British to Hindu masters signified no emancipatory potential for the masses. The fight for a national cause, according to him, misconstrues the role of Swaraj: "In the fight for Swaraj, you fight with the whole nation on your side. In this, you have to fight against the whole nation and that too, on your own... In my opinion, only when the Hindu society becomes a casteless society that it can hope to have strength enough to defend itself. Without such internal strength, Swaraj for Hindus may turn out to be only a step towards slavery."

It is this total programme of societal transformation which constituted his conception of Swaraj. Swaraj was not just freedom from the British, it was a freedom based on distributive justice.

Ambedkar's critical dialogue with some Congress leaders and his struggles to reform Hindu society occurred within a colonial context. His struggle is not with faith but with false brahmanical beliefs, not with religion but with Brahmin domination of Indian society. He portrays the nature of the caste system in our society in particular using it to show that Hinduism was incapable of establishing a just political and social order. His view differed from other nationalist leaders and social reformers in that he never claimed higher caste status for untouchables, nor did he ever invoke another claim – that untouchables were pre-Aryan, the original settlers of the land or claimed spiritual equality for lower castes within the Hindu tradition. And most importantly his reforms were not directed towards the caste- Hindus. Unlike other critiques of Brahmin domination and caste hierarchy which focus on the unity argument, Ambedkar's critique provides a justice argument against the caste system.

Most nationalists argued that their country was fragmented, deeply divided into a large number of castes, sub-castes and local communities; that is why the Hindus had failed to develop a sense of mutual concern and social compassion. Ambedkar's theory of caste oppression focuses not only the distributive paradigm (allocation of material goods such as resources, income, wealth or the distribution of social positions, such as jobs) as many contemporary liberal theories do, but also brings out the issues of decision-making (representative institutions for the dalits) division of labour (occupational mobility), and culture that bear on distributive justice but were often ignored in national assessments of their social structure.

This argument was premised on two views: (a) the problems of dalits would always have a particularity that could not be subsumed under class or national mobilisation; (b) the status of the dalits was 'irreversible' if they remained isolated within Hinduism. Therefore, he formulated Dalit liberation in terms of two solutions–political assertion through separate electorates and ideological liberation from Hinduism by converting to Buddhism.

Unfortunately, the very cogency and persuasiveness of his arguments raise questions as to the broader contours of his thesis. Dissatisfied with the dominant proposals for the reform of the caste system, Ambedkar undertakes a recovery of Buddhism as a religion that relates to individuals with dignity and respect. However, Ambedkar's point that Buddhism provides the needed theoretical framework to understand Indian politics has its weaknesses. Indeed, by spending considerable energy exploring key conceptions in Buddhism such as Ahimsa, rebirth, karma, etc., Ambedkar leaves us wondering how helpful Buddhism is if the terminology is so open to interpretation.

Behind this solution lay the laudable ideal that responsibility for removing group identity status lies with the dalits themselves, not with the larger dominant society. But it is an explanation that completely ignores the pernicious effects of casteism in the Indian social fabric. On the flip side, Ambedkar's 'self-help' ideology perpetuates the mythical notion of a 'monolithic' Dalit community which made it possible for them to confront other parties. But this political legitimisation also pre-empts questions of interest differentiation among the dalits.

This takes us to my final observations. All this is not to deny that in his critique of the caste system, Ambedkar is clearly arguing for expanding the rights of citizenship to the 'untouchables'. At a more substantive level he is pushing the case for a casteless society without oppression. How was this possible in practical politics?

These two perspectives are contradictory if the objectives they focus upon – the promotion of political and social equality, the abolition of the caste system – are conceived as aims in themselves. But unlike the abolition of the caste system, in Ambedkar's writings, that liberal politics with their emphasis on rights, equality of concern and respect, or freedom to associate can sensibly be defended as more than an instrumental objective. He believed that the more an individual's rights are restricted due to his caste location–for example by constricting the mobility in occupation, of residence, of religion, etc.–the less possibility is there of social and distributive justice.

The principles underlying the caste system unlock the mystery to the inegalitarian distributive outcomes in other spheres. It is an important consideration and one that plays a key role in what is regarded as the only cogent justification for removing caste system in Ambedkar's work. He poses the question whether separation, in some fashion, from the larger body politic, may produce more tangible results than have previous strategies (Gandhi's and Shinde's) aimed at integrating them into the system. Hence, his arguments for separate electorates for dalits should be seen as derivative; equal opportunity in liberal politics was not his ultimate goal. In fact, he wishes to achieve much more.

In the most general sense, the Dalit community is reconstructed by analysing the structural antagonism and conflict within the Hindu community: the idea of shared meanings, of normative frames and cultural values is questioned. By developing a theory of oppression of the untouchables by locating their exploitation, marginalisation and powerlessness, he highlights the structural and institutional relations that delimit the lives of the dalits. He also gives prominence to their cultural oppression which means how the dominant meanings of our society stereotype one group. Ambedkar always thought his account of the role of caste system and its ultimate demise was superior to any other. And as history has shown, he was too optimistic in his predictions and not clear enough in this vision. However, mistaken he was in this analysis and however short-sighted he might appear to many scholars, with respect to the discourse of nationalism, the chief application of Ambedkar's political thought may be seen today to reside in his reflections on social and distributive justice. The subsequent course of Indian politics was to prove him correct; it was not the nation state but its opposite, – irreconcilable political clashes between religious communities and caste-wars that would become the order of the day.

## A Visionary's Plans

B. R. Ambedkar is well known as the principal architect of the Indian Constitution, a social reformer and an emancipator of the poor and the deprived. Having studied bar at the Gray's Inn in UK, he had established himself as a legal luminary. He was a great scholar and a prolific writer in diverse areas like sociology, anthropology, history, economics, politics, law and religion.

However, what is not so well known is the fact that he was also an eminent economist. His academic achievements in economics include a Ph.D. degree from Columbia University, Master of Science in Economics from the London School of Economics and Doctor of Science in Economics from the University of London. He contributed a great deal to the formulation of India's postwar economic development plan in general and planning and development of water resources and electric power in particular.

In his book, Abraham elaborates on Ambedkar's economic philosophy and seeks to trace the relevance of his ideas on economic planning and development to the present day problems of the economy. Evidently, Ambedkar's views on Centre-State financial relations, fiscal deficit, necessity to reduce non-plan expenditure, Government's responsibility towards the weaker sections of society, necessity of land reforms, transfer of surplus labour from agriculture to industry etc. are of contemporary relevance.

Ambedkar enunciated the principles of Centre-State financial relations in the Constitution of India keeping in view the need for a strong Centre and proximity of state governments to the people based on his analysis of 'The evolution of Provincial Finances in British India'. No less important is his contribution to incorporate in the Constitution the provision for the appointment of a Finance Commission every five years to decide on the sharing of the tax kitty between the Centre and States. The crucial importance of this provision can be seen from the fact that even after five decades, and 10 Finance Commissions, the financial relations between the Centre and States remain somewhat strained.

During the discussion on the functions of the Comptroller and Auditor General at the time of framing the Constitution in 1949, Ambedkar enunciated that the Governments should spend the resources mobilised from the public not only as per rules and regulations but should also ensure that 'faithfulness, wisdom and economy' have gone into the acts of expenditure by public authorities. Ambedkar's initiative to ensure that electricity is listed in the 'Concurrent List' in the VII Schedule of the Constitution enabled the Centre to take positive steps for intensified growth of the power sector in subsequent years. The subsequent creation of the Central Electricity Authority (CEA) has been singularly instrumental in planning, developing and nurturing the mammoth system of generation, transmission and distribution facilities that span the length and breadth of the country today.

Thanks to Ambedkar's initiatives during pre-independence years, the need to generate more power at a faster pace for accelerating the country's all round development was recognised since the inception of planning process in 1950. In successive Five Year Plans, power development was accorded a very high priority.

Ambedkar had clearly visualised that India should exploit not only the hydropower resources but also all natural resources such as coal and petroleum.

The book clearly brings out Ambedkar's significant contribution to economic planning and development and his emphasis on the need for land reforms, infrastructure development and industrialisation in order to eradicate poverty and improving the standard of living of the people. The author also highlights his vision and agenda for the social and economic emancipation of the Dalits and other weaker sections of the Indian society.

While fighting relentlessly against inequalities, Ambedkar felt that even in a democracy, leaving economic and social matters to be determined exclusively by a political majority could lead to the dictatorship of the 'haves' and perpetuation of age-long tyranny. He, therefore, saw to it that the economic and social objectives were enshrined in the Constitution itself as Directive Principles of State Policy.

Ambedkar also influenced the country's labour policy. His tenure as Labour Member in the Viceroy's Council during 1942-46 was a watershed in the history of labour legislation and labour welfare in India. According to Ambedkar, unemployment and underemployment were the greatest enemies of labour. Hence he tried to formulate a full employment policy for labour and a state supported labour welfare system.

He adopted a multi-pronged approach in the formulation of labour policy with provisions for: providing safeguard and social security measures for workers; giving equal opportunity to workers and employers to participate in the formulation of labour policy; and establishing a machinery for enforcing labour laws and settling disputes.

Abraham has made a commendable effort in piecing together the scatter information from Ambedkar's speeches and writings as also from articles and contributions of eminent political personalities, legal experts and social scientists. His book will be a source of inspiration to the younger generation.

## Ambedkar's Reply to Gandhi

A village was on fire, and the wind that swirled the flames high above the ancient banyan tree carried with it an unmistakable sound: a lone woman crying over a corpse. It was grief at its most elemental, purer than the wind and fire devouring this village in the dark night of southern India. The woman wailed and shuddered while cradling her dead husband. She is an untouchable, and so was her young husband, Perumal Radhakrishnan. An invisible line divides this village, called Karisakulam, and thousands of others like it across India, separating the untouchables—those beneath Hinduism's rigid caste hierarchy—from the upper-castes. Radhakrishnan had crossed that line. As a leader of the village's untouchables, he had dared to defy the higher-caste community of Thevars.

That evening, Radhakrishnan, a thin and bare-chested man, had ambled over to the upper-caste side to watch the evening news on the village's only TV, rigged up under the stars. While he sat there, four men from the Thevar caste pinned him to the dirt while a fifth man pulled out a sword and butchered him. Enraged by the killing, the untouchables burned down the houses of all the Thevars in the village and slaughtered their animals. They even smashed the TV; its fragments lay scattered next to Radhakrishnan's corpse. Then the untouchables took fright—they were afraid the Thevars would rouse the upper-castes from nearby villages and seek revenge—and so they fled into a wasteland of thorn bushes, leaving Radhakrishnan's widow alone, silhouetted against the flames as she rocked her husband's corpse.

A few years ago, these untouchables would have dragged away Radhakrishnan's body and cowered in their mud-huts, resigned to their subhuman status. But now, scenes of defiance like the rampage at Karisakulam are taking place throughout India. The country's more than 150 million untouchables (who prefer to call themselves Dalits, Hindi for "the oppressed") are striking back. They are instigating a social revolution that is long overdue, one whose aim is to topple the 2,500-year-old juggernaut of the Hindu caste system. Increasingly, Dalits are challenging Hinduism's tenets that a person is condemned to his caste—determining whether he becomes a doctor or a scavenger, whom he marries, which village well he drinks from, and his social standing in a complex, ordered hierarchy—all by his actions in a past life. In this rebellion, the Dalit's main weapons are education and the vote. But in some rural areas, where resistance to their demands for equality is entrenched, they are taking up the gun. "Power was gradual

By slipping through the hands of the dominant castes for several decades," says Ashis Nandy, director of the Centre for the Study of Developing Societies in New Delhi. "It had already slipped down to the lower castes and is now reaching the Dalits. This will help democracy." Or will it? Consider the caste warfare and chaos now engulfing the northern states of Bihar and Uttar Pradesh, where Dalits are trying to grab what they believe is theirs after so many centuries.

Dalits make up one-sixth of India's population, yet only a few have managed to occupy top places in society as politicians, lawyers and scientists. A poor Dalit from Kerala, Kocheril Raman Narayanan, encountered discrimination in school and work. And yet this year he rose to become India's President, the first untouchable to hold that post. Before, Dalits had to support their landlords' candidates or they were beaten away from the polling booths when they tried to vote; now they are asserting themselves with the ballot, and their newfound power has jolted all of the national political parties, especially the long-ruling Congress. Ram Vilas Paswan, a Dalit member of the Janata Dal Party, is now serving in the United Front cabinet. Twice now, a Dalit woman, Mayawati, has been elected Chief Minister of populous Uttar Pradesh state, though her last six months in office were squandered in a vendetta against high-caste rivals. Says Mayawati: "Earlier I had thought it would take longer, but change is now so rapid that in a few years we will have a Dalit Prime Minister in New Delhi."

Politicians and their promises offer little, however, to the most radical Dalits. They would prefer an armed insurrection, and they are willing to settle scores with higher-caste landlords using guns and home-made bombs. Says Ram Prit, a 75-year-old Dalit labourer in Bihar: "If you keep pouring water into a rat hole, the rats will come out fighting."

Religious sanction has allowed this apartheid to survive Muslim invasions, British colonialism and even 50 years of democracy. Defenders of the caste system usually cite a verse from the Upanishads, Hinduism's ancient sacred texts: "Those whose conduct on earth has given pleasure can hope to enter a pleasant womb, that is, the womb of a Brahman or a woman of the princely class. But those whose conduct on earth has been foul can expect to enter a foul and stinking womb, that is the womb of a bitch, or a pig, or an outcaste." A hymn from the sacred Rig Veda describes how this human stratification came about: a cosmic giant, Purusha, sacrificed parts of his body to create mankind. "His mouth became the Brahman, his arms were made into the Warrior (Kshatriya), his thighs the People (Vaishiya) and from his feet the Servants (Sudra) were born." Through the centuries, these four main divisions (called varnas), were silvered into more than 3,000 sub-castes, based on the purity of their professions. A goldsmith is higher up the ladder than a blacksmith, and a priestly Brahman, whose rituals bring him in touch with the gods, is highest of all. The untouchables, however, are off the ladder completely. By origin, many were India's dark-skinned first inhabitants, conquered by Aryans and assigned such awful tasks as burning bodies, skinning carcasses and removing "night soil"—human excrement—from latrines. For thousands of years, outcastes were burdened with these denigrating chores.

In many villages, untouchables still live in poverty and subjugation. They are forbidden from entering temples or drinking from the same wells as upper-castes. It was customary for higher-caste landlords to deflower a Dalit bride on her wedding night, before her helpless groom. (To cleanse himself after such a dalliance, according to the more than 2,500-year-old Laws of Manu, an upper-caste man must give alms and make "daily mutterings" of prayers.) These Hindu rules are far from evenhanded: even today in some parts of India, if an untouchable is caught sleeping with a high-caste woman, both he and the woman are executed. A Dalit also can be considered too uppity, and risks a beating, if he wears a wristwatch or trousers instead of a traditional dhoti or loincloth. In some places in the south, Dalits aren't allowed to use an umbrella. Some roadside tea stalls refuse to serve them out of ordinary cups, and often Dalit children are warned not to try sharing classrooms with upper-caste kids. In some villages like Vembakkotai, in Tamil Nadu, the Dalits are forced to live on the leeward side to prevent the wind that touches their bodies from defiling the upper-castes.

Faced with such persecution, Dalits are finally running out of patience. What's surprising is that it took them so long, Their emancipation began only in this century, behind the efforts of India's two great social reformers, Mahatma Gandhi and Bhimrao Ramji Ambedkar, an angry, brilliant Dalit lawyer and politician. Through a scholarship from the Maharajah of Baroda, Ambedkar, an impoverished village boy, was able to study abroad and eventually earned several degrees. He worked as a financial adviser to the Maharajah but quit in disgust because the prince's upper-caste servants would fling documents onto his desk, rather than hand them to him, for fear of contamination. Yet his genius was unstoppable, as was his grit. "Nothing can emancipate the outcaste except the destruction of the caste system," Ambedkar once declared. "Nothing can help to save the Hindus and ensure their survival in the coming struggle except the purging of the Hindu faith of this odious and vicious dogma." As an author of the Indian constitution, he secured guarantees for the advancement of outcastes. For decades, these promises were often blocked by upper-caste bureaucrats, but a new generation of Dalits inside the civil service is helping their downtrodden people. In Uttar Pradesh, for example, 150 positions are held by Dalits in the elite 540-member Indian Administrative Service. The government gives Dalits a lift by reserving 15% of all government jobs and college places for them.

Many of these educated Dalit bureaucrats are infuriated when, on visits to their villages, they are mistreated by upper-caste neighbours poorer and less educated than they. Man Dahima, a Dalit who is one of the most senior civil servants in Bhopal, capital of Madhya Pradesh state, says he still encounters "feudal harassment" when he goes back to his village. "Even today, we're not allowed in some temples," he says. "There are no signs outside, but these things are well understood." Other urbanized Dalits seethe when being served out of coconut shells instead of teacups or when forced to sit at a village Brahman's feet. Says Ezhilmalai, a Dalit politician in Tamil Nadu: "The Dalit would rather die than live without self-respect. And when he prefers to die for honour, what is there to care for?"

Ambedkar wanted to destroy the caste pyramid through democracy, but the rule of law has been slow in reaching many villages where upper-caste landlords, often in league with local police, are keeping the Dalits down. In such places, many Dalits are opting for armed resistance. "The condition of the Dalits in the villages is so bad that the concern for most is how to gain minimum self-respect and security," says a senior state official in Uttar Pradesh. "What they want today is not jobs, but to be able to live without being humiliated and harassed." In Uttar Pradesh, Bihar, Tamil Nadu and Andhra Pradesh, caste conflict is rife, and it has spread to other states such as Madhya Pradesh and Maharashtra. Many Dalits, along with forest-dwelling tribals, have signed up with armed leftist groups like the Maoist Communist Centre, Liberation and People's War Group, which go around shooting or slitting the throats of feudal upper-caste landowners and policemen. This communist insurgency, which flared in the 1970s, still rages in the backward regions of central and eastern India.

Not surprisingly, the upper-castes are hitting back. In Bihar, high-caste landowners raised a private army called the Ranvir Sena, and hardly a day goes by without caste killings. Even Rabindra Chowdhary, a Ranvir Sena leader, concedes that the landlords had cruelly exploited the Dalits. "We were abusive and did not treat these people well," he says. "We do not believe in killing. But if we do not kill, they will think that we are weak." Tension runs high, and even the most nonsensical incident can trigger a bloody outburst. In Tamil Nadu, a game of tag between Thevar and Dalit schoolboys led to the beheading of a Dalit and the revenge killing of 13 people, both Thevars and Dalits, many of them dragged off a bus and hacked to death. In Bihar's Belaur village, a tiff over a pack of cigarettes led to a mini-war between Dalits and the upper-caste Bhumihars that ultimately left 16 dead and dozens wounded. Even today, that feud festers: more than 350 Dalit families have deserted the village, and the Bhumihars—who patrol their village at night with guns and spears, ready for attack—cannot hire labourers for their fields. Some Dalits are even refusing to carry out their repugnant jobs. "My generation is fighting," says Sri Prakash, a Dalit whose house was set ablaze in a caste feud. "We've told the Thevars we're not going to cremate their dead any more. Let them do it themselves." Says Sociologist Nandy: "The Dalits are much more aggressive. Now that they have tasted power, they don't want to be denied it."

A mini-partition based on caste lines is taking shape in areas where Dalits are especially politicized. In some districts, police say, Dalits are probably better armed and organized than their upper-caste adversaries. It has become too dangerous for a Thevar family to live among the Dalits. Thevars are migrating to villages where they are in control, while Dalits are moving to places where they are in the majority. A Thevar knows better than to wander into some villages in the Srivilliputhur district, where Dalits humiliate upper-caste strangers by making them walk through the village with their sandals on their heads, ridiculing Vedic order by putting the lowliest on top. Dalits toiling in stone quarries and match factories have allegedly pilfered enough explosives to gain a lethal edge. Says Mahboob Batacha, a Tamil social worker in Madurai: "There's no village around here where the Dalits aren't armed. Now, more Thevars are getting killed than Dalits."

Envy is often the spark for caste warfare. It is not usually the top-rung Brahmans and Kshatriyas who clash with the Dalits but rather the castes lower down: those slightly above the untouchables, such as the Thevars in Tamil Nadu and the Yadavs in Bihar and Uttar Pradesh. As Dr. K. Krishnaswamy, a prominent Dalit politician in Tamil Nadu, explains, "Some Dalit youth are climbing fast through reserved government jobs. Others have gone to the Gulf for employment, and they are all bringing back TVs, refrigerators and vcrs. This is causing a lot of heartburn among the other castes." Krishnaswamy's own life is an illustration of this jealousy. When he was granted a scholarship to a prestigious college, the upper-caste postman pocketed his admissions letter, and Krishnaswamy never found out that he was accepted until too late.

Eventually he made it to medical school and, after leaving, set up practice near his village. Many of his patients were Dalit women who wanted abortions after being raped by upper-caste landowners. "I went to the upper-caste men and told them this wasn't right. They should marry these girls," he says. It was not a popular idea; a mob of 1,000 upper-caste men besieged the doctor's house one night, attacking him and his family. After a month in the hospital, he returned, full of fight. "It made me angry, more determined than ever," he says. Today, Krishnaswamy is one of only a few Dalits elected to Tamil Nadu's assembly, even though Dalits comprise about 20% of the state's voters. His life has been threatened so often that, while driving through upper-caste-dominated areas of the state, he is accompanied by two armed bodyguards. Says Krishnaswamy: "The political parties are the real culprits for keeping the caste conflict going." But caste politics is alive and well, and is contributing to a stirring-up of anti-Dalit sentiment in Bombay. In July, slum-dwellers awakened to find that their statue of the bespectacled Ambedkar had been garlanded not with the customary flowers but with a wreath of dirty sandals. That was all it took to start a riot. Hundreds of angry Dalits poured onto the streets, hurling stones and setting up roadblocks with burning tires. Fearing the rioters would set fire to a parked gas tanker, police started shooting in the shanty lanes, killing about a dozen people. Once news of the deaths spread, Dalits began protesting in the neighbouring states of Gujarat, Karnataka and in the capital, New Delhi.

The police shootings also revived antagonism between the Dalits and Maharashtra's ruling Shiva Sena party. Its militant Hindu leader Bal Thackeray has often attacked job reservations and the renaming of a university after Ambedkar. The Bombay incident also revealed the Dalits' disillusionment with their own leaders. When a former State Minister and Dalit leader visited the shantytown the day after the killings, he was attacked and had to run for his life. The funeral procession for those shot by police was attended by 150,000 Dalits, but not one Dalit politician dared to show up. Says Savita Ambedkar, the 81-year-old widow of the Dalit leader: "If we can stay together, we have the power to make a party succeed. But it's a great disappointment that the movement has been captured by people who cannot really lead it properly."

A doctor and a Brahman who became Ambedkar's second wife, Savita now lives alone in a shabby house in central Bombay. She has written a biography of her late husband, but because of her high caste, she was never really accepted by Dalits. Ambedkar's grandson Prakash hasn't fared much better. Ambedkar died in late 1956, soon after founding the Republican Party of India, but grandson Prakash, who now leads one of its many factions, lacks his visionary fire.

Desperate, the Dalits in Bombay's slums are flailing for an alternative leadership—or at least a godfather. Shortly after the funeral of the slain Dalits, a lower caste Bombay underworld chieftain named Arun Gawli offered himself as their saviour. When the gangster called a Bombay rally, thousands of Dalits flocked to it. Says social worker Sushoba Barve: "After the killings, many Dalit youth felt that the only way to protect themselves was to ally with someone who could give them protection."

Elsewhere in India, Dalits are feeling equally deceived by the national parties, which are top-heavy with high-caste politicians. Dalits have yet to unite. "All that keeps India from having a bloody revolution is that we Dalits are a divided lot," says civil servant Dahima. Even among the Dalits, strong caste rivalries exist; one study discovered 900 Dalit "sub-castes" in the country. Basically, everyone is squirming not to fall to the bottom of India's massive pile of humanity. Predicts one Dalit official: "As benefits trickle down, the conflicts between sub-castes are bound to sharpen." Lately, a number of regional leaders have been trying to bring unity to lower-caste aspirations. Several could easily cripple their state capitals with 100,000-strong demonstrations. So far, the only Dalit politician to challenge the mainstream parties is Kanshi Ram, a former technician at a government defence laboratory. Armed with wiliness and an ability to survive in the venal world of

Indian politics, Ram has no qualms about forming alliances with his high-caste adversaries if it brings his Bahujan Samaj Party to power. His abrasive protege Mayawati governed Uttar Pradesh for six months in alliance with the Hindu nationalist Bharatiya Janata Party, many of whose followers adhere stoutly to Manu's ancient law.

During her term, Mayawati ordered 13,000 statues of Ambedkar and began work on a $30 million park in Lucknow in honour of the Dalit leader. She also reshuffled 1,400 bureaucrats and police officers. Dalit civil servants, whose promotions had been mothballed by their high-caste superiors, were elevated to top posts. State funds and projects for roads, schools and electricity were channelled to neglected Dalit villages. Above all, Dalits were treated to the spectacle—unimaginable a few years back—of an acid-tongued Dalit like Mayawati ordering around upper-caste grandees in the administration who in the past had either bullied or, at best, ignored them.

## Give Ambedkar His Due

President Bush in his recent trip to India mentioned Gandhi, Tagore and Nehru in that order as thinkers who shaped the destiny of India. These three names indicate a certain mode of representative ideology of the Indian establishment and also the politics of ideological representation. A few years ago the University Grants Commission of India recognized Gautama Buddha, Gandhi, Ambedkar and Nehru as the epoch making thinkers of India. It also directed the Indian universities to institute special chairs and research centres in their names. Evidently these names are a product of intensive deliberations. In these four names one can see the globally known positive system built by Buddha, who established an alternative Sangha system, that gradually emerged as the Buddhist religion in ancient India. As against the names of Kautilya and Manu, Buddha alone was seen as a thinker to be recognized as the epoch making thinker of that period.

In the modern period, Gandhi undoubtedly is credited as one of the epoch making thinkers. Even though one may not agree with many of his ideological positions one does not dispute his role as an epoch maker. Ambedkar occupies the second place in the modern period as an epoch maker because he played a political, ideological and philosophical role to abolish caste- slavery and untouchability in India, a role that is comparable to that of Abraham Lincoln and Martin Luther King. Both Abraham Lincoln and Martin Luther King are seen as epoch makers in American history.

Nehru is recognized as an epoch making thinker because he steered the Indian administrative setup through a colonial phase into an independent one with administrative acumen. Thus, Gandhi, Ambedkar and Nehru are identified as epoch making thinkers of modern India. How does Rabindranath Tagore figure in President Bush's speech and how is Ambedkar ignored?

In Delhi the Bengal lobby is quite strong. It influences the central Government's culture in many ways and Tagore was the tallest figure of Bengal.

Bengali writers project Tagore as the tallest individual of India and deliberately avoid Ambedkar as a significant figure of modern India, leave alone as an epoch making thinker.

The most visible and recent example of such Bengali intellectual tradition is Amartya Sen's international best seller—The Argumentative Indian. In this book Gandhi, Tagore and Nehru figure as the thinkers who shaped modern India. In Sen's scheme in ancient India it was Ashoka, but not Buddha who figures as an epoch making thinker. In early modern India, Akbar is projected as a thinker of unmatched intellect.

### *Theory for Liberation*

The fact that Ambedkar does not merit mention even though he constructed a theory for the liberation of the most exploited underdog of India and sought to liberate that untouchable underdog is a travesty of intellectual representation. Ambedkar's name is mentioned by Sen on only four times and that too for his position as the chairman of the drafting committee of the constitution—but not as a visionary.

Tagore is a poet, but not a thinker with a liberative ideology. No one has any objection if he is recognized as a great poet of modern India. Let us not forget the fact that Bush had to mention Martin Luther King even in his speeches, who has played a similar role like that of Ambedkar in India.

Any nation would have a respectable representation of intellectual tradition if the national psyche recognizes those intellectuals who represented the most oppressed people of a given society.

Why do Americans think that Abraham Lincoln was their greatest president and Martin Luther King was their greatest civil libertarian? Both of them got that national and international stature because they stood for abolition of slavery and racial discrimination. Ambedkar should have got a similar stature if the national elite were to develop any sense of shame of the institution of caste and untouchability which have worse characteristics than the racism of America and Europe. But that was not to be so.

Tagore's greatest poem is Gitanjali. What liberational message does it have for the oppressed Dalit-Bahujans? A philosophically aesthetic poem like the Gitanjali must have got India the first Nobel prize. But that in itself did not reshape India.

The millions of suppressed and exploited masses of India do not revere him. If he does not figure in school text books his name would not have been known among the masses at all.

Ambedkar's name has a different value. That value did not come to him because his name was pushed through the officially written school text books. He is seen as a thinker who keeps on liberating the oppressed masses on a continuous basis.

The projection of this kind of a liberative thinker among the intellectual internationally and sociopolitical circles would have given an impression that this country has an open mind and principled value for human freedom.

If India does not abolish caste and untouchability using all the ideological tools that Ambedkar had handed down to this country what does freedom that Bush is talking from Purana Qila mean to these oppressed masses?

## Dr. Ambedkar with the Simon Commission

Evidence of Dr. Ambedkar before the Indian Statutory Commission on 23rd October, 1928.

Indian Statutory Commission, Poona

Dated 23rd October 1928

*All the members of the Commission, of the Central Committee (except Raja Vawab Ali Khan) and of the Bombay Provincial Committee.*

Dr. B. R. Ambedkar (a member of the Bombay Committee) and Dr. P. G. Solanki (representing the Depressed Classes), called and examined.

***Chairman:*** Just to remind my colleagues, the documents we should have before us are: Dr. Ambedkar's Statement on behalf of the Depressed Classes' Institute of Bombay and the Joint Memorandum of the Depressed Indian Association, Bombay, and the Servants of Somavamshi Society. Dr. Ambedkar has changed his seat, because he is acting for the moment as one of our witnesses. Dr. Ambedkar, of course, we know as a member of the Bombay Committee. I think. Dr. Solanki, you or your Association is responsible for the other document?

***Dr. Solanki:*** I concur in the document submitted by Dr. Ambedkar. I should like you to begin. Dr. Ambedkar, by helping us as to the sort of number of depressed classes in this Presidency. Can you help us about that?

***Dr. Ambedkar:*** I find that the depressed class population, as computed in the Memorandum submitted by the Government of Bombay is estimated at 1,478,390 as may be seen from page 3 of their Memorandum (Vol. VII).

3. They say, "The depressed classes, which include mostly the Dheds, Mangs, Mahars and Holiyas, number, according to the Census of 1921, 1,478,390 approximately." What do you say about that figure?

***Dr. Ambedkar:*** As you will see, the figure I have given on page 39 of my Memorandum is about 28 lakhs.

4. You think the number should be about 2,800,000?

***Dr. Ambedkar:*** Yes.

5. How does the discrepancy arise?

***Dr. Ambedkar:*** The first thing I should like to say is this, that the figures given by the Government of Bombay are taken, I believe, from the Census of India, 1921, Vol. 8, Bombay Presidency, Part II, the tables starting on page 176, while the figures which I give in my memorandum are from Chapter II of Vol. I of the Census of India, 1921. These are the figures estimated by the Director of Census, who has collected the figures of the different Provinces, and his computations, which I have taken bodily, are given on page 39 of my memorandum under the heading "Population of the Depressed Classes in India ", and show the figures for the different Provinces, giving the population of the depressed classes in each.

Now, as we see, there is this discrepancy between the two sets of figures. These figures of course, can never be exact, neither the Provincial nor the Central figures. In fact, if the Conference will refer to the remarks of the Director of the Census of India, which I commence quoting on page 39 of my memorandum, it will be seen that, after giving the total estimated population of the depressed classes he goes on to say (page 39 of memorandum, in italics) , "This, however, must be taken as a low and conservative estimate since it does not include (1) the full strength of the castes and tribes concerned, and (2) the tribal aborigines most recently absorbed in Hinduism, many of whom are considered impure. We may confidently place the numbers of the depressed classes, all of whom are considered impure, at something between 55 and 60 millions in India proper." Then he gives the figures for each province.

6. Would you mind if I just try to clear my own mind, not by reference to precise figures, but by contrasting two conceptions? It is manifest that if some authorities, speaking with the precision of Census returns, give a total like 1,478,000, and other authorities, also speaking with precision, give a

figure like 2,800,000, the second authorities must be including people not included by the first?

***Dr. Ambedkar:*** That is so, and I should, therefore, like to point out to the Conference that the provincial figures do not include certain castes which are, as a matter of fact, untouchable castes.

7. May we put it like this? See if I have it correct, and if I have not please tell me. I have been studying it as well as I can, although I have been looking forward to your help and that of Dr. Solanki. In one sense of the term, by "Depressed Classes "you might mean untouchables in the sense of persons who are Hindus, but who are denied access to the Hindu temples, might you not?

***Dr. Ambedkar:*** Yes.

8. In another sense you might include in the "Depressed Classes "not only those people whom I have described, but also the criminal tribes, the hill tribes and other people who no doubt are very low in the scale, but who are not, perhaps, in the narrower sense untouchables from the point of view of the Hindus hierarchy?

***Dr. Ambedkar:*** Quite.

9. Is not that a possible view?

***Dr. Ambedkar:*** That is a possible view.

10. Is not that the real explanation of why in some connections you get a certain figure for the depressed classes, meaning untouchables, persons who are refused admission to the Hindu temples, whereas on the other hand you sometimes get a bigger figure which would include these criminal and hill tribes?

***Dr. Ambedkar:*** I do not think that is so in this case, because the figures I have given seem to have reference to the depressed classes as distinct from the hill tribes and the criminal tribes.

11. Let me point this out to you. I have before me these three figures. I have got a figure of 1,478,000 odd for

untouchables taken from the Census of 1921, and made up of these Mahars, Dheds and other people. Then I have a long list of criminal tribes and so on, which adds up to 589,000—just over half a million. Then I have a third list of aboriginals and hill tribes- Bhils, and people of that sort—and they add up to another million. If you were to add the aboriginal and criminal tribes in with the first figure, you would get a total approximately like the larger figure you give of 2,800,000?

***Dr. Ambedkar:*** The quotation I reproduce on page 39 of my memorandum from the remarks of the Directors of the Census gives me the impression that his figures are strictly for the depressed classes. My feeling is that the figures computed by the Director of the Census and referred to by him in the paragraph which I quote on page 39 of my memorandum are figures which apply only to the depressed classes.

12. I see that the Director of the Census of India for 1921 says this: "It has been usual in recent years to speak of a certain section of the community as the 'Depressed Classes—so far as I am aware the term has no final definition, nor is it certain exactly whom it covers." Then he refers to some educational criticisms. That is the passage you mean?

***Dr. Ambedkar:*** Yes, and "The total population classed according to these lists as depressed amounted to 31 million persons or 19 per cent of the Hindu and tribal population of British India." That remark would appear to exclude the tribal people from the depressed classes.

13. I do not know. Anyhow, that is one possible explanation, and I think you agree a possible explanation is that the smaller figure is the figure of untouchables in the sense I have tried to define. I think you agree that is a possible view. It is manifest that for many purposes those interested in trying to promote the advancement and elevation of those who are most depressed may very well include in their survey a wider number of persons, including the criminal and hill tribes. That is a possibility?

***Dr. Ambedkar:*** It is a possibility.

14. I should like to suggest to you another possible view. I do not know if it qualifies it. On page 39 of your document

you point out, quite accurately, I think, that if you add the provincial figures together you get something like 55 to 60 millions in India proper?

***Dr. Ambedkar:*** Yes.

15. "India proper "there, I think, would include the Indian States?

***Dr. Ambedkar:*** Yes, I thought of that, but I would point out one thing. He seems to exclude the Indian States, because he gives a separate figure for Baroda.

16. Perhaps he mentions one or two of the larger ones?

***Dr. Ambedkar:*** Probably. Qualification of the figures.

17. We do not, of course, want to spend too long on the statistical point, because, after all, whether the right figure to take is 11/2 million or 2 millions or 21/2 millions, it is obvious, it is a very large number of people, and they are people who deserve our very special consideration?

***Dr. Ambedkar:*** One point I wish to mention is this, that the figures from which the provincial figures are computed are in the table which deals only with the principal Indian castes. It is not an exhaustive table, and I find by going over the different castes which are mentioned in this table that it does not give any figures whatsoever for ten castes, which are undoubtedly castes. They are not included in the principal Indian castes.

18. What I was going to suggest, if it was agreeable to you both, was this. You have called attention to the main considerations with regard to the figures and, without fixing absolutely the right figures, I think it would be well to get rid of this figures point as quickly as possible and then we can get to the question of considering the position and treatment of these classes; otherwise we may occupy a long time on arithmetic. I have asked what I want to put about it, and I am quite prepared to take it that if you apply a narrower test you may get a figure of 11/2 millions, but that with a wider test you will get a figure of between 2 and 3 millions. I accept that from you, as I follow it?

***Dr. Ambedkar:*** Yes, with this qualification, that the Bombay figures do not include ten of the castes.

***Chairman:*** We want to get to the real point, which is their representation. Is there anyone who wants to occupy time on this statistical point? Are you content, Mr. Rajah, that we should take it the figures are something of that sort?

***Rao Bahadur Rajah:*** Which figures?

*Chairman:* Do not you think we might proceed with the really important question, which is their representation, leaving it like this that in the Bombay Presidency the Census of 1921 gives a figure of 11/2 millions, but it would appear that those are the depressed classes in the narrower sense I have mentioned, the untouchables from the point of view of religion, but that, as Dr. Ambedkar has pointed out, the official figures really show, if you take a rather wider but perfectly legitimate view, that the true figure may be between 2 and 3 millions. Is not that fair?

***Rao Bahadur Rajah:*** Yes, that is right.

***Chairman:*** Does anybody want to add anything about that? 19.

***Colonel Lane Fox:*** On which figure are the two memoranda which we have received based? In each memorandum you ask for special representation for the depressed classes. You ask for adult suffrage in one memorandum, and you ask for special recruitment for the army and navy and so on. It is obvious it is a bigger thing if you ask for it for the aborigines and criminal tribes and so on. Are these privileges asked for the bigger figure or for the smaller?

***Dr. Ambedkar:*** I ask for them for the depressed classes.

20. For the aborigines and criminal classes also?

***Dr. Ambedkar:*** No. I do not think it would be possible to allow them the privilege of adult suffrage.

21. But you quote the bigger figure?

***Dr. Ambedkar:*** I am not accepting altogether the fact that the figure which I have given in my memorandum covers the aborigines and the hill tribes. I still hold to the view that on a fair computation the figure I have given is largely the figure for the depressed classes. I admit only the possibility of the other view.

***Chairman:*** There is only one thing I might add. Sir Arthur Froom may be able to confirm it. I notice the Muddiman Committee (Reforms Enquiry Committee, 1925) in the table subjoined to para. 64 of their Report, give the figure at 2,800,000.

22. ***Sir Hari Singh Gour:*** Dr. Ambedkar, would you regard "depressed classes" and "untouchables" "as synonymous terms?

***Dr. Ambedkar:*** Yes.

23. In asking for special representation for the depressed classes you confine yourselves to the untouchables?

***Dr. Ambedkar:*** Yes.

24. You say that some aborigines are not untouchables?

***Dr. Ambedkar:*** In some parts they may be. I do not propose to speak on their behalf.

25. They are not untouchables. The criminal tribes are not untouchables?

***Dr. Ambedkar:*** Some of them are.

26. Some, but as a tribe they are not?

***Dr. Ambedkar:*** The criminal tribes have so little social intercourse with the rest of the Hindus that there is no basis for any definite opinion on that point, but if they did have such intercourse I think they would be retarded as untouchables.

27. There are certain classes which stand midway between touchability and untouchability?

***Dr. Ambedkar:*** I would rather say they were lower down than (be untouchables.

28. No, higher up in the social ladder there is a class which is semi untouchable?

***Dr. Ambedkar:*** I cannot say. My point is this, that with respect to the criminal tribes we have no data for forming an opinion as to whether they are untouchable or not, because there is very little intercourse between the main body of Hindus and the criminal tribes.

29. Leave out of account the criminal tribes and aborigines; I am now dealing with the untouchables. Among the untouchables themselves there are degrees; there are certain among them who may be regarded as only semi untouchable?

***Dr. Ambedkar:*** (Both witnesses) No.

30. I will give you an example. What is the position of the Chambhar?

***Dr. Ambedkar:*** He is entirely untouchable.

31. As much as the Mahar?

***Dr. Ambedkar:*** Yes.

32. Are you certain of that?

***Dr. Ambedkar:*** Yes, if you apply this test of common water, or of entering a temple.

33. No, by untouchability I mean whose touch will pollute a high caste Hindu?

***Dr. Ambedkar:*** Well, you can take entering a temple or taking water as a test.

***Chairman:*** After all, we are engaged here primarily in a constitutional and political inquiry. Social customs and deep-rooted religious traditions are not things which are likely to be removed between night and morning by any commission; that is obvious enough. It really comes to this, that in one sense the depressed classes meaning the untouchables, will be those classes who are denied all access to Hindu temples, and who, it is suggested, are deprived very often of the use of schools, of dharmashalas and things of that sort. In addition to those, speaking politically and constitutionally, we shall all agree there are others, not very advanced in the scale of civilisation, such as Sir Hari Singh Gour has referred to—criminal tribes, hill tribes and so on—who are also inhabitants of India and as such demand our attention.

***Sir Hari Singh Gour:*** The Hindus are divided into four castes. The Sudras cannot get into the temples.

***Chairman:*** I think we all appreciate that. However, we are not engaged in making laws for the Hindu religion, but in considering the structure of the constitution of British India, which is a very different thing.

34. Taking that figure, what is it that you want to represent as the proper way in which the constitution of India, and more particularly the constitution of the Bombay Presidency, should deal with these people?

***Dr. Ambedkar:*** The first thing I would like to submit is that we claim that we must be treated as a distinct minority, separate from the Hindu community. Our minority character has been hitherto concealed by our inclusion in the Hindu community, but as a matter of fact there is really no link between the depressed classes and the Hindu community. The first point, therefore, I would stress before the Conference is that we must be regarded as a distinct and independent minority. Secondly, I should like to submit that the depressed classes minority needs far greater political protection than any other minority in British India, for the simple reason that it is educationally very backward, that it is economically poor, socially enslaved, and suffers from certain grave political disabilities, from which no other community suffers. Then I would submit that, as a matter of demand for our political protection, we claim representation on the same basis as the Mohammedan minority. We claim reserved seats if accompanied by adult franchise.

35. And if there is no adult franchise?

***Dr. Ambedkar:*** Then we would ask for separate electorates. Further, we would like to have certain safeguards either in the constitution, if it is possible, or else in the way of advice in the instrument to the Governor regarding the education of the depressed classes and their entry into the public services.

36. May we just ask Dr. Solanki if he agrees in those points?

***Dr. Solanki:*** I agree with all the points.

37. Then we may take it that is the view of both you gentlemen?

***Dr. Ambedkar:*** Yes.

38. Would it be convenient if I asked a question of two on these points as we go? You claim that the depressed class, although included within Hinduism in a sense, should none the less be regarded from the point of view of the constitution as a distinct and separate community from others who are within Hinduism?

***Dr. Ambedkar:*** Yes.

39. Is that on the ground that in your view the depressed classes cannot expect to have their interests satisfactorily represented by the higher ranks of Hinduism?

***Dr. Ambedkar:*** That is one ground, but a matter of fact, really we cannot be deemed to be part of the Hindu community.

40. You come, I believe from an earlier set of inhabitants of this continent?

***Dr. Ambedkar:*** That is one view, I think.

41. It is supposed—-we will not go into details—that you are pre-Aryan?

***Dr. Ambedkar:*** Well, I do not know. That is a view.

43. I only ask you the question because there are some very distinguished Hindu public men—I do not mention any names—who have undoubtedly exhibited a good deal of interest in the case of the depressed classes. There is no question about that?

***Dr. Ambedkar:*** Yes, there is a great deal of public talk.

44. I know; but, at any rate, that is your view: You say you must be regarded as a distinct and separate community from the constitutional point of view?

***Dr. Ambedkar:*** Yes.

45. As regards representation, I notice that whether there is adult franchise, or whether there is not adult franchise, you seem to be abandoning any idea of nomination, you want election?

***Dr. Ambedkar:*** Yes.

46. Is that the view of both of you?

***Dr. Solanki:*** Yes.

47. That means, of course, that you have to make a list of voters?

***Dr. Ambedkar:*** Yes.

48. And you have to make sure that the man who comes to vote is the man on the list, and nobody else?

***Dr. Ambedkar:*** Yes.

49. Could you give me an estimate at all, Dr. Ambedkar, of what percentage of the population whom you call the depressed classes can read?

***Dr. Ambedkar:*** In a separate memorandum which I have submitted to the Commission on education in the Bombay Presidency I gave the figures.

50. I am afraid it is a very small proportion?

***Dr. Ambedkar:*** Quite.

51. After all, one of the complaints that are made is that they have not had as free access to schools as more fortunate people?

***Dr. Ambedkar:*** Quite so.

52. So it would mean, would it not, if it was done by election, that it would almost entirely have to be done by people voting who could not themselves understand the ballot paper?

***Dr. Ambedkar:*** Yes. That is true of the majority of voters even today.

53. True. Now, would you tell me how many reserved seats in the Bombay Presidency you would suggest classes?

***Dr. Ambedkar:*** In the scheme that I have prepared I say out of 140 we claim 22 seats.

54. What you suggest is that if the total number of members of the Bombay Council, all elected, was 140, then you think that the body for which you wish to speak should have 22 elective seats?

***Dr. Ambedkar:*** Yes.

55. And supposing, to take your other alternative, there is no adult franchise, then you are asking for separate electorates. Do you still want 22 seats?

***Dr. Ambedkar:*** Yes.

56. The only other thing I will ask you is this. I think Mr. Rajah probably will be glad to put a few questions himself to bring out the social condition. At present I think, in the Bombay Legislative Council there are two members, are there not, who are nominated to represent the depressed classes?

***Dr. Ambedkar:*** That is so.

57. You yourself being one of them?

***Dr. Ambedkar:*** Yes.

58. And Dr. Solanki being the other?

***Dr. Ambedkar:*** Yes.

59. Was that based on the Southborough Committee's Report?

***Dr. Ambedkar:*** Yes, I believe so.

60. I believe you gave evidence before the Southborough Committee?

***Dr. Ambedkar:*** Yes.

61. I have been reading your evidence before that Committee, and I was looking to see how many members you said there were of the depressed classes. I think you point out in your memorandum, in a note at the bottom of page 39, that the figure of the depressed classes given by the Southborough Committee for the Bombay Presidency was 5,77,000?

***Dr. Ambedkar:*** Yes.

62. I think your view is that, that was an error?

***Dr. Ambedkar:*** Yes, a very large error.

63. Can you tell me, as a matter of fact, how they arrived at it? Do you know at all?

***Dr. Ambedkar:*** They simply took, I think, a small table with regard to castes which cause pollution.

64. It was taking a still narrower definition of what constituted the depressed classes?

***Dr. Ambedkar:*** Yes.

65. ***Mr. Hartshorn:*** I notice in this note you say, after referring to the figure of the Southborough Committee of 5,77,000. "According to the authority relied upon by the Southborough Committee, the population of the depressed classes in the Bombay Presidency in 1911 was 2,145,000".

***Dr. Ambedkar:*** In the Census.

66. That is the authority they relied upon? That was what I wanted to know.

***Dr. Ambedkar:*** Yes. The authority gave two different figures on two different pages, if I remember correctly. On one page they gave the smaller figure, and they took that up, and as soon as the Report of the Southborough Committee was published we protested against this estimate to the Government of Bombay.

67. *Chairman*: I think it is quite clear what the 2,100,000 was. It was the result of adding together in the Census of 1921 the figure given for the untouchables, which as I have said, was 1,478,000, and the figure given for the criminal tribes, which was something like 623,000. Adding those two together, you would get the 2,100,000?

***Dr. Ambedkar:*** Yes.

68. And it was leaving out the aboriginal and hill tribes. It must have been?

***Dr. Ambedkar:*** Yes.

69. *Mr. Miller:* I should like to ask about the position in some of the Indian States. In Baroda and one other State, I think, where some special facilities are shown, are those special facilities anything beyond education facilities?

***Dr. Ambedkar:*** No, nothing beyond that.

70. Could you obtain service with the State?

***Dr. Ambedkar:*** I should think it would be very difficult.

71. You are particularly anxious to get appointments in the public service?

***Dr. Ambedkar:*** Yes, decidedly.

72. Why is that so?

***Dr. Ambedkar:*** On that point I should like to say this, that our experience so far as the administration of the law is concerned is very bitter. I wish to say most emphatically that in many cases the law is administered to the disadvantage of the depressed class man. I would like to give a concrete case of what actually happened in one of the districts, without, of course, mentioning names. The Bombay Government annually lets out its forest lands for cultivation to the villages on certain stated terms. Now we discovered that in the allotment of those forest lands the depressed class man, who was often a landless labourer or with very little land, and who was clamouring for some sort of economic stability, never came in for a share. The Mamlatdars, who were really in charge of distributing the lands, showed absolute favouritism to the caste Hindu as against the depressed class man. Last year in one district we organised and sent a deputation to the Assistant Deputy Collector of that district, placing before him our grievances with respect to these forest lands. He issued a circular to the Mamlatdars saying that the applications from the depressed classes should be considered.

Now, some of the Mamlatdars, to show they were acting up to the circular, did give some lands to the depressed classes. But we found that they rather fooled us, if I may say so. What they did was, on paper they allotted a very large amount of land to the depressed classes and a very small amount of land to the caste Hindus, but when we came to see actually what was allotted to us we found that the land allotted to the depressed classes was all rocky and unfit for cultivation and the depressed class people would not take it for anything, and the land allotted to the caste Hindus though small, was all rich and fertile. Now I think that is a most fragrant abuse of the administrative power which is entrusted to the officials, and I personally attach far more importance to good administration of law than to more efficient administration of law.

73. *Chairman:* I imagine that the application of what you have told us, which is interesting, to our present inquiry is really this — because, of course, it is no part of the function of this Commission to interfere in day-by-day administration?

***Dr. Ambedkar:*** No.

74. You are using it as an argument to support your view that the depressed classes should have a full representation?

***Dr. Ambedkar:*** In the services.

75. That is your point?

***Dr. Ambedkar:*** That is my point. I will give some instances of what happens in judicial courts actually in this Presidency. I happened to defend a depressed class man in one of the courts, and, to my great surprise, I found that the man had to stand outside the court behind a little window, outside the wall, and he would not come in simply because, he said, "It is all right so far as you are concerned, but after you have left there will be terrible social ostracism if I enter the court."

76. It was the client who did not want to come in?

***Dr. Ambedkar:*** Who dare not come in.

77. What sort of social ostracism had he in mind?

***Dr. Ambedkar:*** The social ostracism would be that if he went back to the village there would be the boycott of the shopkeepers; nobody would sell him grain. The villagers would stop his dues as a village servant. He would not be allowed to come into the village. The depressed class people always live on the border of the village, not in the centre or in the midst.

78. Your point would be that he was timid about coming into court on this occasion because he thought that afterwards the other people of the village, not his own lot but the others, the caste people, would regard him as having pushed himself in where he should not go?

***Dr. Ambedkar:*** Certainly—having exceeded the bounds of his social status.

79. That is a single case, is it?

***Dr. Ambedkar:*** I have had that experience but I think that the existence of a circular of the Bombay High Court to the effect that the depressed classes must be allowed entry in the courts indicates that is often the case. There must be some reason for that circular.

80. *Mr. Miller:* The only other question, I want to ask is this. If you got these 22 seats in the Council do you think you could bring forward 22 suitable men?

***Dr. Ambedkar:*** Yes, I think so.

81. *Khan Sahib Abdul Latif:* Would you please enlighten the members of the Conference as to the fate of the minorities in the Bombay Council, when the official bloc is withdrawn for certain reasons?

***Dr. Ambedkar:*** I quite see that the fate of the minorities would be precarious. It has been precarious.

82. Did the honourable Minister belonging to the advanced class show any consideration to the project, or the feelings of Mohammedans, non-Brahmins, or depressed classes?

***Dr. Ambedkar:*** No, not at all.

83. Do the minor communities stand any chance of getting through any legislation in the Bombay Legislative Council, or get any chance to move it?

***Dr. Ambedkar:*** Their chances would be almost nil.

98. *Sardar Mujumdar:* Is it not a fact that different kinds of castes among the depressed classes are known as the depressed classes; that is to say, there are different kinds of castes even among the depressed classes?

***Dr. Ambedkar:*** Yes, of course.

99. Can you give me approximately the number of those castes?

***Dr. Ambedkar:*** I think you will find them in the Census, the different castes enumerated as untouchables.

100. Can you give me any idea of the number of different castes?

***Dr. Ambedkar:*** About a dozen or so. The Census gives it.

101. How many castes are included in the depressed classes in Bombay?

***Dr. Ambedkar:*** Almost all the castes.

102. Then the members of the different castes are members of your organisation?

***Dr. Ambedkar:*** Quite; it is a general body inclusive of all the depressed classes.

103. So that among the depressed classes are included all those?

***Dr. Ambedkar:*** Yes.

104. Have you taken into consideration the claims of the Bhils and Wadias and other persons?

***Dr. Ambedkar:*** No.

105. What do you say about the protection of those minorities?

***Dr. Ambedkar:*** I think that they also should be allowed some protection by representation.

106. Do you not think that even among the backward classes there are certain communities, who are in a minority?

***Dr. Ambedkar:*** Yes.

106A. Then has the present constitution any provision to protect their interest?

***Chairman:*** Are these castes to which you refer refused admission to the Hindu temples?

***Sardar Mujumdar:*** No, they are allowed to go into them.
*Chairman:* This morning we are really considering the case of untouchables, and persons who are quite outside the Hindu temple scheme. I do not think we can go into the question of the backward classes, who would be admitted to the Hindu temples.

*Sardar Mujumdar:* What I submit is that there are various minorities even amongst the backward classes. We are not concerned with the question of suitability; we are here to safeguard the interests of all the minorities.

*Chairman:* Certainly.

*Sardar Mujumdar:* It was from that point of view that I asked the question.

*Chairman:* Let me relieve you at once. India is full of minorities, and you have mentioned some of them; but this morning we are considering the body of people called the depressed classes.

*Sardar Mujumdar:* Very well. Sir.

107. *Syed Miran Muhammad Shah:* You have just said that you want representation in proportion to what the Mohammedans get?

***Dr. Ambedkar:*** Yes.

108. Do you want them because Mohammedans get them? Do you see any justice in that?

***Dr. Ambedkar:*** I see justice in that, I do not quite accept the principle of representation of minorities according to population of the legislature as though it was a museum in which we have only to keep so many specimens of so many communities. A Legislative Council is more than a museum, it is a place where, for instance, social battles have to be fought, privileges have to be destroyed, and rights have to be won. Now, if that is the conception of a Legislative Council, I do not think it at all in the fitness of things to confine the minority to proportional representation according to population, that means you are condemning a minority to be perpetually a minority without the power necessary to influence the actions in the majority.

109. Would you be satisfied if the franchise was reduced to local boards in the rural areas?

***Dr. Ambedkar:*** Well, I would really insist upon adult suffrage. The lower the franchise the better, on that principle I would accept any lowering, but I certainly would not say I would be content with that.

110. Would you then extend adult suffrage to the aboriginal tribes and to the criminal and hill tribes?

***Dr. Ambedkar:*** Yes, I think so.

111. You would?

***Dr. Ambedkar:*** Yes.

112. Or would you like to exclude them and give them nomination and yourselves adult suffrage?

***Dr. Ambedkar:*** I will say one thing. With regard to the criminal tribes, it might not be a good thing to give them adult suffrage, because by occupation they are a people who have more the interest of their own particular community in their mind, and they are not very particular as regards the means whereby they earn their living; but I do not think there is any harm in giving aborigines the right to vote.

113. They should be given the right to vole, or should their interests be protected by nomination?

***Dr. Ambedkar:*** They should be protected somehow; I do not much mind how. My feeling is that every man is intelligent enough to understand exactly what he wants. Literacy has not much bearing on this point; a man may be illiterate, none the less he may be very intelligent.

114. Do not you think that this separate representation will lead to communal tension? It is stated that communal tension is due to separate representation and separate electorates. Is that your belief?

***Dr. Ambedkar:*** Even assuming it does lead to tension I do not see how you can get rid of it. Whether it does lead to tension is questionable, but I do not see in any case how you can get rid of it, having regard to the fact that society is divided into classes and communities. 115. Do not you think it is the root cause of dissension?

***Dr. Ambedkar:*** I do not think so, but I do say this; as a result of communal representation, the leaders of the communities are less prone to compromise than they would otherwise be. That is my feeling, but I do not! think it leads to communal riots, which are due, I think, to something very different.

116. *Syed Miran Muhammad Shah:* Would you not suggest that by taking away the official bloc, non-officials may be nominated in order?

***Dr. Ambedkar:*** I do not want nomination.

117. *Major Afflee:* Are there members of the depressed classes working in industry, in the cotton mills and so on?

***Dr. Ambedkar:*** All of them. The depressed class men are all labourers.

118. You have not got my point; I am talking of industry. You have members of the depressed classes who work in villages, for the most part in certain occupations. But are there large numbers of the depressed classes engaged in industry?

***Dr. Ambedkar:*** A very large number.

119. You would have a very large number in a place like Bombay City?

***Dr. Ambedkar:*** Yes.

120. Do they cease in any degree to be untouchable?

***Dr. Ambedkar:*** No, I should like to point out this. The depressed class man is entirely kept out of the weaving department, the most paying department. He can only enter departments like the throstle department and others.

121. Why?

***Dr. Ambedkar:*** On account of untouchability.

122. When he is working there he is working alongside people of all castes?

***Dr. Ambedkar:*** Not quite. The departments are discriminated according to castes. One department is entirely manned by the depressed classes; another—say the weaving department—by Mohammedans and caste Hindus.

123. Do they take part in the trade unions?

***Dr. Ambedkar:*** Yes, they are beginning to do so.

124. With members of the classes above the depressed classes?

***Dr. Ambedkar:*** Yes.

125. I wanted to get this point from you. You put forward a claim for representation of the depressed classes on the basis of numbers. Now, we have claims put forward on a different

basis altogether; on, say, the labour basis. You get a cross-division in that way, because a man can be a depressed class man and he can also be a labourer?

***Dr. Ambedkar:*** He is usually, if not always, a labourer.

126. That is rather a play on words, is not it? I am speaking of capital and labour, of labour in big industries, not of the ordinary un-organised labour. I am speaking of organised labour. How are you going to get over the difficulty? If you are going to have representation by social status in one case and by industry in another, you are going to get a cross division. How will you get over that?

***Dr. Ambedkar:*** There will be some provision for organised labour, and the majority of the depressed classes are labourers.

127. *Mr. Hartshorn:* I think. Dr. Ambedkar, you have made it pretty clear that you are in favour of adult suffrage. You say on page 41 of your memorandum, however, "The Sabha would, however, be content if the franchise for the Legislative Council is fixed at the same level as that for the Taluka Local Board in the rural parts and Rs. 3 rental per month in the urban parts of the Presidency." Have you formed any opinion, or are any statistics available to enable us to know to what extent the franchise would be extended on that qualification?

***Dr. Ambedkar:*** I may tell you that I am myself shaky about that statement. I do not mind admitting that. Such information as I have been able to gather from the depressed classes in the mofussils, however, leads me to believe that the existing taluka local franchise does produce a certain number of voters from the depressed classes.

128. I was not quite thinking of that. Could you tell us the increase in the number of persons who would become voters in the Bombay Presidency if this qualification rather than the present one were adopted?

***Dr. Ambedkar:*** I do not think I can give you any very definite information on this point.

129. May I revert to a question put to you by Major Attlee? I gather the depressed classes work in the factories in isolation?

***Dr. Ambedkar:*** In isolation, yes.

130. They have their own shed and their own department?

***Dr. Ambedkar:*** Their own department; there are no sheds.

131. Whatever it is, they are separated from the other workers in the factory?

***Dr. Ambedkar:*** I would rather put it in this way, that certain departments are exclusively assigned to the depressed classes and certain departments are departments into which they are not allowed to enter.

132. Certain kinds of occupations are forbidden to them?

***Dr. Ambedkar:*** In the mills, yes.

133. I think you said they are not allowed to go into the weaving department?

***Dr. Ambedkar:*** Yes.

134. If they became members of the same trade union, would the workers in the weaving department decline to allow them in?

***Dr. Ambedkar:*** They would decline to allow them in. If I may mention one thing, in the recent Bombay strike this matter was brought up prominently by me. I said to the members of the union that if they did not recognise the right of the depressed classes to work all the departments, I would rather dissuade the depressed classes from taking part in the strike. They afterwards consented, most reluctantly, to include this as one of their demands, and when they presented this to the millowners, the millowners very rightly snubbed them and said that if this was an injustice, they certainly were not responsible for it.

135. It is not altogether merely a case of the employers wanting to get cheap labour and confining certain departments to the depressed classes for economic reasons?

***Dr. Ambedkar:*** No, it is untouchability.

136. Would there be anything of this in the situation? The better-paid Indian, say, declines to allow the untouchable to come into his department for fear that the effect of their lower wages would be to depress wages in his department?

***Dr. Ambedkar:*** No. There is no distinction on the basis of wages.

137. That does not come into it at all?

***Dr. Ambedkar:*** No, not at all.

138. It is merely a question of untouchability?

***Dr. Ambedkar:*** Quite so.

139. *Mr. Cadogan:* They can be members of the trade union?

***Dr. Ambedkar:*** Yes.

140. *Mr. Premchand:* Can you give me a strict definition of the classes who will be on a special register of the electorate as the depressed classes?

***Dr. Ambedkar:*** Castes which cause pollution. 141. Is the principle that the lower the standing of a community the greater the electoral advantage it should command over others, justifiable?

***Dr. Ambedkar:*** Yes. 142. If all minorities are granted additional seats, what then will constitute the majority?

***Dr. Ambedkar:*** If minorities put together make up a majority there is no majority and the question does not arise. There may be class distinctions among the minorities. I can quite conceive the Mohammedans in the Bombay Presidency being divided into two groups, one favouring the capitalists and one the labourers.

143. Is not it true that people who are not politically minded or trained are frequently led astray by professional leaders?

***Dr. Ambedkar:*** I do not know. I have never been a professional leader, so I cannot say.

144. Would not the extension of the franchise to the large majority of the uneducated section of society be fraught with danger and render it liable to abuse?

***Dr. Ambedkar:*** No, I do not think so.

145. Can you tell me why it is not possible to admit members of the depressed classes to our present schools and colleges without the necessity for a charge on the revenue of the Province?

***Dr. Ambedkar:*** Because they are hopelessly neglected under the present system.

146. Why is not it possible to admit members of the depressed classes to our present schools and colleges without the necessity for a charge on the revenues of the Province?

***Dr. Ambedkar:*** You should ask those who refuse what their reason for resfusal is.

147. Refusal of what?

***Dr. Ambedkar:*** To admit them.

148. To the colleges and schools?

***Dr. Ambedkar:*** Yes.

149. Do you know the Bombay Municipality has passed a rule now?

***Dr. Ambedkar:*** And you know also of the protest meeting which was held in Bombay.

150. There may have been a protest by one section, but the Municipality has removed all those restrictions?

***Dr. Ambedkar:*** It remains to be seen how far they will stick to it at the next election.

151. But they have done it, you know?

***Dr. Ambedkar:*** Yes.

152. *Chairman:* Might we know what is the protest meeting to which he refers?

***Dr. Ambedkar:*** The position is this. Hitherto the Bombay Municipality has had separate schools for the depressed classes in the City of Bombay. Now, under the scheme of compulsory primary education, the Bombay Municipality is compelled to limit the number of schools and bring together the scattered children of the depressed classes into the schools of the caste Hindus as a measure of economy. Naturally, some provision has to be made for water and other amenities for the children who attend. The question arose whether there should be a distinction in the drinking arrangements, whether the untouchables should have separate pots for drinking from the caste Hindus. The Municipality passed a resolution saying "We cannot recognise untouchability in our own schools," and they issued a circular that there should be no distinction as to drinking pots in their schools. This protest meeting was a meeting held under the presidency of an important Hindu leader of Bombay to protest against that kind of uniform arrangement being made, as being against the Hindu religion.

153. *Mr. Premchand:* Do you know the depressed classes are employed in the weaving departments of the Ahmedabad mills?

***Dr. Ambedkar:*** I did not know that.

154. I can tell you they are.

***Dr. Ambedkar:*** There again I should like to say one thing, probably they are employed exclusively. I can quite conceive of a situation where, for instance, so many looms are exclusively handed over to the depressed classes. Today there is a proposal also in certain mills that the depressed classes should take charge of the whole of the weaving department, that the mill owners should hand it over to them, but you cannot have part depressed classes and part caste Hindus.

155. *Chairman:* The difficulty is the mixture?

***Dr. Ambedkar:*** Yes.

156. *Sir Hari Singh Gour:* What is the view of your Institute in regard to the general scheme of constitutional reform? Have you formulated any views at all on the subject?

***Dr. Ambedkar:*** I may tell you this. The depressed classes as such, of course, are not very much interested in constitutional questions; they are more interested in obtaining the guarantees and protection they require, under whatever form of Government that may come to be. Therefore, I do not think that the depressed classes as such have any definite views as to the form of Provincial Government or the form of the Central Government; but, of course, I have my own individual views as a member of the depressed classes, without these being the views of the depressed classes themselves. It is on that account that nothing is said about the constitution in my memorandum.

157. I am aware of that, and that is why I asked you that question. What are your personal views?

***Dr. Ambedkar:*** *So* far as the Provincial Government is concerned, I am in favour of Provincial autonomy. 158. Qualified or unqualified?

***Dr. Ambedkar:*** I think there might be some safeguards with regard to the transfer of law and order. It is not that I object to the transfer of law and order; I am in favour of the transfer; but still I should like some safeguard. I am not certain today what it should be, but there might be with advantage some safeguard in that respect. Barring that, I am in favour (speaking personally) of full Provincial autonomy.

159. What about the Central Government?

***Dr. Ambedkar:*** I think we might start with dyarchy there.

160. As regards adult suffrage, I suppose you are in favour of adult male and female suffrage?

***Dr. Ambedkar:*** Yes.

161. Do you think that is a practical proposition?

***Dr. Ambedkar:*** Very practical.

162. Do you think the masses have attained any degree of political consciousness, so as to be able to use that political suffrage with any advantage to their own community?

***Dr. Ambedkar:*** Speaking only on behalf of the depressed classes. I emphatically maintain that the depressed classes will exercise their vote in a most intelligent manner, speaking for the Bombay Presidency. Having regard to the fact that the canker of untouchability is before their minds every minute of their lives, and having regard to their being alive to the fact that political power is the only solvent of this difficulty, I emphatically maintain that the depressed class voter would be an intelligent voter.

163. Do not you think that, following the example of other countries, those who pay no taxes, having a political existence and possessing political power, will tax those who are already oppressed with heavy taxes?

***Dr. Ambedkar:*** I think that should be so. I do not see anything wrong in it.

164. You see no wrong in the exploitation of the tax paying community? Is this your own opinion or the opinion of the Institute which you represent?

***Dr. Ambedkar:*** My own opinion. The Institute has said nothing about it here.

---

165. Do you think you reflect the general opinion of your Institute in conveying this view to the Commission?

***Dr. Ambedkar:*** I think that would be the view of all poor communities.

167. *Sir Hari Singh Gour:* In answer to the Chairman, you said the depressed classes must be regarded as a distinct community, a community distinct from the Hindu community. Do you apply that only for electoral purposes, or for all purposes?

***Dr. Ambedkar:*** They are distinct for all purposes, as a matter of fact. 168. Would you class the depressed classes as real Hindus?

***Dr. Ambedkar:*** I do not care about the nomenclature. It does not matter whether I call myself a Hindu or a non-Hindu, as long as I am outside the pale of the Hindu community.

170. It makes all the difference in the world. If you were outside the pale of Hinduism you would not be subject to Hindu law. You could not, for instance, contract a marriage under the Act 30 of 1923, which has completely abolished all castes so far as the marriage law is concerned between a Hindu and a Mahar, touchable and untouchable. Now, if you go out of that community, out of that social system, and call yourself a non-Hindu, you will be outside the pale of Hindu law to that extent?

***Dr. Ambedkar:*** It might be.

171. Then by what law would you be governed?

***Dr. Ambedkar:*** We are governed by the Hindu law, just as, for instance, the Khojas, who are Mohammedans, prefer to be governed by Hindu law so far as the devolution of property is concerned.

172. And you are under the Act 30 of 1923; you are under Hindu law?

***Dr. Ambedkar:*** I do not know what the depressed classes would think about marriage.

173. Would you kindly turn to your memorandum? You say at page 39, and you also repeated it today in answer to my friend Mr. Kikabhai, "the standing of the community must mean its power to protect itself in the social struggle. That

power would obviously depend upon the educational and economic status of the community."

***Dr. Ambedkar:*** Quite.

174. It follows from the recognition of the principle that the lower the standing of a community, the greater electoral advantage it must get over the rest. Do you adduce this last sentence as a logical deduction from the premises, from the previous two sentences?

***Dr. Ambedkar:*** Yes.

175. You regard that as a logical deduction?

***Dr. Ambedkar:*** Yes, quite.

176. I wish to draw your attention to the fact that you say: "In addition to the demand for adequate representation, the Sabha feels that it must also demand the inclusion of clauses in the constitution of the country." Now, amongst these clauses you find things like this mentioned: "the right of every depressed class to the appointment of a special inspector of police from amongst themselves"?

***Dr. Ambedkar:*** Yes.

177. Do you expect that an Act of Parliament should contain a clause to this effect, that the depressed classes in India shall have an inspector of police in every district from amongst themselves?

***Dr. Ambedkar:*** I really do not see anything strange in that.

178. Supposing there was a provision to that effect relating to all communities (because if you have got certain constitutional guarantees it follows by necessary implication that other communities have an equal right), then you parcel out all the official posts and you parcel out all the other things amongst the various communities, and that is the constitution that you foresee for India?

***Dr. Ambedkar:*** I do not know that. I am only speaking for the depressed classes. May I just make one thing clear?

179. May I just complete my sentence? That is a contingency that does not arouse any apprehension in your mind?

***Dr. Ambedkar:*** Just let me explain before you go further. I think we must be very careful in using the word "minority "". I do not think simply because a community happens to be a community composed of small numbers it is therefore necessarily a minority for political purposes.

A minority which is oppressed, or whose rights are denied or the majority, would be a minority that would be fit for consideration for political purposes.

180. Wherever you have these minorities in other countries, there is provision made, there is sometimes a minister for the protection of minorities. Have you thought about that?

***Dr. Ambedkar:*** Yes.

181. Supposing we gave you the protection—the protection might he given in any form, and if I may say so?

***Dr. Ambedkar:*** I am sorry to interrupt you—I do find that the new constitutions that have been framed after the peace for the various European countries composing the bulk of the Slavonic nations very largely embody this principle. I have devoted some special attention to this subject, if you will permit me to say so.

182. *Lord Burnham:* And carried out?

***Dr. Ambedkar:*** And made part of the Constitution.

183. And carried out in practice too?

***Dr. Ambedkar:*** Carried out in practice; and the point is this, that if a minority feels that the guarantee has not been fulfilled, it has the right of appeal to the League of Nations.

186. I am not quarrelling with the principle?

***Dr. Ambedkar:*** And I may say T am not very particular about the form.

187. If the details of the scheme which you have adumbrated were to be introduced into the constitution of this country, would it not lead to a perpetual class war?

***Dr. Ambedkar:*** It might, but that would depend upon the attitude of the majority.

188. Therefore you would not, as a sagacious statesman?

***Dr. Ambedkar:*** If you will permit me to say so, all these things, though T insist upon them, I admit to be provisions of a transitory character. T do contemplate and I do desire, the time when India shall be one; and T believe that a time will come when, for instance, all these things will not be necessary; but all that would depend upon the attitude of the majority towards the minority.

198. Now, you mentioned a case that you conducted on behalf of a member of the depressed class, who, from fear of social ostracism, stood outside near the window. What district was it?

***Dr. Ambedkar:*** Khandesh district.

199. Ordinary Magistrate's Court?

***Dr. Ambedkar:*** The stipendiary Magistrate's Court.

200. What caste was the Magistrate?

***Dr. Ambedkar:*** A Hindu.

201. He did not object to the accused coming into the court?

***Dr. Ambedkar:*** No. I say the accused himself would not come in.

202. The accused himself was terrorised by the past acts of the Hindus?

***Dr. Ambedkar:*** Yes.

203. The fear had been engendered in the minds of the depressed classes on account of the oppression of the caste Hindus that he would not get a square deal thereafter if he was to trench upon the limited rights which he had been given by the caste Hindus?

***Dr. Ambedkar:*** Yes.

204. *Sir Hari Singh Gour:* I think you will admit. Dr. Ambedkar, that during the last few years there has been a forward movement in the way of removing untouchability and removing all disqualifications from the path of the depressed classes?

***Dr. Ambedkar:*** Yes.

205. I admit that the reforms have not been commensurate

with your desires and mind, but at the same time, we have to recognise that there is a growing feeling that there must be a consolidation of the Hindu people by removing all these barriers that stand between the caste and the non-caste Hindus. You recognise that?

***Dr. Ambedkar:*** Yes, there are speeches from the platform.

206. There are positive actions?

***Dr. Ambedkar:*** Speaking for my part of the country, the Bombay Presidency, I would rather hesitate to accept your proposition.

207. Therefore, I will give you examples. Every year, for instance, wherever there is a caste and no-caste society, Hindus hold annual dinners, and they all sit together for the purpose of making one class of people accustomed to the other class of people?

***Dr. Ambedkar:*** I am not aware of it in this Presidency.

208. I have attended several of them.

***Dr. Ambedkar:*** In this Presidency?

*Sir Hari Singh Gour:* No, in Nagpur.

209. There is no such movement here?

***Dr. Ambedkar:*** No.

210. But you admit that there is recognition of the fact that oppression and untouchability must go, and that every effort to suggest anything in that way receives sympathetic consideration from the caste Hindus, and particularly from the Reformers?

***Dr. Ambedkar:*** I would hesitate, again, to answer that.

*Chairman:* Would you agree, in order to get this witness's view of the facts, that I should ask two or three questions on your line?

*Sir Hari Singh Gour:* Yes Sir, certainly.

211. *Chairman:* Mr. Rajah would be, in many ways, the best person to do it, but I wish you would tell us your own view. Compare twenty years ago with now in the Bombay Presidency. How many years, if I may ask, have you been here?

***Dr. Ambedkar:*** Five or six years.

212. You have, of course, taken an interest in your own community since long before that? ***Dr. Ambedkar:*** Yes.

213. You can look back twenty years and give us some ideal?

***Dr. Ambedkar:*** Yes.

214. Let me take two or three things. First of all I imagine that there is no change at all so far as regards the admission of the depressed classes to the interior of a Hindu temple. That, of course, is a matter of religious practice and teaching. I do not criticise it, but there is no change at all?

***Dr. Ambedkar:*** No, there is no change at all in that respect.

215. What I want to know is this. Let us take two or three definite things in this Presidency. In the country districts, you have told us that as a rule the depressed classes, the untouchables, live in a place for themselves. Of course, we have seen it many times. Sometimes they live in a corner of the village, if it happens to be a Hindu village, and sometimes in a hamlet of their own. Now is there any change in the last twenty years as regards their living among the general communities?

***Dr. Ambedkar:*** No change.

216. We saw some of the villages the other day. We understand some of them can draw water from the river, but I suppose there are other villages that rely on wells?

***Dr. Ambedkar:*** Even in the case of rivers they can take water only from a portion of the river. A point on the river is appointed for them.

217. That is to say, the depressed classes will draw water at a point lower down than the caste Hindus?

***Dr. Ambedkar:*** Yes.

218. Now let us take the case of villages that rely on wells. It is not uncommon?

***Dr. Ambedkar:*** No, not; uncommon.

219. I am anxious to know and I hope you will tell me quite frankly, is there in that respect any improvement in the last twenty years?

***Dr. Ambedkar:*** No.

220. Your attention has been called to the fact that there have been resolutions passed on this subject?

***Dr. Ambedkar:*** Yes, only resolutions.

221. It is suggested that untouchability sometimes goes to such a length that the actual contact with the man (or sometimes his shadow itself) is regarded socially by those of the higher castes as a pollution?

***Dr. Ambedkar:*** Yes.

222. Is there an improvement in that respect?

***Dr. Ambedkar:*** There is an improvement in that respect.

223. I am glad to hear that. That is, whereas 20 years ago a caste Hindu who found himself in close contact with an untouchable would possibly think it his religious duty to purify himself, it is not viewed with so much strictness now; is that correct?

***Dr. Ambedkar:*** Yes.

224. Then, of course, as compared with twenty years ago I imagine that there are some members of the depressed classes who have in fact risen very much in the professional scale. Twenty years ago were there depressed classes who were practising at the Bar in Bombay?

***Dr. Ambedkar:*** No.

225. How many members of the depressed classes practise at the Bar now?

***Dr. Ambedkar:*** I am the only man.

226. I think we were told yesterday that in the list of voters for the Sardars and Inamdars there were two members of the depressed classes?

***Dr. Ambedkar:*** Only one. His position is different. His jagir was granted by the Peshwas for the services rendered on the battlefield. His title was not given by the British Government.

227. What one notices is that in India there is gradually being introduced the motor bus connecting the town with the village and I see them going along the road. Are those public vehicles open to the depressed classes?

***Dr. Ambedkar:*** Not in villages. There are a great many villages where the depressed classes are not allowed to travel in these buses.

228. Who prevents them?

***Dr. Ambedkar:*** The driver would not take them.

229. One would expect the driver to take anybody who pays. Why does he not take them?

***Dr. Ambedkar:*** Because if he takes them the other people will not come into his car. For instance, the barber here would not shave my head even though I offer him a rupee.

230. *Rao Saheb Patil:* According to law the driver would be prosecuted if he refuses to take any passenger?

***Dr. Ambedkar:*** That can be evaded by saying that all seats are booked. 231. Are matters improving in that respect?

***Dr. Ambedkar:*** Yes, they are improving; but still there are numerous cases where the depressed classes would not be allowed to enter into these buses.

232. Let us take the depressed classes who are employed in the mills in Bombay. Some of them go in trams, I suppose. Do you suggest that they are not allowed to use the trams?

***Dr. Ambedkar:*** There was a case two years ago where a Bhungi was not allowed to board a tram.

233. When you speak of the case two years ago it suggests to me that it is rather exceptional than a rule?

***Dr. Ambedkar:*** I have seen, for instance, when I was travelling by the B.B. & C.I. Railway hundreds of cases where the passengers obstructed the depressed classes coming into the compartments.

234. *Sir Hari Singh Gour:* With regard to the case of the Bhungi which you mentioned, are you sure if he was not properly attired and therefore be was not allowed to get into the tram?

***Dr. Ambedkar:*** I do not know about that.

235. Before a man gets into the tram he is not asked to which caste he belongs; they only ask him whether he has got the fare, is it not?

***Dr. Ambedkar:*** But people can easily recognise him.

236. That is on account of his dress?

***Dr. Ambedkar:*** But he will be dealt with very badly when once he is recognised to belong to the depressed classes.

237. Apart from the question of caste there is also the question of costume?

***Dr. Ambedkar:*** Yes, but some of the members of the depressed class are very well dressed.

238. In the Bombay Presidency you have no such thing as to consider it a pollution to walk in the shadow of a depressed class member?

***Dr. Ambedkar:*** Yes, it exists in some parts of the Konkan and in Kathiawad.

239. It is on the wane?

***Dr. Ambedkar:*** Yes.

240. With regard to the Ambalal Sarlal School in Ahmedabad, has not his sister started the school for depressed classes?

***Dr. Ambedkar:*** That is the only honourable exception.

241. Is not the school maintained for the depressed classes from public funds?

***Dr. Ambedkar:*** I do not know that, but I know that lady is taking interest in the elevation of the depressed classes.

242. *Chairman:* I understand it is an exceptional case?

***Dr. Ambedkar:*** Yes, it is quite an exceptional case.

243. *Dr. Suhrawardy:* In view of the instances of social ostracism and tyranny which you have just stated, do you not think that in a general election members of your community will be frightened out of the polling booths?

***Dr. Ambedkar:*** Yes, it may happen.

244. Also there is the further apprehension that the high caste-Hindus may refuse to come and participate in the elections where the untouchables go to record their votes?

***Dr. Ambedkar:*** They might; it is very difficult to say what might happen. We have cases, for instance, where the caste-Hindu members of district boards have left the premises because the depressed class members have claimed to sit at the table.

245. Do you not think that, in view of this state of affairs, it will be better for you to have a separate electorate because in practice it will mean a separate electorate even if you reserve your seats in a general electorates?

***Dr. Ambedkar:*** Yes.

246. *Rao Bahadur Rajah:* With reference to the question put by my friend, Sir Hari Singh Gour, regarding the costume of the depressed classes, did the barber refuse to shave your head because you were not well dressed?

***Dr. Ambedkar:*** No; it is because I belong to the depressed class.

247. Not on account of the dress you were wearing?

***Dr. Ambedkar:*** No.

248. With regard to another question put by another member of the Committee, may I ask you whether it is easy for a depressed class member in a village to file a suit against the owner of a bus because he has refused to take him?

***Dr. Ambedkar:*** It is not possible.

249. I understand that you have been taking very much interest in the uplift of the depressed classes. What has been your experience during your propaganda as to the help you receive in this work from the higher classes? Do they help you to impress upon the depressed classes the need for greater sanitation, hygiene and such like things?

***Dr. Ambedkar:*** My experience, unfortunately, is rather very bitter in this matter. The depressed classes have been dubbed to be unfit for association because of certain unclean habits. That is the allegation of the upper classes. That is to say, they eat the meat of the dead animals and they are not clean, and so on. In this Presidency during the last two years I started a campaign to purify the depressed classes, so to say, and to persuade them to give up some of their dirty habits.

But, to my great misfortune, I found the whole caste-Hindu population up against me when in a matter like this I expected the utmost cooperation from them. But when I began to analyse the basis of their opposition I found that they insisted upon the depressed class people doing the unclean things because giving up doing these things meant that the depressed classes were exceeding their social status and rivalling the upper class. For instance, in the Colaba and Ratnagiri districts the whole of the Mahar population have given up the eating of the meat of dead animals, but the tyranny and social oppression that is going on against them is simply unspeakable; there is a complete economic and social boycott. The lands they had been cultivating for years past have been taken away from them by their caste-Hindu landlords.

Every sort of pressure, social and economic, has been brought to bear upon the depressed classes in order to compel them to resume their dirty habits. The officials, who are all caste-Hindus, give no protection to the depressed classes, whose condition has really become pitiable, and all this because they sought to give up their dirty habits. Instead of getting cooperation I find that the members of the upper classes are up against me, and they say "these evil habits of the depressed classes are all insignia of their inferiority and they must remain."

250. The other day we heard a witness say that there is not a single depressed class member on the sanitary boards. If what you have said just now with regard to the higher castes is true, is there any good in the depressed class members, being on these boards so far as their sanitary improvement is concerned?

***Dr. Ambedkar:*** I think the depressed class people ought to be represented on every local authority.

251. You told us just now that in the courts in this Presidency witnesses belonging to the depressed classes have no access. I want to be clear on that point. Do you mean to say that the members of the depressed class are not admitted into some of the courts?

***Dr. Ambedkar:*** Yes.

252. And I understand you to say that in a case the man did not dare go into the court, is that so?

***Dr. Ambedkar:*** The thing is the depressed class man is looked upon by the caste people as having a particular station in life, he exceeds that station in life when he enters the court, and if he exceeded that station in life they would begin to harass him. The man, if he exceeded the social limits, would subsequently suffer at the hands of the caste people. My protection in that particular case was only temporary protection and he knew it would cease as soon as the case was over.

253. If you had not been there and if he attempted to go into the court, what would have happened to him?

***Dr. Ambedkar:*** I think the same thing would have happened to me when I tried to enter a temple in Bombay.

254. Coming to medical relief, will you kindly enlighten us as to the kind of medical relief the depressed class men are getting?

***Dr. Ambedkar:*** They are not allowed entry into the dispensary, unless the case is a very very serious one; such as, for instance, the non-admission would bring the officer's conduct to the notice of the higher authorities. Ordinarily the medicine is dispensed out.

255. *Chairman:* I suppose you are talking of dispensaries in the mofussil?

***Dr. Ambedkar:*** Yes, Government dispensaries.

256. They are, of course, in the department of the Minister of Medical Administration?

***Dr. Ambedkar:*** Yes.

257. I imagine that the regulations of the Minister provide that these dispensaries are open to everybody who goes?

***Dr. Ambedkar:*** Yes.

258. But you say that in the mofussil in fact it does not work out like that?

***Dr. Ambedkar:*** No.

*Dr. Solanki:* The Hindu medical man who is orthodox always takes objection to examine a man belonging to the depressed classes. There have been instances in Gujarat where the men have actually died from the want of medical relief. I know of instances where doctors have actually refused even to touch the patient when he was suffering from pneumonia. The doctor would hand over the thermometer to a Mohammedan who does not know how to hold the thermometer and the Mohammedan would hand over the thermometer to the patient. This is a fact and it has happened.

259. What is important, I think, as I said before and I may repeat it, is to get a true picture. The thing may happen occasionally. I want to know whether what you are describing is quite an exceptional thing due to some particular doctor's objection or whether you think it is an everyday happening?

*Dr. Solanki:* Doctors who are orthodox do it.

260. The difficulty about this thing is that the objection that is taken by the medical man is an objection based on his own religious views?

*Dr. Solanki:* Yes.

261. *Rao Bahadur Rajah:* Have these facts been brought to the notice of the authorities concerned?

***Dr. Ambedkar:*** Yes.

262. What was the action they took?

***Dr. Ambedkar:*** The reply the Minister gave was that we had better depend on persuasion; that was the word he used.

*Chairman:* Would you do this for us, Rao Bahadur? One hears of different aspects of this and I want to know the facts. What is the position about the depressed class children in the ordinary public schools in this province? Would you ask the witness about that for me?

263. *Rao Bahadur Rajah:* Will you kindly enlighten us as to the attitude of the schoolmasters or the Education Department or the managers of schools towards the children of the depressed classes?

***Dr. Ambedkar:*** There is a circular issued by Dr. Paranjpye when he was Minister of Education in this Presidency to the effect that children of depressed classes should be admitted in all schools. But our experience is that circular has not been carried out at all. It is true that in the report of the Director of Public Instruction it is stated that circular has been carried into effect; but I beg to differ from that view. It is not a correct statement of facts as they exist today. There is an incident here at Poona which took place only a few days ago, at Deoo, where the children of the depressed classes were refused admission and when they insisted on it the village proclaimed social boycott against the depressed classes.

264. *Chairman:* The memorandum refers to that report?

***Dr. Ambedkar:*** Yes, that is not a correct statement of facts as I said. I beg to differ from that.

265. *Rao Bahadur Rajah:* I understood from Mr. Griffith that in his view there are reasons why the depressed classes could not be taken into the police department as the duties of the police involved house searches and arrests. Supposing, for the sake of argument, that is true, would there be similar objection to the recruitment of the depressed class members to other subordinate and provincial services?

***Dr. Ambedkar:*** Find that there are so many objections raised.

266. You are a member of the Local Legislative Council?

***Dr. Ambedkar:*** Yes.

267. What is your experience as regards the attitude of the higher caste members of the local Council towards your community?

***Dr. Ambedkar:*** One cannot say it is favourable to the depressed classes.

268. What is the attitude of the Government towards the members of your community in your Provinces?

***Dr. Ambedkar:*** Very apathetic.

269. I suppose you have got honorary bench magistrates' courts in this Presidency. Are there any members of the depressed classes on these boards?

***Dr. Ambedkar:*** There are none and we are trying to get some on the bench of magistrates, but without effect. Perhaps it might be interesting to the Conference if I read in this connection a letter written by the Collector of the Khandesh district to a member of the depressed classes when he applied for an appointment on the bench. This letter also gives the reasons why he should not be appointed to the place, and it reads thus:

> *"The Collector has every sympathy with the aspirations of the depressed classes and is glad to recognise and appreciate Mr. Medhe's good work in the various fields of public activities; but in his opinion time has not yet come when a member of the depressed classes can be given a seat on the bench of magistrates, and, until the Government makes some pronouncement favourable to the aspiration of the depressed classes in this Presidency he must regretfully express his inability to recommend such an appointment." This letter is dated 25th September 1928.*

270. I am sure you will agree with me that appointments to these bodies have nothing to do with the progress of the communities?

***Dr. Ambedkar:*** Nothing.

271. The sole consideration should be whether the individual candidate can discharge his duties with a sense of responsibility?

***Dr. Ambedkar:*** Yes.

272. *Lord Burnham:* I understood you to say that of all the methods to protect the interests of the depressed classes, you preferred the universal suffrage?

***Dr. Ambedkar:*** I would rather say adequate representation in the Legislative Council.

273. I understand you to say you were in favour of universal suffrage?

***Dr. Ambedkar:*** Yes.

274. If you have not got that you go in for separate electorates? Supposing you cannot get either, are you still in favour of the principle of nomination?

***Dr. Ambedkar:*** No. I would insist on our representative being elected.

275. If you cannot get the election on the terms proposed, you would prefer adult franchise?

***Dr. Ambedkar:*** Yes.

276. *Chairman:* You have spoken of your strong preference for the representation of the depressed classes being secured by the method of election. Are you satisfied, supposing the method was the method of election, that the result would be that you will get elected those who were really the best spokesmen for the depressed classes?

***Dr. Ambedkar:*** I believe so.

277. You do not feel anxious that influences which were really against the interests of the depressed classes will get to work?

***Dr. Ambedkar:*** I admit that and that is why I want adult suffrage.

278. You think that the influence will cease because of the adult suffrage?

***Dr. Ambedkar:*** That will be counterbalanced.

279. Supposing that a member of the depressed classes has the necessary qualification, does he vote in a general constituency?

***Dr. Ambedkar:*** He does.

280. Taking your case you will have a qualification to vote in some general constituency?

***Dr. Ambedkar:*** Yes; I vote for the University constituency as also my friend.

281. How does the position stand about the paying of taxes? A suggestion was made that depressed classes do not pay the taxes. Of course, it follows that, as regards the Customs duties and other indirect taxes which may raise the price of the articles, I suppose the depressed classes will have to pay the increased price like anybody else?

***Dr. Ambedkar:*** Yes. Also the depressed class men,

particularly the Mahar community, is always in possession of some land of ordinary tenure or watan tenure at any rate, and they pay what is called the judi, that is the assessment, as anybody else.

282. I suppose that a good many Mahars follow the occupation of waiters in private service?

***Dr. Ambedkar:*** Yes, very few. But they mainly work in industries in the cities.

283. Take, for instance, a European private house or a club, they employ Mahars?

***Dr. Ambedkar:*** Yes.

284. Are those people qualified to vote in a general constituency or not?

***Dr. Ambedkar:*** That will depend on the pitch of franchise.

285. As a rule the waiters would not have any qualification?

***Dr. Ambedkar:*** Yes, under the existing circumstances.

286. *Sardar Majumdar:* Are you aware that saints from the depressed classes are revered by all classes, and high-class persons bow down before them as much as before such saints from higher classes?

***Dr. Ambedkar:*** There is only one case so far as I know.

287. But do they do so?

***Dr. Ambedkar:*** Yes, as they do the Mohammedan Pir.

288. Are you aware that untouchability is not observed in the Warkari Panth, *i.e.* the devotees of the God Vithoba at Pandharpur?

***Dr. Ambedkar:*** That is entirely incorrect.

289. Do you agree that there is a vast change during the last 25 years in the treatment accorded to the depressed classes, that the educated higher classes are trying to remove this evil of untouchability and mix with them quite freely and that there is a gradual change in the condition of the depressed classes and in the treatment accorded to them by the general educated public?

***Dr. Ambedkar:*** Yes, it is so, though the sympathy is only in words and is seldom translated into action.

290. Are you aware that in almost all villages the depressed class people are provided with wells meant only for their own use?

***Dr. Ambedkar:*** No.

291. Are there not such wells?

***Dr. Ambedkar:*** Not in every village.

292. Who are the depressed classes? Will you please name the castes?

***Dr. Ambedkar:*** There is the census.

293. Do inter-marriages take place between the Mang and the Mahar castes?

***Dr. Ambedkar:*** No, the caste Hindus have spread their poison to the rest.

294. Do they dine together?

***Dr. Ambedkar:*** Yes, nowadays. The movement for consolidation is going on and there is now a case of intermarriage between a Mang and a Mahar.

295. Are there not two Inamdars in my constituency who belong to the depressed classes?

***Dr. Ambedkar:*** I do not know.

## Nomenclature

14. The revision of the electoral rolls consequent upon the proposed changes in the constitution is a very good occasion for considering the question of having a proper and appropriate nomenclature for the depressed classes. I therefore propose to express my opinion on this question. There is considerable objection on the part of the communities which are now called "depressed classes" to the use of that term in describing them. Several witnesses who have appeared before the Committee have given expression to this sentiment. Besides the term 'depressed classes' has led to a great deal of confusion in the census because it includes

others who are not strictly untouchables. Secondly, it gives the impression that the depressed classes are a low and helpless community when as a matter of fact in every Province numbers of them are both well-to-do and well-educated, and the whole community is acquiring consciousness of its needs, is charged with ambition for securing a respectable status in Indian society and is making stupendous efforts to achieve it. On all these grounds the term 'depressed classes' is inappropriate and unsuitable. Mr. Mullan, the Census Superintendent of Assam, has brought into use a new term called 'exterior castes' to cover the untouchables. This designation has many advantages. It defines exactly the position of the untouchables who are within the Hindu religion but outside the Hindu society and distinguishes it from Hindus who are economically and educationally depressed but who are both within the pale of Hindu religion and Hindu society. The term has two other advantages. It avoids all the confusion that is now caused by use of the vague term depressed classes and at me same time is not offensive. Our Committee did not feel competent to make recommendation in this behalf. But as a representative of the depressed classes I have no hesitation in saying that until better nomenclature is found the untouchable classes should hereafter be described by the more expressive term 'Exterior Castes or 'Excluded Castes' and not as depressed classes.

## Reservations

15. Before concluding this note I would like on my part to make the same reservation which my Muslim colleagues on the Committee have made namely that the allocation of seats to labour women, and other special interests must not affect the proportion of seats which the depressed classes have claimed in the Minorities Pact submitted to the Round Table Conference.

The 1st May 1932.

B. R. Ambedkar

# Bibliography


Agarwal, S. P., and Aggarwal, J. C.: *Educational and Social Uplift of Backward Classes: At What Cost and How? Mandal Commission and After,* Concept Publishing Co., New Delhi, 1979.

Ahir, D.C.: *Dr. Ambedkar, Buddhism and Social Change*, BR Publishing, Delhi, 1993.

Aluwalia, B.K. & Shashi B.R.: *Ambedkar and Human Rights*, KK Publishers, New Delhi, 1981.

Ambedkar, B. R.: *Annihilation of Caste: An Undelivered Speech,* Arnold Publishers, New Delhi, 1990.

Asghar Ali.: *Mandal Commission Controversy*, Ajanta Publications, Delhi, 1991.

Bakshi, S. R.: B.R. *Ambedkar: His Political and Social Ideology*. New Delhi: Deep & deep publications, 2000.

Barill, C.: *Social and Political Ideas of B.R. Ambedkar*, Aalekh Publishers, Jaipur, 1977.

Benjamin, Joseph: *Scheduled Castes in Indian Politics and Society*, Ess Ess Publications, New Delhi, 1989.

Bhagat Ram: *Educating Harijans*, Academic Press, Haryana, 1981.

Bhatia, K.L.: *Dr. B.R. Ambedkar: Social Justice and the Indian Constitution,* Deep & Deep, New Delhi, 1994.

Chanchreek, K.L., Prasad, S. & Kumar, R.: *Dr. Ambedkar. Social Justice and Political Safeguards for Depressed Classes,* Shree, New Delhi, 1991.

Chatterjee, Partha: *Caste and Subaltern Consciousness*, Oxford University Press, Delhi, 1994.

Danda, A.K.: *Weaker Sections in Indian Villages*, Inter-India, New Delhi, 1993.

Deshpande, Vasant: *Towards Social Intergration: Problems of Adjustment of SC Elites*, Shubhada- Saraswat, Pune, 1978.

Engineer, Asghar Ali.: *Mandal Commission Controversy*, Ajanta Publications, Delhi, 1991.

Epstein, T. S.: *Economic Development and Social Change in South India*, Manchester University Press, Manchester, 1962.

Fiske, A.: *The Untouchables in Contemporary India*, University of Arizona Press, Tucson, 1972.

Galanter, Marc.: *Competing Inequalities: Law and the Backward Classes in India,* University of California Press, CA, 1984.

Glen, M. and Johnson, S. B.: *Social Mobility Among Untouchables*, Vikas, New Delhi, 1979.

Ishwaran, K.: *Shivpur: A South Indian Village*, Routledge, London, 1968.

Jadhav, N.: *Dr. Ambedkar's Economic Thought and Philosophy*, Popular Prakashan, Bombay, 1993.

Jaffrelot, Christophe: *Dr. Ambedkar and Untouchability: Fighting the Indian Caste System*, New York, Columbia University Press, 2005.

Johnson, Glen and Bose, Sipra: *Social Mobility Among Untouchables,* Cohesion and Conflict in Modern India, New Delhi, 1978.

Jose, K.: *Constitutional Provisions for the Scheduled Castes*, Indian Social Institute, New Delhi, 1984.

Joshi, B.R.: *Untouchable! Voices of the Dalit Liberation Movement*, Zed and MRG, London, 1986.

Juergensmeyer, Mark: *Religion as Social Vision: The Movement Against Untouchability in 20th Century Punjab*, University of California Press, Berkeley, 1979.

Khairmode, C.B.: *Dr. Bhimrao Ramji Ambedkar*, Pratap, Bombay, 1978.

Khare, R. S.: *The Untouchable as Himself: Ideology, Identity and Pragmatism Among the Lucknow Chamars*, Cambridge University Press, London, 1984.

Krishnaiah Chetty, V.B.: *Scheduled Castes and Development Programmes in India,* Vohra, Allahabad, 1991.

Kshirsagar, R. K.: *Dalit Movement in India and Its Leaders (1857-1956)*, MD Pub. Pvt. Ltd., New Delhi, 1994.

Lannoy, Richard: *The Speaing Tree*, Oxford University Press, London, 1971.

Majumdar, D. N.: *Caste and Communication in an Indian Village*, Asia Publishing House, Bombay, 1958.

Mann, K.: *Tribal Women in a Changing Society*, Mittal Publications, Delhi, 1987.

Marriott, Mckim: *Village India: Studies in the Little Community*, The University of Chicago Press, Chicago, 1955.

Meyer, Mark J.: *Religion as Social Vision: The Movement Against Untouchability in 20th Century in Punjab*, University of California Press, Berkeley, 1982.

Michael J.: *The Untouchables in Contemporary India*, University of Arizona Press, Arizona, 1972.

Mumtaz Ali: *Human Rights and the Dalits*, Uppal Publishing House, New Delhi, 1995.

Naidu, Ch. M.: *Salt Satyagraha in the Coastal Andhra*, Mittal Publications, Delhi, 1986.

Nath, Trilok: *Politics of the Depressed Classes*, Deputy Publications, Delhi, 1987.

Nim, H.L.: *Thoughts on Dr. Ambedkar*, Siddhartha Educational and Cultural Society, Agra, 1969.

O'Malley, L. S. S.: *Indian Caste Customs*, Vikas Publishing House, Delhi, 1974.

Pantavane, G.: *Patrikar Dr. Babasaheb Ambedkar*, Abhijit, Nagpur, 1987.

Paranjpe, A. C.: *Caste, Prejudice and the Individual*, Lalvani Publishing House, New Delhi, 1970.

Parmaji, S.: *Caste Reservations and Performance*, Mamata Publications, Warangal, 1985.

Partha, C.: *Caste and Subaltern Consciousness*, Oxford University Press, Delhi, 1994.

Prabhu, P. N.: *Report of the Seminar on Casteism and Removal of Untouchability*, Indian Conference of Social Work, Bombay, 1955.

Pradhan, A. C.: *The Emergence of the Depressed Classes*, Bookland International, Bhubaneshwar, 1986.

Prahlad G.: *Dalit Movement in Maharashtra*, Kanak Publications, New Delhi, 1991.

Rajasekharaiah, A.M.: *B.R. Ambedkar: the Politics of Emancipation*, Sindhu Publications, Bombay, 1971.

Raju, G.G.: *The Life of B.R. Ambedkar*, Babasaheb Dr. Ambedkar Memorial Society, Hyderabad, 1979.

Ram, Jagivan: *Caste Challenge in India*, Vision Books, New Delhi, 1980.

Rege, Sharmila: *Sati: A Critical Analysis,* University of Poona, Poona, 1989.

Rodage, S.: *Subhedar Ramji Ambedkar*. Ramaji Prakashan, Wakvali Dapoli, 1989.

Sarkar, J.: *Caste, Occupation and Change*, B. R. Publishing Co., Delhi, 1984.

Shah, Ghanshyam: *Caste Association and Political Processes in Gujarat*, Popular Prakashan, Bombay, 1975.

Sharma, Kusum: *Ambedkar and Indian Constitution*, New Delhi, Ashish Pub. House, 1992.

Shashi B.R.: *Ambedkar and Human Rights*, KK Publishers, New Delhi, 1981.

Silverberg, James: *Social Mobility in the Caste System in India*, Mouton Publishers, The Hague, 1968.

Singh, K. K.: *Patterns of Caste Tensions*, Asia Publishing House, Bombay, 1967.

Singh, S. N.: *Reservation: Problems and Prospects*, Uppal Publishing House, New Delhi, 1987.

Tope, T.K.: *Dr. B.R. Ambedkar, A Symbol of Social Revolt*, Maharashtra Information Centre, New Delhi, 1964.

Varale, B.H.: *Dr. Babasaheb Ambedkarrancha Sangaki*, Shrividya Prakashan, Pune, 1988.

Venkateshwarlu, D.: *Harijan-Upper Class Conflicts*, Discovery, New Delhi, 1990.

Wolf, G.: *Re-inventing Tradition,* Indian Institute of Advanced Studies, Shimla, 1992.

Yogesh, A.: *The Changing Frontiers of Caste*, National Publishing House, Delhi, 1968.

# Index

## A



## B



## C

D



E



F



G



H



I

□□□